"Fr. Paul Turner's *Inseparable Love* is one of those rare books that is both scholarly and pastoral. For scholars he offers deep background on the reformed rites of marriage, particularly by making available the discussions and debates among the drafters of the reformed rites on various aspects of the theology and practice of Christian marriage. For those with pastoral responsibilities he offers a host of practical suggestions, born of years of experience, for carrying out the rites with fidelity and grace. This is a splendid and indispensable resource."

—Deacon Frederick C. Bauerschmidt
    Professor of Theology
    Loyola University Maryland

"Paul Turner is a sure and reliable commentator on the newly translated *Order of Celebrating Matrimony*. This paragraph-by-paragraph commentary is comprehensive, including in its view liturgy, history, translation, and custom. It is readable, pastorally useful, and delightfully interesting. Highly recommended."

—Fr. Anthony Ruff, OSB
    Associate Professor of Theology
    Saint John's University and School of Theology-Seminary

"*Inseparable Love* is Paul Turner at his best. Historical study is perfectly integrated into a theological account of the new translation of *The Order of Celebrating Matrimony*. The commentary on the various texts and rubrics are both pastorally and theologically rich. Even someone who has spent a lifetime studying the theology of the sacrament of marriage will discover something new in this volume. This in-depth commentary should be read by liturgical theologians, graduate students, those involved in marriage formation, and every member of the clergy."

—Timothy P. O'Malley, PhD
    Associate Professional Specialist
    Director, Notre Dame Center for Liturgy
    Institute for Church Life

D1496228

"This book is a must-read for those who wish to seriously study and understand *The Order of Celebrating Matrimony* in all its intricate details. Pastors, deacons, catechists, liturgists, and musicians who prepare the engaged couple for the liturgy of marriage and prepare the liturgy for the worshiping community would benefit from this highly annotated and scholarly work. Fr. Turner leaves no stone unturned; he gives a thorough historical background to each and every paragraph of the OCM while at the same time providing a pastoral examination of present-day realities in the celebration of marriage."

    —Dolores Martinez
      Liturgist and Music Minister, San Antonio, Texas

Paul Turner

Inseparable Love

A Commentary on
The Order of Celebrating Matrimony
in the Catholic Church

A PUEBLO BOOK

Liturgical Press   Collegeville, Minnesota
www.litpress.org

A Pueblo Book published by Liturgical Press

Cover design by Jodi Hendrickson. Image courtesy of W. P. Wittman Photography.

1	2	3	4	5	6	7	8	9

Library of Congress Cataloging-in-Publication Data

Names: Turner, Paul, 1953– author.
Title: Inseparable love : a commentary on the Order of celebrating matrimony
 in the Catholic Church / Paul Turner.
Description: Collegeville, Minnesota : Liturgical Press, 2017. | "A Pueblo
 book." | Includes bibliographical references.
Identifiers: LCCN 2016040579 (print) | LCCN 2016048568 (ebook) | ISBN
 9780814663530 (pbk.) | ISBN 9780814663783 (ebook)
Subjects: LCSH: Catholic Church. Ordo celebrandi matrimonium (1991) |
 Catholic Church—Liturgy—Texts—History and criticism. |
 Marriage—Religious aspects—Catholic Church.
Classification: LCC BX2035.6.M373 T87 2017 (print) | LCC BX2035.6.M373
 (ebook) | DDC 264/.02085—dc23
LC record available at https://lccn.loc.gov/2016040579

AMICITIÆ MEMOR
TAM MARCI QVAM MICHELÆ AVERY
IN MVSICA NATÆ
IN VOCATIONE ALITÆ
IN MATRIMONIVM EORVM SIGILLATÆ
IN PVERIS EORVM ADORNATÆ
IN DOLORIBVS CONFIRMATÆ
IN FIDE, CONVIVIO, CIBO, RISO, AMOREQVE SVSTENTÆ
DEO GRATIAS DANS
HOC VOLVMEN DEDICAT AVCTOR

Contents

Acknowledgments   xi

Abbreviations   xii

Prologue   xiii

Preface   xv

The Title   1

Introduction   7

I. The Importance and Dignity of the Sacrament
of Matrimony   8

II. Duties and Ministries   14

III. The Celebration of Marriage   28
The Preparation   28
The Rite to Be Used   33

IV. Adaptations to Be Prepared by the Conferences
of Bishops   41

I. The Order of Celebrating Matrimony within Mass   51

The Introductory Rites   52
The First Form   52
The Second Form   68

The Liturgy of the Word   74

The Celebration of Marriage   78
The Questions before the Consent   82
The Consent   88
The Reception of Consent   97

The Blessing and Giving of Rings   102
The Blessing and Giving of the *Arras*   111
The Universal Prayer   116

The Liturgy of the Eucharist   120
The Blessing and Placing of the *Lazo* or the Veil   123
The Nuptial Blessing   125

The Conclusion of the Celebration   154

II. The Order of Celebrating Matrimony without Mass   163

The Introductory Rites   168
The First Form   168
The Second Form   171

The Liturgy of the Word   175

The Celebration of Matrimony   176
The Questions before the Consent   178
The Consent   178
The Blessing and Giving of Rings   180
The Blessing and Giving of the *Arras*   180
The Universal Prayer   181
The Blessing and Placing of the *Lazo* or the Veil   182
The Nuptial Blessing   183
Holy Communion   187

The Conclusion of the Celebration   192

Editio typica altera **III. The Order of Celebrating Matrimony
in the Presence of an Assisting Layperson**   195

The Introductory Rites   197

The Liturgy of the Word   198

The Celebration of Marriage   198
The Questions before the Consent   199
The Consent   199
The Reception of the Consent   200
The Blessing and Giving of Rings   200

The Universal Prayer   201
The Nuptial Blessing   201
Holy Communion   202

The Conclusion of the Celebration   205

III. The Order of Celebrating Matrimony between a Catholic and a Catechumen or a Non-Christian   207

The Rite of Reception   212

The Liturgy of the Word   213

The Celebration of Matrimony   214
The Questions before the Consent   214
The Consent   215
The Reception of the Consent   216
The Blessing and Giving of the *Arras*   217
The Universal Prayer   217
The Blessing and Placing of the *Lazo* or the Veil   218
The Nuptial Blessing   219

The Conclusion of the Celebration   220

IV. Various Texts to Be Used in the Rite of Marriage and in the Mass for the Celebration of Marriage   223

I. Biblical Readings   223
Readings from the Old Testament   225
Readings from the New Testament   228
Responsorial Psalms   234
Alleluia Verses and Verses before the Gospel   237
Gospel Readings   238

II. Collects   241

III. Other Prayers for the Blessing of Rings   246

IV. Prayers over the Offerings   247

V. Prefaces   249

VI. Commemoration of the Couple in the Eucharistic Prayer   252

VII. Other Prayers of Nuptial Blessing 255

VIII. Prayers after Communion 261

IX. Blessings at the End of the Celebration 263

Appendices 267

I. Examples of the Universal Prayer 267

II. The Order of Blessing an Engaged Couple 270
The Introductory Rites 271
Reading of the Word of God 273
Prayers 275
Prayer of Blessing 276
Conclusion of the Rite 278

III. The Order of Blessing a Married Couple within Mass
on the Anniversary of Matrimony 278
The Blessing of Rings 283

Afterword 289

Bibliography 291

Index 295

Acknowledgments

I wish to thank

The staff of the Conception Abbey Library, which housed

Members of the Secretariat of the International Commission on English in the Liturgy, who shared

Michael Witczak and Michael Driscoll, who catalogued

Bishop Brian Dunn, who clarified

Nicholas Denysenko and Irene Nowell, who answered

Ken Riley, who scoured

The staff at Liturgical Press, who conspired

The people of St. Anthony Catholic Church, who waited

God, who loves.

P. T.

Abbreviations

BB	*Book of Blessings*
CB	Ceremonial of Bishops
CCC	Catechism of the Catholic Church
CCT	Consultation on Common Texts
ETA	*Editio typica altera*
FC	*Familiaris Consortio*
GIRM	*General Instruction of the Roman Missal*
GS	*Gaudium et Spes*, Pastoral Constitution on the Church in the Modern World
IO	*Inter œcumenici*
LG	*Lumen Gentium*, Dogmatic Constitution on the Church
LM	Lectionary for Mass
OCM	Order for Celebrating Matrimony
OCMAUS	Order for Celebrating Matrimony (Australia)
OCMEW	Order for Celebrating Matrimony (England and Wales)
OM	Roman Missal, Order of Mass
PL	Patrologia Latina
PRG	The Roman-Germanic Pontifical
RCIA	Rite of Christian Initiation of Adults
SC	*Sacrosanctum Concilium*, Constitution on the Sacred Liturgy

Prologue

Love has measures. It always delights. It also demands.

Some love is transitory. It fascinates, then fails.

The greatest love penetrates the soul and expands the self. It blossoms unbidden, like a flower at dawn.

Love dismays reason. It defies explanation. People do not will love. They fall into it like gravity.

When two individuals against incalculable odds discover a mutual love, they lose its measure. Love's expression eludes their grasp. In vain they riffle the books of eternity searching for words.

They resort to symbols.

Since God is love, they ascribe their love to God. A church provides a finite venue to hold for an hour their immeasurable hearts.

There they will consent to love. There they will celebrate matrimony. There they will seal the bond that makes them one. Inseparable. As they are with God.

Preface

The Catholic Church numbers matrimony among its seven sacraments, ceremonies in which the people of God especially experience the presence of Christ. Engaged couples seeking marriage in the church find other arrangements inadequate for the love they intend to express. All weddings invite stress, and the parish that opens its doors to the engaged extends a much-needed sign of hospitality, mercy, and love.

The Second Vatican Council's Constitution on the Sacred Liturgy, *Sacrosanctum Concilium* (SC), authorized a revision of the sacramental ceremonies of the church, including its order of matrimony. After Pope Paul VI established his Consilium for implementing the constitution, its members created a number of study groups to carry out the work in specific areas. Groups 22 and 23 received the charge to revise the Roman Ritual.

The members of group 22 on the sacraments were Balthasar Fischer (relator), Xavier Seumois (secretary), Jacques Cellier (additional relator), Louis Ligier (additional secretary), Emil Lengeling, Frederick McManus, Ignacio Oñatibia, Boniface Luykx, Alois Stenzel, Joseph Lécuyer, and Jean-Baptiste Molin.

The members of group 23 on sacramentals were Pierre-Marie Gy (relator), Secondo Mazzarello, Jairo Mejia, Jean Rabau, Johannes Hopfinger, François Vandenbroucke, Damien Sicard, Antoine Chavasse, Bruno Löwenberg, and Korbinian Ritzer.[1] Other experts included bishop and theologian Carlo Colombo, who served on the advice of the Secretariat of State; Gianfrancesco Arrighi, who helped resolve ecumenical problems; Seumois, who

---

[1] Annibale Bugnini, *The Reform of the Liturgy, 1948–1975*, trans. Matthew J. O'Connell (Collegeville, MN: Liturgical Press, 1990), 579.

brought the voice of mission lands;[2] and Luigi Ciappi, theologian of the papal household.[3]

These two study groups began their work with the Rite of Christian Initiation of Adults and the Order of Christian Funerals. They then took up matrimony together with the Rite of Baptism for Children.[4] The two study groups functioned as one for their work on matrimony and will be considered one study group for the sake of this commentary.

The members started with the expectations of SC, which addressed the celebration of matrimony in two short paragraphs. The council requested that the present rite "be revised and enriched in such a way that the grace of the sacrament is more clearly signified and the duties of the spouses are taught."[5] As the Council of Trent had done, the Second Vatican Council allowed regional adaptations to celebrating matrimony while stressing that "the rite must always conform to the law that the priest assisting at the marriage must ask for and obtain the consent of the contracting parties."[6]

SC moved the celebration of matrimony inside the Mass between the homily and the prayer of the faithful.[7] Furthermore, "The prayer for the bride, duly amended to remind both spouses of their equal obligation to remain faithful to each other, may be said in the mother tongue." This caused surprise and debate not

---

[2] Ibid., 697.

[3] Ibid., 698.

[4] *Consilium ad exsequendam Constitutionem de Sacra Liturgia, Coetus a Studiis* 22–23, Schemata 157, p. 1. Hereafter, all citations from the postconciliar reports sent to the Consilium are labeled "Schemata." Copies of the original reports (mostly in Latin, some in modern languages) are held by ICEL and by the University of Notre Dame. All English translations of excerpts from these reports and other footnoted original sources in Latin, Italian, French, Spanish, and German are by the author.

[5] Second Vatican Council, *Sacrosanctum Concilium* (Constitution on Sacred Liturgy) 77, hereafter SC, http://www.vatican.va/archive/hist_councils/ii _vatican_council/documents/vat-ii_const_19631204_sacrosanctum-concilium _en.html. All translations from the documents of the Second Vatican Council come from the Vatican Website.

[6] Ibid.

[7] Ibid., 78.

because of promoting the vernacular but for including the groom in the traditional blessing of the bride.

For marriages without Mass, SC called for the reading of the epistle and the gospel;[8] prior to this time, Catholic weddings included no readings from Scripture. Finally, the council asked that the blessing "always" be given to the spouses.[9] In the past, the bride alone received her blessing only during Mass. In the discussions preparing these paragraphs of SC, it was Bishop Luigi Carlo Borromeo of Pesaro, Italy, who stated, "I would add, 'And the blessing of the couple should always be given even if matrimony is celebrated without mass.'"[10]

The study group and its advisers worked for two years (1966–1968) on the *Ordo celebrandi matrimonium*, which the Sacred Congregation of Rites approved on the Solemnity of St. Joseph, March 19, 1969. It was among the earliest of the revisions; the decree for the ordination ceremonies preceded it by a few months on August 15, 1968. The congregation's decree for celebrating matrimony explained that the revision happened in accord with SC so that the rite in force "might be enriched."[11] As Gy wrote in his first communication from the study group,

> There certainly are parts of the Roman liturgy in which greater simplicity, brevity—I do not say "impoverishment"—may be desired. On the other hand, many people consider today's Roman liturgy of matrimony too sober, undernourished. A "richer" result as to meaning and perhaps even as to an expansion of rites will better sanctify human life and turn it toward God.[12]

On the Solemnity of St. Joseph in 1990, the Vatican's Congregation for Divine Worship and the Discipline of the Sacraments (CDWDS) approved the second edition of the same book, with a

[8] Ibid.

[9] Ibid.

[10] Francisco Gil Hellín, *Concilii Vaticani II synopsis in ordinem redigens schemata cum relationibus necnon Patrum orationes atque animadversiones: Constitutio de Sacra Liturgica Sacrosanctum concilium* (Vatican City: Libreria Editrice Vaticana, 2003), 491.

[11] Benno Cardinal Gut, Decree, Prot. N. R 23/969, 19 March 1969.

[12] Schemata 157, p. 6.

further "enrichment"[13] of its introduction, rites, and prayers and complying with some changes in the Code of Canon Law, which had been revised in 1983. Among those who worked on the revision were Gy and Mazzarello, who had also contributed to the first edition, along with members of the CDWDS.[14]

Whereas the English translation of the first edition was published almost immediately, the English translation of the second edition was delayed for many reasons, largely due to a change in the Vatican's translation policy[15] and the primacy given the work on the third edition of the Roman Missal. The United States Conference of Catholic Bishops (USCCB) requested a number of local adaptations, some to put the book in conformity with the Spanish translation approved for use in the United States in 2010.[16] The conferences of Australia and of England and Wales published their revised books ahead of the USCCB, whose adaptations required more consideration.

The new book, then, is new for two reasons: it includes material that the first book did not contain, and the translation of the material that had already appeared in the first book was revised according to new norms.

The historical evidence for the liturgical celebration of matrimony is scattered through many sources, notably the Verona,[17] Gelasian,[18] and Gregorian[19] sacramentaries of the sixth, seventh, and

[13] Eduardo Cardinal Martínez, Decree, Prot. N. CD 1068/89, 19 March 1990.
[14] Jean Evanou, "Commentarium," *Notitiae* XXVI (1990): 310–11.
[15] Congregation for Divine Worship and the Discipline of the Sacraments, "Fifth Instruction 'For the Right Implementation of the Constitution on the Sacred Liturgy of the Second Vatican Council'," in *Liturgiam authenticam* (On the Use of Vernacular Languages in the Publication of the Books of the Roman Liturgy), http://www.vatican.va/roman_curia/congregations/ccdds/documents/rc_con_ccdds_doc_20010507_liturgiam-authenticam_en.html.
[16] *Ritual del Matrimonio* (Collegeville, MN: Liturgical Press, 2010). The paragraph numbers match those in the English edition for the United States, so this commentary makes no further footnote to this source.
[17] *Sacramentarium Veronense*, ed. Leo Cunibert Mohlberg, Rerum Ecclesiasticarum Documenta (Rome: Herder Editrice e Libreria, 1978). Hereafter Verona.
[18] *Liber Sacramentorum Romanae aeclesiae ordinis anni circuli*, ed. Leo Cunibert Mohlberg (Rome: Casa Editrice Herder, 1981). Hereafter Gelasian.
[19] *Le Sacramentaire Grégorien, ses principals forms d'après les plus anciens manuscrits*, ed. Jean Deshusses (Freiburg: Éditions Universitaires, 1979). Hereafter Gregorian.

eighth centuries, respectively, though some elements originated from more obscure origins. After the Council of Trent, the Roman Missal was revised in 1570,[20] but the Roman Ritual was not completed until 1614.[21] The ritual covered a variety of circumstances, from Sunday Mass to baptisms to exorcisms. At times, though, its organization strains logic: weddings are found after funerals. The Missal included a Mass for spouses, one of the options for Mass on a wedding day.

Prior to the post–Vatican II revision, a couple's wedding took place first, and then, if there was a Mass, it followed, and the nuptial blessing took place only within Mass. The ritual contained the rubrics and words of the wedding, while the Missal contained the rubrics and prayers of the Mass and nuptial blessing. Even today, a priest needs two books: the Missal for the wedding Mass and the *Order of Celebrating Matrimony* (OCM) for specific parts of the wedding.

The OCM contains much more than elements of a wedding Mass. For example, it includes directions for a wedding without Mass, as well as prayers for an engagement and wedding anniversary.

This book offers a paragraph by paragraph commentary on the English translation of the second edition of the Vatican's OCM. The reader will derive most benefit with a copy of the ritual book at hand. Although this book traverses the academic fields of liturgy, history, translation, and custom, it hopes to help the church celebrate well, in meaning and in symbol, the immeasurable mystery of inseparable love.

---

[20] *Missale Romanum ex decreto SS. Concilii Tridentini restitutum summorum pontificum cura recognitum* (Vatican City: Typis Polyglottis Vaticanis, 1962). Hereafter *Missale Romanum*. All translations of excerpts of this work into English are by the author. The last section of the 1962 edition puts the page numbers within brackets. Subsequent footnotes referencing this section reflect this usage.

[21] *The Roman Ritual in Latin and English with Rubrics and Plainchant Notation: The Sacraments and Processions*, trans. and ed. Philip T. Weller, vol. 1 (Boonville, NY: Preserving Christian Publications, 2007). Hereafter *Roman Ritual*. All translations of excerpts of this work from Latin into English are by the author.

The Title

The revised English translation carries a new title. The first edition was called *Rite of Marriage*,[1] and the second is *The Order of Celebrating Matrimony*. There has been no change to the Latin title of the post–Vatican II book; both editions are *Ordo celebrandi matrimonium*.[2]

Prayers and rubrics for the ceremony have appeared in liturgical books under many different titles. The sixth-century Verona Sacramentary called it *Incipit uelatio nuptialis*,[3] or "The Veiling of the Bride Begins [Here]." The custom of veiling the bride was known as early as Popes Siricius (+399) and Innocent I (+417), whereas Paulinus of Nola (+431) told of veiling both the bride and the groom.[4] Isidore of Seville (+636) says that the very word that has come into English as "nuptial" refers to the veil: "The verb *obnubere* means 'to cover.' Hence, . . . [these] women are called *nuptae*, because they veil their faces, just as clouds [*nubae*] cover the sky."[5]

By the seventh century, the Gelasian Sacramentary included a collection of prayers titled *Incipit accio nupcialis*, or "The Nuptial Act Begins [Here]."[6] The eighth-century Gregorian Sacramentary's

---

[1] *The Rites of the Catholic Church* (Collegeville, MN: Liturgical Press, 1990), 715. Hereafter *The Rites*.

[2] *Editio typica* (Vatican City: Typis Polyglottis Vaticanis, 1972); and *Editio typica altera* (Vatican City: Typis Polyglottis Vaticanis, 1991).

[3] Verona 1105 supra.

[4] Kenneth W. Stevenson, *To Join Together: The Rite of Marriage* (New York: Pueblo Publishing Company, 1987), 22–23.

[5] Mark Searle and Kenneth W. Stevenson, *Documents of the Marriage Liturgy* (Collegeville, MN: Liturgical Press, 1992), 118.

[6] Gelasian 1443 supra.

Hadrian Supplement used the heading *Orat[io]n[es] ad sponsas ve-landas*,[7] or "Prayers for Veiling Women Who Have Been Promised." The English word "spouse" comes from the Latin word for making a promise.[8] The Roman Ritual of 1614, a product of the Counter-Reformation, changed the title to defend the doctrine that there are seven sacraments, not two, as the Protestant Reformers held. It called the ceremony *Ritus celebrandi matrimonii sacramentum*,[9] or "The Rite of Celebrating the Sacrament of Matrimony." Some editions called it *Ritus administrandi matrimonii sacramentum*, or "The Rite of Administering the Sacrament of Matrimony," stressing the juridical nature of the ceremony and the active role of the priest.[10]

After the Second Vatican Council, the Consilium's study group approved its first draft of the revised ceremony on August 25, 1966, under the title *Ritus celebrandi matrimonii sacramentum intra missam*, or "The Rite of Celebrating the Sacrament of Matrimony within Mass."[11] The second draft of February 8, 1967, changed the title to *De sacramento matrimonii*,[12] or "On the Sacrament of Matrimony." The third draft of March 24, 1967, simplified the title to *De matrimonio*, or "On Matrimony."[13] The final draft of March 21, 1968, changed it back to *De sacramento matrimonii*,[14] explaining that "the title de Matrimonio [sic] follows the traditional arrangement of the Roman Ritual, which has been done for the rite of funerals"[15] by the same study group.

---

[7] Gregorian 833 supra.

[8] Adrien Nocent, "The Christian Rite of Marriage in the West," in *Handbook for Liturgical Studies IV: Sacraments and Sacramentals*, ed. Anscar J. Chupungco (Collegeville, MN: Liturgical Press, 2000), 277.

[9] *Roman Ritual*, 460.

[10] Michael Driscoll, "Marriage and Mozart: Ritual Change in Eighteenth-Century Vienna," in *Ars Liturgiae: Worship, Aesthetics and Praxis: Essays in Honor of Nathan D. Mitchell*, ed. Clare V. Johnson (Chicago: Liturgy Training Publications, 2003), 89.

[11] *Consilium ad exsequendam Constitutionem de Sacra Liturgia, Coetus a Studiis* 22–23, Schemata 183, p. 1. Hereafter, Schemata.

[12] Schemata 204, p. 1.

[13] Schemata 221, p. 1.

[14] Schemata 280, p. 1.

[15] Ibid., p. i.

In the end, the Vatican's Congregation must have decided that including the word "sacrament," appropriate for a catechetical book, was unnecessary for the title of the liturgical book.

The Congregation made an early distinction between "rites" and "orders." An order was an entire book containing a series of rites. Thus the subheading "The Rite of Matrimony" refers to the marriage ceremony that takes place within the entire *Order of Celebrating Matrimony*. The second edition makes this change in English. The book used to be called *Rite of Marriage*, but now it is called an "order," in keeping with other liturgical books.

Considerable discussion concerned the best English translation for the word *matrimonium*. The International Commission on English in the Liturgy (ICEL) has been charged with working out the translations for submission to the conferences of bishops and the subsequent approval of the Vatican.[16] ICEL preferred to keep the word "marriage" in the title. It distinguished "matrimony" as a sacrament from "marriage" as a ritual. The *Catechism of the Catholic Church*, for example, consistently uses the Latin word *matrimonium* for its treatment of the sacrament,[17] but the English translation has "matrimony" for the title of that section[18] and in every reference to the sacrament,[19] but it favors "marriage" as a translation throughout the rest of the section, especially in paragraphs pertaining to married life and to the wedding.[20] Similarly, the Code of Canon Law consistently uses the word *matrimonium*, which is rendered "marriage" in English.[21]

---

[16] See http://www.icelweb.org/whatis.htm. The author of this book serves as a facilitator for the biannual meetings of the commission, and information about ICEL's commission meetings comes from his personal experience; hence, such remarks carry no footnotes.

[17] *Catechismus Catholicæ ecclesiæ* (Vatican City: Libreria Editrice Vaticana, 1997), 1601–1666.

[18] *Catechism of the Catholic Church*, 2nd ed. (Washington, DC: United States Conference of Catholic Bishops, 1997), 1601 supra. Hereafter CCC.

[19] Ibid., 1620, 1623, 1638 supra, 1641 supra, 1641, 1642, 1644, 1647, and 1661.

[20] 1621, for example.

[21] *The Code of Canon Law Latin-English Edition*, trans. Canon Law Society of America (Washington, DC: Canon Law Society of America, 1983), canons 1055–1165. Hereafter Canon.

The USCCB, however, which received the translation from ICEL as *The Order of Celebrating Marriage*,[22] wanted a change. As reported in the newsletter of the USCCB's Committee on Divine Worship, "It was recommended that the title use 'Matrimony' to highlight the book as a liturgical ritual (*i.e.*, the Sacrament of Matrimony) for the beginning of a lifelong commitment of one man and one woman."[23] Indeed, according to other news coverage, the American bishops sought a way to show that the trend toward the legalization of unions between two men or two women, commonly called "gay marriage," was different from the Catholic definition of marriage.

> Springfield, Illinois, bishop Thomas Paprocki rose to make an amendment that the bishops revise the texts to replace each use of the word "marriage" with the word "matrimony," saying that was a closer translation of the Latin original.
>
> Referencing the approval of marriage equality in fifteen states, Paprocki also said what the bishops mean when they say the word "marriage" is "different than what our society is saying now."
>
> "The word marriage has now been co-opted," he said. "I think we have to recognize that reality . . . and then make some distinctions about what we mean by matrimony."
>
> New Orleans archbishop Gregory Aymond, who leads the bishops' committee responsible for spearheading the translations, said his divine worship committee did not support making that change.
>
> "We believed it was better to use [the words] interchangeably, otherwise it could be construed that we are admitting defeat" on the redefinition of the term marriage, Aymond said.
>
> Paprocki's initial amendment was voted down by the bishops in a firm voice vote. Paprocki then proposed they change the word "marriage" to "matrimony" in the title of the rite, which the bishops approved by 114–95.[24]

---

[22] *Newsletter: United States Conference of Catholic Bishops Committee on Divine Worship* XLIX (November–December 2013): 48.

[23] Ibid., 47.

[24] Joshua McElwee, "Bishops Overwhelming Approve Continuing Liturgy Translations," *National Catholic Reporter*, November 12, 2013, http://ncronline .org/blogs/ncr-today/bishops-overwhelmingly-approve-continuing-mass -translations.

Father Andrew Menke, associate director of the USCCB's Secretariat for Divine Worship, observed, "The bishops felt that the word 'matrimony' has a more sacred connotation than 'marriage.' They thought the change was important in the American context, where we've seen attempts to redefine what marriage even means."[25]

Apparently the CDWDS agreed, and in all the official versions sent to all English-speaking conferences of bishops, the word in the title changed from "Marriage" to "Matrimony."

This creates a discrepancy with the revised English translation of the Missal's third edition, where one finds the prayers and antiphons for the Mass "For the Celebration of Marriage." The prayers are located in the collection of ritual Masses, a section that did not exist in the pre–Vatican II Missal because so few sacraments of the Catholic Church were celebrated during Mass. Instead, that missal put its Mass *Pro sponsis* among the Votive Masses.[26] At first, the post–Vatican II Lectionary and the first editions of the missal retained the title *Pro sponsis* in their new section of ritual Masses. The first English translation of the Missal, which favored a recognizable vocabulary, called it the "Wedding Mass."[27] The third edition of the Missal changed the title to *In celebratione matrimonii*,[28] which now appears in English as "For the Celebration of Marriage."[29] The English word "matrimony" has never appeared in the title until the second edition of the post–Vatican II ritual.

Throughout its history, then, the title of this celebration has stressed different points: the mystical veiling of the bride, her

[25] Barry Hudock, "Changes Coming to Marriage Rite in the U.S.," *Our Sunday Visitor*, December 16, 2015, https://www.osv.com/OSVNewsweekly/Perspectives/Columnists/Article/TabId/797/ArtMID/13632/ArticleID/18852/Changes-coming-to-marriage-rite-in-the-US.aspx.

[26] *Missale Romanum*, p. [75].

[27] *The Sacramentary* (New York: Catholic Book Publishing Co., 1974), 840.

[28] *Missale Romanum ex decreto sacrosanti ecumenici Concilii Vaticani II instaurato auctoritate Pauli PP. VI promulgata Ioannis Pauli PP. II cura recognitum*, Editio Typica Tertia (Vatican City: Typic Vaticanis, 2008), 1023.

[29] *The Roman Missal Renewed by Decree of the Most Holy Second Ecumenical Council of the Vatican, Promulgated by Authority of Pope Paul VI and Revised at the Direction of Pope John Paul II* (Collegeville, MN: Liturgical Press, 2011), 1177. Hereafter Roman Missal.

promised status, the doctrine of sacramentality, the role of the priest, the sacredness of the quotidian, and opposition to same-sex marriage.

Introduction

The second edition's expanded introduction is one of its most important features, especially the first eleven paragraphs, which can serve as a foundation for premarital catechesis on the Catholic Church's theology of matrimony.

The 1952 edition of the Roman Ritual devoted a comparable introduction to juridical concerns about marriage—the publication of the banns and the search for impediments, for example.[1] The post–Vatican II study group took a new approach.

> After a certain general expression of the mystery of Christian matrimony, as was often done in different sections of the post-Tridentine Roman Ritual, it must certainly treat special problems of the pastoral liturgy of matrimony, as well as adaptations that may be useful or necessary.
>
> For if certain episcopal conferences desire to use a future Roman Ritual in their own territory, that Ritual will have to preserve and keep intact local customs, and resolve difficulties pertinent to certain cultures, and offer sufficient space all over for adaptation.[2]

As Annibale Bugnini explained, this introduction was the Consilium's first, so it lacked some of the style, content, and scope evident in later contributions.[3] The previously published *Ordo* for ordinations did not include an introduction, so the one for

---

[1] *The Roman Ritual in Latin and English with Rubrics and Plainchant Notation: The Sacraments and Processions*, trans. and ed. Philip T. Weller, vol. 1 (Boonville, NY: Preserving Christian Publications, 2007), 454–60. Hereafter, *Roman Ritual*.

[2] Schemata 182a, pp. 3–4.

[3] Annibale Bugnini, *The Reform of the Liturgy 1948–1975*, trans. Matthew J. O'Connell (Collegeville, MN: Liturgical Press, 1990), 699.

matrimony was the first among the revised liturgical books. These introductory paragraphs went through several drafts before the publication of the first edition, and the second edition has completely expanded the contents, even rearranging some paragraphs. It has four sections that now match the introductions of other ritual books: The Importance and Dignity of the Sacrament of Matrimony (1–11), Duties and Ministries (12–27), The Celebration of Marriage (28–38), and Adaptations to Be Prepared by the Conferences of Bishops (39–44). This diligent work has made a more satisfying introduction to the book.

In the commentary that follows, the heading numbers match those in the OCM. Although they usually include more than one paragraph, the numbers are considered "paragraphs" for the sake of this commentary. The first paragraph of the commentary usually summarizes the relevant content of the ritual book.

I. THE IMPORTANCE AND DIGNITY OF THE SACRAMENT OF MATRIMONY

The first eleven paragraphs treat the importance and dignity of marriage. In addition to their reliance on the Pastoral Constitution on the Church in the Modern World (*Gaudium et Spes*),[4] they derive insight from the apostolic exhortation *Familiaris Consortio* of Pope John Paul II.[5]

1.

Matrimony has its origins in creation itself, yet it has a higher degree among Christians who number it among the sacraments. This is a new opening paragraph to the entire book. The original opening has been moved to paragraph 6.

---

[4] Second Vatican Council, *Gaudium et Spes* (Pastoral Council on the Church in the Modern World), hereafter GS, http://www.vatican.va/archive/hist _councils/ii_vatican_council/documents/vat-ii_const_19651207_gaudium -et-spes_en.html.

[5] John Paul II, *Familiaris Consortio* (On the Role of the Christian Family in the Modern World), hereafter FC, November 22, 1981, http://w2.vatican.va /content/john-paul-ii/en/apost_exhortations/documents/hf_jp-ii_exh _19811122_familiaris-consortio.html.

The new paragraph 1 describes marriage as a covenant and a partnership between a man and a woman, and places it within the spheres of natural and canon law. Its first footnote stands upon canon law's definition of marriage.[6] The revised Code of Canon Law came into force over a decade after the first edition of the OCM. The second edition thus links these books at the very first opportunity.

One of the earliest testimonies to marriage among Christians is from the second-century "Letter to Diognetus," which simply states that Christians marry like everyone else.[7] This opening paragraph makes a similar point: the Christian practice is based on natural law.

2.

Marriage is established by the free, irrevocable consent of both spouses. It requires complete fidelity and indissoluble unity. This paragraph 2 consists of only the first two sentences of the original paragraph 2, whose final sentence has been moved to the second half of the new paragraph 5.

As noted in the original edition, the ideas come from GS, one of the last documents of the Second Vatican Council. Its number 48 breaks into four paragraphs. The first of these opens with the idea of the conjugal covenant of irrevocable consent and closes with the expectation of total fidelity and unbreakable oneness in marriage.[8]

According to Gy, the original first four paragraphs of the OCM were written by Lécuyer,[9] a member of the Congregation of the Holy Spirit, a theology teacher at the Lateran University in Rome,[10] and an original member of group 22.[11] Lécuyer had placed a heading on each of these paragraphs. This one he called "The Nature of

---

[6] Canon 1055, §1.
[7] "Office of Readings, Wednesday, Fifth Week of Easter," in *Liturgy of the Hours*, vol. 3 (New York: Catholic Book Publishing Co. 1976), 840–41.
[8] GS 48.
[9] Schemata 204, p. [i].
[10] Bugnini, *Reform of the Liturgy*, 947.
[11] Ibid., 579.

Matrimony."[12] The headings were removed from the final draft[13] and never appeared in the published book.

ICEL had discussions about the word "spouses," which appears many times in the translation, sometimes referring to the bride and groom before they are married as wife and husband. The Latin uses words for the couple in both senses—the bride and groom about to be married and the couple that have now been married. Here and in other places of the OCM, the English word "spouses" has remained.

3.

Both marriage and conjugal love are ordered toward the procreation and education of children. Children even contribute to the good of the parents. This new paragraph 3 is the first half of the original paragraph 4. Hence, it was also authored by Lécuyer, who gave it the heading "On Matrimonial Fecundity."[14]

The footnote from the end of this paragraph in the first edition has been moved here in the second edition, showing that these ideas also derive from GS. The final section of GS 48 states that children contribute to making their parents holy.[15] The second edition, however, does not properly credit an additional source, GS 50. Ciappi, the theologian of the papal household and adviser on the final draft of the OCM, shared a few pertinent thoughts with the cardinal secretary of state Amleto Giovanni Cicognani, who agreed with him, prompting Ciappi to write to the Consilium.[16] Ciappi was suggesting a reference to GS 50: "Children are really the supreme gift of marriage and contribute very substantially to the welfare of their parents."[17] This idea was added to Lécuyer's draft and included in the original paragraph 4 in the same place where it now concludes paragraph 3. The paragraph in the first edition used one final footnote to cite both numbers from GS. In

---

[12] Schemata 204, p. [1].
[13] Schemata 280, p. 2.
[14] Schemata 204, p. [1].
[15] GS 48.
[16] Schemata 280 addendum, p. 2.
[17] GS 50.

shortening that paragraph to create this one for the second edition, the connection between these lines and GS 50 was lost.

4.

God the creator established marriage with laws and a blessing. Its existence is not the product of human decision but of its divine origins.

This new paragraph has no equivalent in the first edition. Having established the natural origins of marriage, its nature and expectations, the introduction now stresses its divine establishment. Footnotes show the influence of Jesus' teaching in the Gospel of Matthew, the words of the nuptial blessing, and GS once again. Perhaps the editors of the second edition felt that changes in society's practice of marriage erroneously presumed that people and governments were free to redefine a divine institution.

5.

Christ willed that marriage be restored to its primordial form and raised it to the dignity of a sacrament. This paragraph has been built from the final sentence of the original paragraph 2 along with new material based on two biblical passages.[18] The introduction makes here its first direct reference to Christ. Building on arguments from natural law and from fundamental theism, the exposition now becomes explicitly Christian.

The second half comes from the paragraph in the first edition that Lécuyer had called "The Nature of Matrimony." Breaking open his paragraph in this way permits a more expansive treatment of its themes.

6.

At Cana, Christ foreshadowed the hour of his new and eternal covenant, in which he offers himself to the church as Spouse.

This paragraph is new to the second edition. It develops the theme of the Christian view of human marriage, a sacrament of the union of Christ and the church. The paragraph dips once again

[18] 2 Cor 5:17 and Matt 19:6.

into GS 48. This is the only paragraph in the OCM that refers to the paschal mystery, a concept much prized by the documents of Vatican II.

7.

The marriage between two baptized persons is always a sacrament. This new paragraph is inspired by GS,[19] but it especially comes from ideas in the 1981 apostolic exhortation of John Paul II, FC.[20] There he states that Christ sacrificed himself on the cross for the sake of his bride the church. Marriage is specifically a sacrament of the covenant in the blood of Christ. Interestingly, this paragraph does not state that the marriage of someone who is unbaptized is not a sacrament. As will be noted below in the commentary on Chapter III, those who prepared the revised marriage ceremony after the council did not take a position on that point.

8.

Christian spouses participate in the unity and fruitful love of Christ and the church. They help each other become holy.

This is the former paragraph 1, the very beginning of the first edition of the same book—word for word, with identical footnotes. It has been moved here where the previous paragraphs better prepare for it. Lécuyer drafted this and gave it the heading "On Matrimony and the People of God."[21]

9.

Through the Holy Spirit Christian spouses nurture and foster their union in dignity and charity. This is the former paragraph 3, relocated and expanded.

In this location, the argument of the introduction flows more logically, as it tells more of the responsibilities of spouses. The paragraph has been expanded both at the beginning and at the end. The reference to the Holy Spirit is new, along with the intimation of Ephesians 5:25, that Christ loved the church and gave

[19] GS 48.
[20] FC 13.
[21] Schemata 204, p. [1].

himself up for her. This balances with the new conclusion to the paragraph that focuses on unity and commitment, avoiding adultery and divorce. The allusion to GS 49, which mentions these two ways that marriage can be "profaned," is also new.

Lécuyer drafted the original paragraph, which he called "On Conjugal Love."[22] His draft was abbreviated before the publication of the first edition and then was expanded with the second. Ironically, Lécuyer had included GS's allusion to adultery and divorce at the end of his paragraph, where it had been removed, and where now it has been reinserted.

10.

Couples glorify the Creator as they carry out procreation with generous, human Christian responsibility. This is the second half of the former paragraph 4 drafted by Lécuyer and given the heading "On Matrimonial Fecundity."[23] The first half now stands as paragraph 3.

The second half of this paragraph is new. It alludes to Paul's exhortation that couples should develop a spirit of sacrifice or self-control.[24] It also makes a final reference to GS.[25]

11.

God called the couple and continues to call them to a marriage that is united and bears witness to the world. This is a new paragraph, and it concludes the first section of the revised introduction.

Two references build the content. It opens with another nod to John Paul's FC.[26] It concludes with a generous quotation from Tertullian (+225). Whereas John Paul's ministry postdates the first edition of the OCM, Tertullian's work was well known at the time. This citation supports arguments for the existence of an early Christian marriage ceremony. After all, Tertullian mentions the joining in the context of an offering and a blessing. The English

[22] Ibid.
[23] Ibid.
[24] 1 Cor 7:5.
[25] GS 50.
[26] FC 51.

translation expands the Latin word *oblatio* into the term "sacrificial offering," which invites a eucharistic interpretation. It would be dangerous, however, to extrapolate too much from this because evidence for early Christian wedding ceremonies is scarce. The same quotation appears in the CCC, without the word "sacrificial" and with other minor differences.[27] Tertullian's lovely words to his wife deserve their honored place here.

II. DUTIES AND MINISTRIES

This entire section of the introduction is new to the second edition of the OCM. Nearly all its footnotes come from two works that appeared after publication of the first edition: FC and the Code of Canon Law. The introduction has been restructured to imitate the outline of those in other ritual books, which all include a section on duties and ministries.

12.

Many people share responsibilities for the preparation and celebration of marriage—the couple, the clergy, and the entire community. This new paragraph footnotes John Paul II again,[28] where he explores the importance of lifelong and proximate preparation for marriage. But it could also have cited *Lumen Gentium*, the Dogmatic Constitution on the Church from the Second Vatican Council. Its development of the people of God explains the sacramental responsibilities of the collective whole of those who have been baptized.[29]

13.

The bishop regulates the celebration and pastoral care of marriage throughout the diocese. This paragraph refers back to the same place in FC where John Paul II challenges the church to

---

[27] CCC 1642.

[28] FC 66.

[29] *Lumen Gentium* (Dogmatic Constitution on the Church) 11, hereafter LG, http://www.vatican.va/archive/hist_councils/ii_vatican_council/documents /vat-ii_const_19641121_lumen-gentium_en.html.

offer fitting marriage preparation.[30] Its more specific source is the section from the Code of Canon Law that treats the pastoral care and preparation for marriage.[31] Although the OCM does not say so explicitly, canon law suggests that the bishop consult men and women of proven experience and skill.[32]

This is the first usage of the term "engaged couples," the translation of which ICEL had discussed along with the word "spouses" in paragraph 2. Noting that the *Book of Blessings* includes a blessing for an "engaged couple,"[33] the term was retained.

14.

Pastors provide assistance by preaching and catechesis, marriage preparation, the liturgical celebration of marriage, and continued support of married couples. This paragraph is nearly a complete re-presentation of one in the Code of Canon Law.[34] This section of the introduction is moving through the hierarchy of the church from bishops through pastors.

15.

Couples should allow sufficient time for preparation. This paragraph contains no footnotes and received no comments from anyone reviewing the translation. It offers practical advice growing from the previous paragraphs about preparation. No period of time is specified because the needs change from one country to another, one diocese to another, one parish to another, and even one couple to another.

The author of this paragraph surely realized that few couples would actually read the introduction to the OCM. Hence, it takes the slant that the engaged should be made aware of a timetable in advance. In practice, parishes often make their expectations known on the cover of the weekly bulletin or on their website.

---

[30] FC 66.

[31] Canons 1063–1072, especially 1063–1064.

[32] Ibid., 1064.

[33] *Book of Blessings* (Collegeville, MN: Liturgical Press, 1989), 195–214. Hereafter BB.

[34] Canon 1063.

16.

Pastors should welcome engaged couples and nourish their faith. Although this entire section on duties and ministries is new to the second edition, this brief paragraph appeared in the first edition as paragraph 7. It, however, was even shorter there. The second edition adds a motive for pastors: They are to be led by the love of Christ. Whereas the preceding paragraph garnered no comments, this one has a long history of controversy.

This paragraph argues that the sacrament of matrimony demands faith, but it footnotes a paragraph in SC, which says that all sacraments presuppose faith.[35] It is true that matrimony does but no more than the rest.

Due to the rearrangement of paragraphs in the introduction, this has become the OCM's first footnote to SC, and to a very significant spot: not the section that laid out the council's plans to revise the marriage ceremony, but its overview of the spiritual nature of sacraments.

Hidden within the opening words is the fear that pastors will not conduct preparation with love, yet this is what they are called to do. Many pastors feel inconvenienced by marriage preparation and weddings. Hurt by years of experience, some feel that couples take advantage of them and the church. Yet here and—as will be seen at OCM 45—in the introductory rites, the liturgy reminds pastors of their human and ministerial responsibility to show love, kindness, and mercy to those who are entering a life based on the same virtues. Blessed are those couples planning to profess their love publicly who meet happiness and support from the pastor and parish staff.

Today's pastors are not alone. Their predecessors, those who prepared the postconciliar marriage ceremony, expressed concern that some couples lacked faith.

The first draft of this paragraph in 1967 added the opinion that if faith was lacking, it was not permitted to celebrate marriage.[36] A redraft the same year went further: If there is no faith, "even if there is no doubt concerning validity, it is not permitted to cele-

---

[35] SC 59.

[36] Schemata 204, p. 2. It first appeared as paragraph 6.

brate the sacrament of matrimony."[37] The preparatory group added a footnote:

> See in another historical context these words of Pope Benedict XIV *De Synodo Dioeces.* VIII, 14, 15: "Since Matrimony between faithful Christians is one of the seven sacraments of the new law instituted by Christ the Lord, and one of their number that is called sacraments of the living, no one may celebrate it in a state of mortal sin without grave sacrilege."[38]

In prefatory comments to this draft, the study group explained matters this way:

> For the most part this introduction is taken whether by word or intention from the conciliar Constitutions on the Sacred Liturgy (n. 11), on the Church (n. 1), and on the Church in the Modern World (nn. 2, 3, 4). Nevertheless, n. 7 deserved special consideration because the gravest difficulties may be found in some nations concerning the defect of faith of many who are engaged.
>
> The doctrine of this paragraph number, namely concerning the conditions required for receiving any sacrament of the living, seems to be common and is exposed with great clarity by Pope Benedict XIV. Attending to the pastoral difficulty, the text was edited most carefully, by the work of the most excellent Bishop Carlo Colombo, with the approval of the most excellent Bishop Pericle Felici.[39]

Colombo was the bishop recommended for theological questions on the advice of the Secretariat of State. Felici was a member of the Consilium who eventually became a cardinal.

When the final draft was prepared in 1968, the prefatory notes restated the problem.

> There are given then some indications of the principal pastoral difficulties that arise in relation to Matrimony, especially when the spouses have been baptized but do not believe, a case particularly

---

[37] Schemata 221, p. 6. It became paragraph 7 here.

[38] Ibid.

[39] Ibid., 3.

pressing in certain countries (cf. art. 7 and the particular Note on this article), or when Matrimony is celebrated between one party who is Catholic and another who is not (art. 8: text proposed by the Secretariat for Christian Unity).[40]

Even this explanation seemed insufficient, so Colombo added in Italian an extraordinary three-page "Special Note on Article VII," concerning the pastoral problem of faith.

1. The Roman Ritual, published in 1614 by Pope Paul V, in force up to our own age, carries an important doctrinal, canonical and pastoral "Introduction," which has been in particular one of the fonts of the Code of Canon Law of 1917 for the sacraments. The Constitution *Sacrosanctum concilium* underlines at article 63 the importance of an "Introduction" of this type, and in particular its "social moment," and it establishes what should apply also to the rituals prepared by the episcopal conferences, with appropriate adaptations.

2. As the constitution *Sacrosanctum concilium* recalls in the preamble of the chapter "On the Sacraments," the fact of being sacraments "of faith" pertains to the nature of the sacraments: "They do not only presuppose faith, but they also nourish, strengthen and express it with words and actions; therefore, they are called sacraments of faith" (art. 59). If the sacraments presuppose faith, each one in the manner particular to it, it is necessary that priests in the preparation of those betrothed to matrimony nourish their faith, and, if necessary, commit themselves to the effort of reawakening it or giving it rebirth.

3. But one needs to take account at this point of a difficulty, perhaps rather rare in the regions that have remained more Christian, but on the other hand frequently in dechristianized countries: the existence of persons, baptized in the Catholic Church, who not only have abandoned every religious practice, but been notoriously "nonbelievers," or who, before matrimony, formally declare to the priest that they renounce the faith, still demanding that their matrimony be celebrated in the church. This can happen with one of the engaged or with both.

---

[40] Schemata 280, p. i.

4. This problem is grave, and it has been considered such by faithful and clergy. The faithful are scandalized in seeing that the liturgical texts, which, above all when they are said in the vernacular language, express and presuppose faith, have been used also for the matrimony of those who have renounced it. Non-Catholics wonder if the Church attributes true importance to its own liturgy and even its own faith. Priests have been profoundly disturbed by the fact of having to exercise their ministry under these conditions. It seems indispensable then to remedy this difficulty at the time of the revision of the marriage Ritual.

5. When only one of the two parties, both having been baptized in the Catholic Church, renounces the faith, while the other is a believer, it seems advisable, in the interest of the believing party, that the sacramental rite be celebrated in church according to the liturgical rules. The following observations pertain therefore only to the case in which both parties renounce the faith.

6. If the priest has not been able in any way to awaken or sustain the faith of the betrothed, it is desirable that they not be obliged "to follow the Catholic form of matrimony" (see Code of Canon Law 1099), because that would be contrary to their conscience (see the Declaration on Religious Liberty, 2), which renounces the faith expressed in the liturgy of the sacrament.

It would even seem appropriate in this case to refuse the betrothed the "Catholic form of matrimony," so as not to cause scandal to the faithful and an obstacle to the evangelization of non-Christians.

7. In this case two baptized Catholics, who have both renounced the faith, if they marry, would find themselves in the same situation of two baptized non-Catholics who renounce the sacramental value of matrimony: Matrimony thus realized, *when it possesses all the conditions necessary to be a true matrimony, is a sacrament*, even if the spouses do not know its exact religious meaning.

However, there is a close difference between the situation of two baptized Protestants who deny the sacramental value of matrimony and two baptized, non-believing Catholics: In reality, for the first, marriage is a religious act, while for the second this religious meaning is totally absent.

8. Article 7 of the "Introduction" is the following: "First of all, pastors should foster and nourish the faith of the engaged, for the sacrament of matrimony presupposes faith (see the Constitution on the Sacred Liturgy, 59).

"However, if it is established that both spouses renounce their faith, even if the serious intention of contracting matrimony is established, it is not permitted to celebrate the rite of the sacrament of matrimony."

The second paragraph pertains to the problem above. Because it touches not only the pastoral aspect of matrimony in its celebration, but the doctrine and the discipline of the Church, this problem should eventually be treated by the competent dicasteries, *examining the possibility of matrimony for unbelieving Catholics without the obligation of the canonical-liturgical form.*[41]

Predictably, the complete text of the draft of the rite that accompanied this note contains the same wording for paragraph 7.[42]

Ciappi, who had already opposed earlier drafts of paragraph 7, objected: "The Church always has an obligation to remind 'unbelieving Catholics' of their duties as *de iure* 'subjects,' even if they behave as though they were not such."[43] He wrote this formal response:

> Given that the most eminent Cardinal Secretary of State has proposed a correction, I would think it appropriate to agree with him. Also in the Sacred Congregation for the Doctrine of the Faith it is preferred to examine individual cases, rather than give a general dispensation, which one could easily abuse. On the part of the Church, in fact, there always remains the obligation to invite "unbelieving Catholics" back to their duty as "subjects" *de iure*, even if they are such *de facto*, but behave as if they are not.[44]

When the much-debated paragraph 7 appeared in the first edition of the OCM, the Vatican's lighter touch prevailed: "First of all, pastors should foster and nourish the faith of the engaged, for the sacrament of matrimony presupposes and demands faith." The sentence carried then—as it does in the second edition—a footnote to SC 59. It removed the controversial statements about refusing

[41] Schemata 280, pp. iii–v. Colombo's authorship is established in Schemata 180 addendum, p. 1, and in Bugnini, *Reform of the Liturgy*, 701.
[42] Schemata 280, p. 3.
[43] Letter of May 3, 1968, cited by Bugnini, *Reform of the Liturgy*, 701.
[44] Schemata 280 addendum, p. 2.

to celebrate the rite of the sacrament and that unbelieving Catholics might contract a valid marriage outside the canonical-liturgical form. The only hint of the debate was in the insertion of the word "demands."

Omitting the controversy did not end it. Several years later, John Paul II returned to the theme of the engaged unbelieving Catholic,[45] which gave the editors of the second edition of the OCM a source for addressing the pastoral dilemma. It appears in paragraph 21.

When the second edition repositioned paragraph 7 as paragraph 16, it also clarified its structure and identified the love of Christ as a motivation. The result is the fruit of much care. It reminds those involved with ministry for the engaged that they are helping people with spiritual preparation, not merely wedding preparation.

17.

The engaged couple should be given catechesis about marriage and the family, as well as the rites, prayers, and readings of the wedding ceremony. This paragraph has reworked and relocated the former paragraph 5.

In its original placement, it came after the four paragraphs drafted by Lécuyer. The second edition has amplified those into a broader presentation of the church's teaching on marriage through eleven paragraphs. This paragraph suggests that those eleven may serve as the foundation for catechesis.

The first draft from 1967 had only one sentence here.[46] It primarily pertained to the homily, suggesting that it make a connection to the Scriptures, in accord with SC[47] and *Inter œcumenici*,[48] a 1965 instruction by the Sacred Congregation of Rites on implementing SC, which came at an early stage of the renewal; many of its sections were superseded by later documents. There was nothing wrong with the original paragraph 5 of the first edition of the OCM, but

---

[45] FC 68.

[46] Schemata 204, p. 2.

[47] SC 52.

[48] *Inter œcumenici* 54, hereafter IO, https://www.ewtn.com/library/CURIA/CDWINOEC.HTM.

its treatment of the homily was already contained in what became the second edition's paragraph 57, so the focus of paragraph 17 has shifted from the homily to catechesis.

The second half of the original paragraph 5 came from the last draft of the study group.[49] Most of this was retained in the second edition, though moved to this paragraph. It fits better within a presentation of duties and ministries.

18.

Before marriage, Catholics should receive the sacrament of Confirmation unless they face some grave inconvenience. The engaged are also encouraged to receive the sacraments of penance and the Eucharist.

This paragraph, entirely new, fits the spirit of paragraph 16, which sees marriage as a time to nourish faith through the sacraments. It also turns to the Code of Canon Law, still unrevised at the time of the first edition of the OCM, to explain the requirements concerning confirmation.[50]

Surprising to some will be the statement that confirmation completes initiation because, in practice, many receive confirmation after baptism and before first communion. The 1971 decree of the Sacred Congregation for Divine Worship announcing the new post–Vatican II Order of Confirmation says that initiation is brought to completion with the help of confirmation.[51] The CCC notes in several places that confirmation completes baptismal grace, or that it completes *baptism,* but not "initiation."[52] Even so, the usage of this term probably means that confirmation brings baptism to greater perfection; it cannot imply that anything is somehow lacking in baptism.

In practice, many Catholics go unconfirmed, and many of them get engaged. Confirmation is not absolutely required for a Catholic wedding, though some people think it is. The definition of a

---

[49] Schemata 280, p. 3.

[50] Canon 1065.

[51] Sacred Congregation for Divine Worship, "Decree" Prot. n. 800/71s., in *Order of Confirmation* (Washington, DC: USCCB, 2016), v.

[52] CCC 1285, 1288, 1290, 1291, 1304.

"grave inconvenience" is a matter of judgment. It probably means some chronic reason why the Catholic was unable to be confirmed, not a persistent carelessness on the part of the potential candidate for confirmation. Still, the past is past. If being confirmed before the wedding would cause a grave inconvenience, then the Catholic(s) may have to wait to be confirmed. Nonetheless, they should strive to receive confirmation at the earliest opportunity.

Another "grave inconvenience" could be that the unconfirmed person is already married outside the church. Which sacrament should come first? Canon Law forbids anyone in "manifest grave sin" to receive communion.[53] By extension, a person married outside the church is ineligible for confirmation. Hence, the marriage should be convalidated first, and then the person, being in a valid marriage, becomes eligible for confirmation.

Advice to celebrate the sacrament of penance is modified by the expression "if necessary." Only those in mortal sin are obliged to confess in the sacrament of penance.[54] Nonetheless, confession is advisable for venial sins.[55]

19.

For a valid and licit celebration of marriage, no canonical obstacle can stand in the way. Those responsible conduct a reasonable investigation of the couple's background.

The paragraph turns again to the revised Code of Canon Law,[56] published after the OCM's first edition. Hence, this paragraph is new, though it restates word for word the content of the pertinent canon.

20.

Pastors should evangelize the couple's love in the light of faith, showing how even the canonical requirements promote faith and love, as well as the Christian family.

---

[53] Canon 915.
[54] Canon 988 §1.
[55] Canon 988 §2.
[56] Canon 1066.

This paragraph is entirely new and does not quote any other document. It builds on the theme of fostering faith in marriage preparation. Perhaps, in a section that is steeped in canons, this paragraph reminds pastors of the spiritual good toward which the canons aspire.

ICEL considered several options for the translation of the phrase "prevailing attitudes." At first, using a cognate from the Latin, it had proposed "popular attitudes." Some objected to the word "popular" because it seemed to have a positive connotation, whereas the sentence warns about such mentalities. The commission agreed and proposed several alternatives, including "widespread," "common," "different," "differing," and "various." In the end, "prevailing" seemed best to catch the meaning.

21.

If the couple reject what the church intends, the pastor is not permitted to celebrate the sacrament. This paragraph squarely returns to the themes put forth in the draft of the first edition's paragraph 7.

In the second edition, the topic became easier to address because John Paul II had elaborated the difficulties in FC.[57] There, he reviewed many of the themes that lay behind the first paragraph 7, making it seem that he had reviewed the material previously discussed. The pope's conclusion is what the new paragraph 21 cites: A pastor refuses to celebrate the sacrament of marriage only when the couple have prevented it. The spirit of John Paul's exhortation, however, is to avoid the predicament and to disdain laying down further criteria. He knew the pastoral, canonical, ecumenical, and spiritual problems.

Anecdotally, many pastors will say that the number of marriages has decreased in the early part of the twenty-first century. Indeed, perhaps some couples have realized that they do not want what the church offers, and they are seeking a wedding elsewhere.

ICEL wondered if saying pastors "must" take note of the situation was too strong. Other proposals were made, including "should" and "ought," but in the end the strong word remained.

---

[57] FC 68.

22.

Other special cases exist. A Catholic may marry another Christian, a catechumen, an unbaptized person, or a person who has rejected faith. Such cases deserve pastoral care and have recourse to competent authority.

This paragraph gives more detail on the pastoral situations that arise especially with Catholic marriage. It echoes the concerns that surfaced during the 1960s. Instead of presenting solutions as the study group was hoping, however, it wisely directed the reader to the basic principles of pastoral care and church authority. This paragraph is new to the second edition.

23.

It is appropriate for the same priest to prepare the couple, celebrate the Mass, preach, and receive their consent.

This new paragraph offers practical advice for pastors. Their work will bear better fruit if they work individually with couples from their preparation through the celebration of the wedding. Special mention of the homily here implies that his familiarity with the couple will inspire the message he delivers. This paragraph presumes that there will be a wedding Mass, but even in cases when there is not, the same advice holds.

The Ceremonial of Bishops suggests that bishops should occasionally bless marriages.[58] It uses the verb "bless" because it foresees the possibility that a priest will celebrate the Mass, whereas the bishop in choir dress presides.[59] He may of course celebrate the Mass and, in either case, he offers the nuptial blessing.[60] The church especially encourages the bishop to celebrate the weddings of the poor.[61] His ministry should show no favoritism to the wealthy.

Normally the bishop is assisted by the parish priest and a deacon, along with other ministers.[62] In practice, few bishops can take

[58] *Ceremonial of Bishops* (Collegeville, MN: Liturgical Press, 1989), 598. Hereafter CB.

[59] CB 601.

[60] CB 611.

[61] CB 598.

[62] CB 600.

an active part in marriage preparation, but for those who can, the advice of paragraph 23 holds. Every priest (and deacon for that matter) will exercise better ministry by guiding the couple's spiritual formation before preaching and presiding at the wedding.

24.

A deacon with faculties may preside at weddings and give the nuptial blessing.

The second edition pays greater attention to deacons, whose ministry flowered after the publication of the first edition. (The third edition of the Roman Missal similarly treats the diaconate more expansively than its predecessors did.) This new paragraph affirms two points that developed in the postconciliar church. In dioceses, deacons widely received the faculty to preside at weddings. In the universal church, deacons were authorized to give the nuptial blessing. In the past, as will be seen, this blessing was given only by the priest and only during Mass. Also, as will be seen in the commentary to Chapter II, the practice of having a deacon witness a marriage during a Mass has been questioned.

ICEL's first draft said that the deacon presided at the celebration, "including" the nuptial blessing. The wording in Latin is stronger, however, so the translation matches it: He presided "without omitting" the blessing.

25.

A bishop may delegate a layperson to assist at marriages under the correct circumstances. These include a vote by the conference of bishops and permission from the Apostolic See. The layperson should be capable of offering instruction to the engaged and of performing the liturgy.

This new paragraph comes almost completely from the Code of Canon Law, which authorizes lay witnesses to receive the consent of the couple.[63] This pastoral consideration assists parts of the world where priests and deacons are scarce, yet faithful Catholics desire a sacramental marriage. The couple still manifest their

---

[63] Canons 1112 §2; 1108 §2.

consent, and the assisting layperson receives it in the name of the church.

ICEL chose the words "a shortage" of priests and deacons, even though the Latin says *Ubi desunt sacerdotes et diaconi*. More literally, this means "Where priests and deacons are lacking." One could argue that it could mean a circumstance where they are not present for other reasons. The historical, canonical, and pastoral sense of the original, however, probably does refer to a shortage of numbers.

26.

Other laypersons and indeed the entire Christian community may participate in the preparation and celebration of matrimony. They bear witness to the faith and show God's love to the world.

Although this paragraph is new, its intention is shared by other postconciliar liturgical books. Their introductions contain sections showing how the entire Christian community is involved in all the rituals. Here, the faithful are expected to participate through preparing the couple and in bearing witness to God's love. This brief paragraph could prompt a good brainstorming exercise within any parish: How do all the members prepare, celebrate, and bear witness to matrimony?

27.

The wedding usually takes place in the parish church of the engaged persons, but the bishop or pastor may permit another location.

Even in Latin, this sentence does not prejudice the parish of the bride or the groom. Neither is listed first. The parish of either one of the engaged is considered the normal place. By custom the church of the bride held preference, but not here.

Exceptions are permitted by law, and indeed this paragraph was put into place after the revised Code of Canon Law explained the possibility.[64] A summary of the canon now appears here as paragraph 27.

---

[64] Canon 1115.

Regarding the place of a wedding, a bishop should not prefer the use of a private chapel or a home but rather the cathedral or a parish church.[65] This will avoid any appearance of favoritism or outward show. By celebrating in a public space the bishop demonstrates the ecclesial nature of the wedding and grants ready access to the local community's participation.[66]

III. THE CELEBRATION OF MARRIAGE

The third section of the revised introduction takes up liturgical matters for the celebration of the sacrament. This parallels a similar section in other introductions developed after the first edition of the OCM.

The Preparation

The first part of this section treats the preparation for the wedding. It focuses less on the couple's preparation for married life, which the previous sections have addressed. The introduction now turns attention to what is most on the mind of most of the engaged: the wedding.

28.

Marriage is ordered to the increase and sanctification of the People of God, so it is fitting that members of the community participate. More than one couple may be married in a single ceremony. A wedding may take place during Sunday Mass.

This new paragraph introduces the section with a focus on the participation of the community. Marriage is an intimate, personal experience, but it has an effect on the entire community.

The first edition's paragraph 11 presumed the possibility of weddings taking place at a parish Sunday Mass. That paragraph has been reworked and re-presented as 31 in the second edition. But the possibility of celebrating at the parish Mass is now introduced here.

---

[65] CB 598.
[66] Ibid.

The French translation of the OCM in Canada carries this same paragraph; however, its lectionary, published as a separate slim volume, differs in order to account for the widespread custom that forbids weddings there on Sundays:

> According to the custom established in Canada, marriage can only be celebrated on a weekday, whether with or without the eucharist. As to the possibility of celebrating marriage on Sunday, one must hold to diocesan directives.[67]

The first edition's paragraph 38 included directions for how a wedding of more than one couple may take place. Its parallel still appears as number 58 in the second edition. But the option is now first presented here in the introduction to the OCM.

29.

The celebration must be diligently prepared with the engaged couple. Weddings normally take place at Mass, but the pastor may propose a celebration outside of Mass. The couple should help choose the readings, the form of consent, the blessing of rings, the nuptial blessing, the intentions for the universal prayer, and the music.

The final draft of the former paragraph 5 included a section that carried into the first edition.[68] It called for the catechesis of the couple on the sacrament and its rites, prayers, and readings, as expressed in the second edition's paragraph 17. The new paragraph 29 does more. It urges not only the catechesis of the couple but also their participation in choosing texts for the wedding.

No other ritual book so urges the inclusion of those celebrating the sacrament in its preparation. Some parish leaders have long encouraged couples to select the readings for the wedding with the help of published aids.[69] Other publications have enlisted the

---

[67] *Lectionnaire pour la célébration du mariage* (Ottawa: Conférence des évêques catholiques du Canada, 2011), 3.

[68] Schemata 280, p. 3.

[69] For example, Paul Turner, *Preparing the Wedding Homily: A Guide for Preachers and Couples* (Chicago: Liturgy Training Publications, 2003).

couple's help in selecting presidential prayers and blessings. Many couples have strong opinions about the music. Perhaps some couples will take the time to review all the options presented in this paragraph, but many will not know about them. Nonetheless, the OCM encourages their engagement in the liturgical planning of parts of the wedding.

This paragraph is one of many that mentions the homily based on the readings. The former paragraph 5 also made this recommendation. The introduction to the Lectionary for Mass says of every homily that it should be based on the sacred text.[70] Nonetheless, the General Instruction of the Roman Missal says that it may also draw from the Ordinary or the Proper of the Mass.[71]

Paragraph 29 does not encourage the couple to choose from the presidential prayers—the collects, prayers over the offerings, prefaces, and prayers after communion. These apparently are left to the discretion of the celebrant.

The forms of consent are few, but the couple should have a voice in which one they will say. If they pray over the nuptial blessings, they may find one that speaks more directly to them. They may certainly have ideas about the intentions for the universal prayer. Part of their marriage preparation could include identifying groups and needs for whom they wish everyone to pray on their wedding day.

The final sentence of this paragraph says that local customs may be observed if they are appropriate. This opens the door to a variety of customs such as deeply rooted Hispanic and Filipino traditions (the *lazo*, the *arras*, and the *velación*, for example), persistent customs such as the unity candle, and future trends inconceivable at the publication of the OCM. Pastors and parishes will probably establish limiting policies that interpret words such as "local," "customs," and "appropriate," but the OCM has created a space for some personalization of the wedding ceremony beyond the contents of the liturgical book.

---

[70] *Lectionary for Mass*, Second Typical Edition (Collegeville, MN: Liturgical Press, 1998). Introduction to the *Lectionary for Mass* 24. Hereafter LM.

[71] *The General Instruction of the Roman Missal* 65. Hereafter GIRM.

New to the postconciliar church is that marriage would take place at Mass. In the past the ceremony happened just before Mass or completely outside of Mass. To have the wedding *during* the Mass was an innovation found in paragraph 6 of the first edition of the OCM. It has become such a deep tradition within the post–Vatican II church that the freshness of this approach may be overlooked.

30.

The chants of the Mass, especially the responsorial psalm, and all the other music should express the faith of the church.

The emphasis on the responsorial psalm is curious but welcome. Many couples hire soloists for the music at their wedding without thinking much of congregational music, which is important. Perhaps the psalm is mentioned because it forms part of weddings both within and without Mass, whereas other chants of the Mass do not.

Many couples want to hear popular secular music at their weddings, especially songs that have come to represent their love because of the text or the occasion on which they have enjoyed them. In a culture where prerecorded music dominates live music even for the national anthem, many parishes struggle to convince couples that live congregational singing should be constitutive of a Catholic wedding. This new paragraph should help because it holds up faith as the criterion for judging wedding music. If those planning the wedding think of the typical parish Sunday Mass as a guide, they will find a path to appropriate wedding music.

31.

Church decorations should express the festive nature of the celebration, yet no favoritism should be shown to individuals or classes of persons.

The first part of this paragraph is new, a welcome agreement with the general practice that a church will be decorated for a wedding. Many parishes establish limiting guidelines because some couples have specific or extravagant desires that may conflict with the usage of the space or its immediate reconversion to an appearance suitable for the Sunday Mass. In some countries, wedding decorations are fairly standard, but in the United States the variety can be substantial, if not competitive. The caution seems apt, then, that decorations should not give the ostentatious appearance of wealth. Most churches already carry some decoration for their observance of a given season, and the couple may consult with parish decorators to learn how the church will look at the time of year chosen for the wedding.

As noted in paragraph 23, the bishop should also avoid showing favoritism to certain groups. Even so, weddings are a place where societal expectations are high, and a couple who chooses not to spend lavishly on clothes and decorations will be taking a countercultural stand. They will need a strong spiritual center.

The second part of this paragraph is based on the concerns of favoritism expressed in the first edition of the OCM. There, paragraph 10 quoted directly from SC 32, which now appears only as a citation in the footnote. The revised paragraph instead expresses specific concerns about decorations and the role of bishops in limiting shows of favoritism.

32.

Weddings that take place on days of penitence, especially during Lent, should take account of the nature of the day. Weddings are not permitted on Good Friday or Holy Saturday.

The CB offers the same advice,[72] which is somewhat surprising in that the book concerns the liturgies of bishops, whereas this paragraph from it pertains to pastors. Perhaps the CB realizes that pastors do more preparation and conversation with the couple than bishops typically do. Although the OCM only mentions Lent as a penitential season, the CB adds Advent to its concern.

Some Catholics still have the mistaken impression that weddings cannot take place during Lent. They may. The only days prohibited are Good Friday and Holy Saturday, when the sacraments are not to be celebrated, except for reconciliation and the anointing of the sick.[73] In the past, some priests have conducted convalidations of weddings on Holy Saturday for couples who were married outside the church but are now eligible for sacraments. The practice is prohibited. Pastorally, a priest should convalidate a couple's

---

[72] CB 604.

[73] "Friday of the Passion of the Lord [Good Friday]," in Roman Missal, 1.

marriage at the earliest opportunity. Normally in this situation, one of the parties is a Catholic, and that party could return to the sacraments as soon as the convalidation takes place. The other party may be baptized or received into the church later.

Regarding the penitential nature of certain days and their impact on the splendor of wedding arrangements, pastors may advise the couple, but they may not get very far. Unless the couple are already long in the habit of conducting a Lent of penance and sacrifice, for example, the concept of a less extravagant wedding will seem strange to them. For the sake of the parish, however, the conversation is worth having. A parish that has decorated the church for repentance should still be able to recognize the character of the season.

The Rite to Be Used

The third part of the introduction carries two subheadings—one on the preparation of the celebration and the second on the rite to be used. These divisions did not appear in the first edition of the OCM, and that may have contributed to widespread ignorance about the rules governing which rite should be used on which occasion. Many pastors and parish staffs have overlooked these out of a desire to help the couple celebrate a meaningful ceremony. Every wedding takes place within the context of a liturgical year and a liturgical day. From the parish's perspective, this will govern some of the choices open to the couple.

33.

Marriage may be celebrated within or without Mass, and the appropriate chapter of the OCM is used. A wedding without Mass still includes a Liturgy of the Word.

This brief paragraph is new to the second edition. The edition actually includes chapters treating some other circumstances, but the primary concern here is the decision pertaining to the celebration of Mass. If the wedding includes Mass, the liturgical calendar comes more strongly into play.

34.

When the ritual Mass "For the Celebration of Marriage" is used, white or festive vestments are worn. In 1965, the Vatican had already permitted the use of this Mass during "closed times."[74] The nuptial blessing, not the votive Mass, was forbidden during Advent and Lent. Now, however, on the Table of Liturgical Days, any celebration listed under the first four paragraphs supersedes the ritual Mass of marriage with its presidential prayers and readings. The ritual Mass may be celebrated on Sundays in Ordinary Time except at parish Masses. (The same is true of the Second Sunday of Christmas in those conferences that retain the Epiphany of the Lord as a holy day on January 6.) The rules restricting the use of the ritual Mass pertain to the lectionary as well as the Missal. On some occasions, however, when the ritual Mass is set aside, one of its readings may replace a reading of the stronger day.

This paragraph now makes an important link to the Table of Liturgical Days. The first edition of the OCM listed specific days of conflict in its paragraph 11, but it did not account for everything in the Table. The CB lists the information accurately but differently.[75] Happily, the third edition of the Roman Missal now matches paragraph 34 of the OCM.[76] This link to the Table of Liturgical Days, found in the front of the Missal among the Universal Norms on the Liturgical Year and the Calendar, provides better cohesion between these liturgical books.

The celebrant wears vestments that are white or of a festive color when he uses the ritual Mass. The CB concurs.[77] When a wedding takes place within a celebration of higher rank, however, the vestment color for that day takes precedence.

Here is how the Table of Liturgical Days ranks the first four categories:

1. The Paschal Triduum ranks first. This should be obvious, but no special wedding Mass may take place between the evening of Holy Thursday and the night of Easter Sunday. In fact, no Mass may take place on Good Friday or Holy Saturday. There is no law forbidding a couple to exchange their consent during the Evening

---

[74] IO 75.

[75] CB Appendix 3.

[76] Roman Missal, "Ritual Masses: V. For the Celebration of Marriage." Hereafter Roman Missal, Marriage.

[77] CB 603.

Mass of the Lord's Supper or during a Mass on Easter Sunday or its Vigil. Pastorally, though, there would have to be a very good reason for this to happen during a parish's celebration of the Triduum. Baptisms often take place during the Easter Vigil or even at Mass on Easter Sunday. Theoretically, a wedding could as well. But it is probably not the best way for the couple or the parish to celebrate the Triduum.

2. Ranking second on the table are several specific days: Christmas, Epiphany, Ascension, and Pentecost; then Sundays of Advent, Lent, and Easter; Ash Wednesday; weekdays of Holy Week from Monday through Thursday before the evening Mass; and finally the days within the Octave of Easter.

This greatly affects any wedding Mass scheduled on the Saturday evening of Epiphany or of Advent, Lent, and Easter. It even applies to a wedding during the day on the Saturday after Easter. All those days rank second on the Table, well ahead of weddings. If a wedding Mass takes place on a Saturday night in Advent or Lent, for example, the prayers and readings of the season take precedence; the celebrant wears purple. If the wedding is on the first Saturday afternoon after Easter, the readings and presidential prayers from Saturday of the Octave of Easter are proclaimed.

This applies to a wedding Mass. If the wedding takes place outside of Mass, there is no conflict, and the readings and prayers of the wedding may be used.

3. Solemnities appear in two groups. The first is the collection of solemnities that appear on the general calendar, as well as All Souls' Day.

This would affect, for example, a Saturday afternoon wedding Mass on the following days: Mary Mother of God (January 1), Saint Joseph (March 19), the Annunciation (March 25), the Nativity of John the Baptist (June 24), Saints Peter and Paul (June 29), the Assumption of the Blessed Virgin Mary (August 15), All Saints' (November 1), All Souls' (November 2), and the Immaculate Conception (December 8).

It also would affect a Saturday night wedding Mass on solemnities of the Most Holy Trinity, the Most Holy Body and Blood of Christ (Corpus Christi), and Our Lord Jesus Christ the King of the Universe.

The Solemnity of the Sacred Heart of Jesus always falls on a Friday, but if a wedding Mass were scheduled for that day, the Sacred Heart readings and prayers would take precedence.

4. The second group of solemnities pertains to the location: the principal patron of the place, city, or state; the dedication or anniversary of dedication of the church where the wedding is scheduled; the title of one's church; or the title, founder, or patron of a religious order or congregation.

If the parish is named St. Anthony, for example, then a wedding Mass that takes place on June 13 in that church uses the readings and prayers of the Mass for St. Anthony. If a wedding Mass takes place on August 25 anywhere in the city of St. Louis, the saint's day trumps the ritual Mass for marriage. Every parish is supposed to observe the anniversary of its dedication as a solemnity each year with a special Mass, using the readings and prayers of the solemnity. Often this goes unobserved because of ignorance of the day or of the custom. If a wedding Mass is scheduled on that day, however, the couple should hear the collect for the anniversary of the dedication of the building where they have gathered for the wedding. If the parish is staffed by Franciscans, and the wedding takes place on October 4, then the prayers and readings for St. Francis are to be used.

This may strike many people as incomprehensible, but the sacrament of matrimony takes place within a living parish community that participates in a general church calendar. Although the couple will tell you that this is the most important day of their lives, certain elements of the day are subject to other forces. There are secular conflicts as well—weddings take place on somebody's birthday, on Valentine's Day, or unexpectedly in the midst of the local baseball team's championship series. No wedding takes place in isolation. It is always part of the fabric of church and social life.

No matter which Mass is used, the nuptial blessing is included. This was important to note because in the preconciliar liturgy the nuptial blessing was forbidden at Mass during Advent and Lent, on All Souls' Day, and during the Triduum.[78] In those cases the

---

[78] *Missale Romanum*, p. [75].

blessing transferred to a more convenient Mass after the wedding had taken place.

Participating at a Saturday evening wedding Mass always fulfills a Catholic's Sunday obligation. The Code of Canon Law says that the precept is satisfied by assistance "at a Mass" either on the day or the evening of the preceding day.[79] Any Mass will suffice. It is up to the priest to provide the correct Mass. On a Sunday in Ordinary Time, he chooses the ritual Mass of marriage (as long as it is not a parish Mass). On other occasions he should celebrate the appropriate Sunday Mass. A Saturday night wedding without Mass, of course, does not fulfill the precept; Catholics who participate at such a service are expected to participate at Mass the same weekend.

The paragraph concludes with a pastoral note about the readings at a Mass that takes precedence over the wedding Mass. Because of the importance of the word of God for understanding matrimony, one of the readings from the marriage lectionary may replace a reading assigned to the liturgical day. Comparing this with OCM 56, however, this permission refers only to the preceding sentence about Sundays in Ordinary Time, and not to every celebration in the first four numbers of the Table of Liturgical Days. When these paragraphs, composed in 1991, were copied into the third edition of the Missal for its ritual Mass of marriage in 2002, the final paragraph permitting the substitution of one reading was omitted. Its retention here is probably an oversight, corrected in OCM 56.

Most of this information is repeated in OCM 54 and can be found in the Missal's ritual Mass for marriage.

35.

The main elements of the wedding are the Liturgy of the Word, the consent of the engaged, the nuptial blessing, and communion. The paragraph footnotes two documents of the Second Vatican

---

[79] Canon 1248 §1.

Council, but both references pertain to the sacraments in general, rather than matrimony in particular.[80]

This is the former paragraph 6, moved into a section of the introduction that deals with the liturgy, carefully edited. The original remarked that marriage usually takes place within Mass; that is now part of paragraph 29. The first edition said that the priest asks and receives the consent, and that he gives the nuptial blessing; both mentions of the priest have been omitted because a deacon may also perform these functions. The first edition referred to the special blessing on the bride, but the second edition more correctly calls it the nuptial blessing (over both bride and groom). The final phrase was clarified to show that not just any charity, but "their" charity is nourished, referring to communicants. The second edition also changed the unusual usage of the first person plural in the original paragraph ("lifts us up") to the third person plural ("they are raised up").

Couples who look forward to the exchange of consent and the rings, the nuptial blessing, and the *lazo* may consider these alone to be the "main elements" of the celebration. Nonetheless, many will take an interest in the Liturgy of the Word when given an opportunity, and Catholics asking for a nuptial Mass generally do anticipate sacramental communion.

36.

When a Catholic marries a baptized non-Catholic the ceremony without Mass should be used. The local ordinary may permit the celebration within Mass. The universal norms for sharing eucharistic communion still apply. Marriage between a Catholic and a catechumen or non-Christian uses the appropriate rite in Chapter III.

Many Catholic weddings take place at Mass even if one party is a baptized non-Catholic. A bishop may grant this permission in general to the priests to whom he gives faculties.

The Rite of Matrimony without Mass often provides the better environment. Many of those participating will not know when to stand, sit, or kneel. They will be unfamiliar with the responses to

---

[80] *Apostolicam Actuositatem* (Decree on the Apostolate of the Laity) 3, http://www.vatican.va/archive/hist_councils/ii_vatican_council/documents/vat-ii_decree_19651118_apostolicam-actuositatem_en.html; LG 12.

the dialogues. They will not be sharing eucharistic communion. A wedding without Mass puts the entire congregation on more equal footing and invites a fuller sign of unity.

This paragraph updates the former paragraph 8, which declared that the general law does not allow communion to a non-Catholic. The norms for sharing communion with non-Catholic Christians, however, were revised after the first edition of the OCM. As found in the Vatican's Directory for the Application of Principles and Norms on Ecumenism,[81] they are not so exclusive.

The directory first addresses cases involving danger of death; otherwise, it refers a diocesan bishop to norms established by the conference and in consultation with the local competent authority of the other church or ecclesial community. "Catholic ministers will judge individual cases and administer these sacraments only in accord with these established norms, where they exist. Otherwise they will judge according to the norms of this Directory."[82]

Regarding eucharistic communion at a wedding, the directory states, "Although the spouses in a mixed marriage share the sacraments of baptism and marriage, Eucharistic sharing can only be exceptional and in each case the norms stated above concerning the admission of a non-Catholic Christian to Eucharistic communion as well as those concerning the participation of a Catholic in Eucharistic communion in another Church, must be observed."[83]

The conditions are "that the person be unable to have recourse for the sacrament desired to a minister of his or her own Church or ecclesial Community, ask for the sacrament of his or her own initiative, manifest Catholic faith in this sacrament and be properly disposed."[84]

In short, the circumstances when a baptized non-Catholic may receive communion at a Catholic wedding exist, but they are quite few, primarily because they would require a situation in which the

[81] The Pontifical Council for Promoting the Unity of Christians, http://www.vatican.va/roman_curia/pontifical_councils/chrstuni/documents/rc_pc_chrstuni_doc_25031993_principles-and-norms-on-ecumenism_en.html.
[82] Ibid., 130.
[83] Ibid., 160.
[84] Ibid., 131.

non-Catholic Christian does not have persistent access to a minister of his or her own community.

The Mexican edition inserts two more paragraphs to the introduction at this point.

> 37. This ritual includes the rite of the blessing and giving of the *arras*, a great tradition in Mexico, which serves to express unity of life and of possessions established between the couple.
>
> 38. Because the "imposition of the *lazo*" is customary in many regions of Mexico, this ritual proposes that this take place immediately after the universal prayer (or the creed, when it is said), but it may be kept until the nuptial blessing. The giving of a bible, for those regions in which this custom exists, may be done at the end of the giving of the *arras*.[85]

As will be seen, most of these appear in the US edition in OCM 67B, 71B, and their parallels: 101A, 103B, 133, and 137.

37.

Pastors, who care for all people, should give special attention to those who never or rarely take part in celebrations of matrimony or of the Eucharist. If one or both of the spouses are among those at the margins of faith, this norm applies first to them.

This reworks and repositions the material in the former paragraph 9. It started as an outreach to those who participate rarely or who have lost faith.[86] The wording was taken almost directly from the first chapter of the most recent draft of the Order of Christian Funerals, which had been approved in 1966.[87] That paragraph was slightly reworked and moved to the introduction. In English editions of the funeral order, it can be found in the appendix.[88] The version in the second edition of the OCM includes nonpracticing spouses as those for whom pastors should especially be solicitous.

---

[85] *Ritual del Matrimonio* (México, D. F.: Obra Nacional de la Buena Prensa, A. C., 2011), 35. Hereafter Ritual (Mexico).

[86] Schemata 204, p. 2, there as paragraph 8.

[87] Schemata 142, p. 1 (paragraph 3). The reference is footnoted in Schemata 221, p. 6 (paragraph 9).

[88] "*Ordo Exsequiarum* Introduction" 18, *Order of Christian Funerals* (Collegeville, MN: Liturgical Press, 1990).

38.

For a wedding within Mass, the usual arrangement of a sanctuary should include the placement of the OCM and the rings for the couple. Optional are a bucket of blessed water and a sprinkler, as well as a chalice of sufficient size for sharing the blood of Christ at communion.

This new paragraph provides information similar in content to other liturgical books. It offers practical advice for preparing the sanctuary before the celebration. Although it appears that the rings are obligatory, if they are incompatible with a particular culture, they may be omitted or replaced by another sign.[89]

A bishop will need his miter and pastoral staff, even if he is just presiding and not celebrating the Mass.[90] The English translation of the CB misspeaks when it says that these will be necessary for the nuptial blessing. Rather, they are needed for the final blessing.[91] If he is presiding, the bishop wears an alb, pectoral cross, stole, and white cope,[92] though presumably the color of the cope would change if the Mass requires a different one. The CB, which was republished in 2008 long after the second edition of the OCM in Latin, does not note here that the blessed water is optional.

This paragraph updates information from the preconciliar ceremony. Because the marriage took place before Mass, the only items needed for the ceremony were the book, the vessel for blessed water, and the sprinkler.[93]

IV. ADAPTATIONS TO BE PREPARED BY THE CONFERENCES OF BISHOPS

This final section of the introduction collects and expands information from paragraphs 12–18 of the first edition concerning adaptations. Introductions to other liturgical books conclude in a similar way.

---

[89] OCM 41, 5.
[90] CB 599.
[91] CB 611, 613.
[92] CB 601.
[93] *Roman Ritual*, 460.

39.

Conferences of bishops may adapt this ceremony according to regional needs with the approval of the Apostolic See.

The need for such adaptations has always been acknowledged. Even the pre–Vatican II book noted that praiseworthy customs and ceremonies could be retained wherever they were in use.[94]

This is the first of several paragraphs that Seumois had originally edited because of his expertise in the needs of mission countries and the value of adaptation.[95] His draft cited SC 77 and 78, which dealt specifically with adaptations to the marriage ceremony.[96] The study group's commentary on this paragraph explained,

> Since the Constitution on the Sacred Liturgy itself grants special importance to adaptations as to the administration of the sacraments (art. 39) and especially as to the rite of matrimony (art. 77), a place has been left for "legitimate adaptations to different . . . peoples, especially in the missions" (art. 38), whether "in the structures of the rites," or "in the rubrics." (art. 38)[97]

This second draft of the introduction also included a reference to SC 63, which gave additional guidelines for cultural adaptations.[98] The third draft contained a further clarification:

> The second chapter of the Introduction gives some directives on the preparation of rituals particular to matrimony, especially in mission countries, according to articles 63 and 67 of the Constitution on the Sacred Liturgy, and recalls the faculty given by the conciliar Constitution to episcopal conferences to prepare their own ritual of matrimony.[99]

The second edition of the OCM has trimmed paragraph 12 and repositioned it here as paragraph 39. It has clarified the canonical language and put the references to SC 63 and 77 in a footnote.

---

[94] Ibid., 464–66.

[95] Gy, [Letter to the Consilium], Schemata 204, [i]. Bugnini, *Reform of the Liturgy*, 697.

[96] Schemata 204, p. 3, there as paragraph 11.

[97] Schemata 221, p. 3.

[98] Ibid., p. 7, there as paragraph 12.

[99] Schemata 280, p. i.

40.

The conferences of bishops formulate adaptations, adapt and supplement the introduction as necessary, in order to foster the participation of the faithful, to prepare versions of the texts and music to accommodate languages and cultures, and to arrange the materials in a usable form.

This new paragraph gathers into one place the responsibilities of the conferences of bishops. Their work still needs the approval of the Apostolic See.

SC famously called for the full, conscious, active participation of the people.[100] That call found its way into the introductory material here, as it did in the introductions of other liturgical books, such as the Rite of Baptism for Children,[101] the Rite of Confirmation,[102] the Rite of Pastoral Care of the Sick,[103] and in the congregational catechesis expected for the Rite of the Dedication of a Church and an Altar.[104]

The introduction permits conferences to rearrange the material in the book to make it more user-friendly for the celebrant. The translations in force for the episcopal conferences of England and Wales,[105] French Canada,[106] and Colombia,[107] for example, have moved some of the material such as alternative collects from the appendices into the body of the book, where they are more accessible to the presider. Other conferences did not receive permission for that particular change, such as those of Australia[108] and Mexico.[109]

[100] SC 14.

[101] Rite of Baptism for Children 32, in *The Rites*, 376.

[102] Rite of Confirmation 3, in *The Rites*, 479.

[103] Pastoral Care of the Sick 38, in *The Rites*, 787.

[104] Dedication of a Church and an Altar 20, in *The Rites of the Catholic Church*, vol. 2 (Collegeville, MN: Liturgical Press, 1991), 365.

[105] *The Order of Celebrating Matrimony* (London: Catholic Truth Society, 2016). Hereafter OCMEW.

[106] *Rituel Romain de la célébration du mariage* (Ottawa: Conférence des évêques catholiques du Canada, 2011). Hereafter *Rituel Romain*.

[107] *Ritual del Matrimonio* [Cali: Comisión Episcopal de Liturgia, 2004]. Hereafter Ritual (Colombia).

[108] *The Order of Celebrating Matrimony* (Strathfield: St. Pauls, 2015). Hereafter OCMAUS.

[109] Ritual (Mexico).

41.

Regarding adaptations, (1) the formulas may be adapted and supplemented; (2) where options exist, more may be added; (3) the order of the parts may be adapted; (4) the consent may be obtained through questions; (5) the crowning of the bride or the veiling of the spouses may take place; (6) the joining of hands and the use of rings may be omitted or replaced; (7) elements of tradition and cultures may be adopted.

This combines material from several of the first edition's paragraphs. The first two points come from paragraph 13; the third point comes from 14; the fourth point comes from a pastoral note from the original paragraph 45 within the rite; the fifth point comes from paragraph 15, as does the sixth. The seventh is new.

Basic principles had been laid out in the study group's communication that accompanied its first schemata. As the Second Vatican Council had done, the groups looked back to a much-cited paragraph from the Council of Trent. It also looked around at variations already in force.

> Concerning local liturgical customs, the Second Vatican Council repeats the words of the Council of Trent: "If certain provinces use other praiseworthy customs and ceremonies, the Holy Synod strongly desires that these be completely retained" (Constitution on the Sacred Liturgy 77 B = Council of Trent Session XXIV, concerning the Reformation, 1; see Roman Ritual 1952, VIII, II, 6). Indeed from the famous Council of Trent until now, there can be found local usages in the rituals of Matrimony, which often repeat an original one from the Middle Ages: in the expression of consent, in the words of the priest after the consent, in certain prayers and even in the place for blessing and giving the ring to be bestowed; other words of consent are found and contained in the Roman Ritual, for example, in German- or Slavic-speaking nations, in dioceses of Belgium, in the Toledo Ritual, and in English-speaking nations the words of consent are carried out through that most famous formula, which will be treated later under no. 18; the formula "I join you" is not precisely found in the Toledo Ritual, nor has it been accepted anywhere in Germany or in Poland.[110]

[110] Schemata 182a, p. 4.

Paragraph 41 ultimately descends from the draft first edited by Seumois to answer the need for adaptations in missionary countries.[111] For the subsequent draft, immediately following its remarks on SC 38's call to adapt structures and rubrics,[112] the study group further explained,

> As to the structure of the rite of matrimony, a fitting flexibility is proposed in numbers 14 and 15; as to the texts, flexibility is proposed in number 13, whose second part has already been approved by the Fathers for the Order of Funerals.[113]

The introduction to the Order of Funerals had been approved in 1966, and it still includes permission for conferences of bishops "to add different formularies of the same type whenever the Roman Ritual provides optional formularies."[114] Hence, when the ritual provided two or three options, even without specifying "in these or similar words," the Congregation's intent was to permit the free composition of further variations. This principle applied to the OCM whenever it presented multiple options.

The second draft of the introduction added a footnote about adapting and supplementing the formulas. This became the first point in OCM 41 (second edition):

> There may be present, for example, particular difficulties (like polygamy), of which mention will have to be made in the questions before the consent. The actual formula of consent that is proposed, although it may be very favorable among the English-speaking nations where it has been in use for a long time, may perhaps seem too long to other nations and ought to be abbreviated.
>
> In the prayer over the bride, certain adaptations will be useful in some places; for example, in the *Collection* of rites in Germany the omission of the names of the holy women in the Old Testament was

---

[111] Gy, [Letter to the Consilium], Schemata 204, [i]. Bugnini, *Reform of the Liturgy*, 697. In this Schemata, the paragraphs ultimately numbered 14 and 15 for the first edition appear as 16 and 17.

[112] See comments on OCM 39.

[113] Schemata 221, p. 3.

[114] *Order of Christian Funerals*, Appendix, Introduction 22, 3.

seen appropriate; but the words "joined to one bed," which ought to be retained where the danger of polygamy is present, finds perhaps less favor elsewhere.[115]

The fifth point of OCM 41 concerns the option of crowning the bride or veiling the couple. A remnant of the ancient custom of veiling persists in Hispanic and Filipino traditions. The USCCB has made provision for it in OCM 67a.

Crowning, however, is more common in churches of the East. (Veiling also occurred in the East but was probably borrowed from Roman usage.[116]) The Armenian Rite included the blessing and wearing of crowns as early as the fourth century.[117] Gregory Nazianzen (+389) was familiar with the custom of crowning,[118] and he interpreted it as a celebration of victory over concupiscence.[119] John Chrysostom (+407) likewise interpreted the crowns as symbols of the couple's victory over passion.[120] By the tenth century prayers for crowning included formulas such as "The Father blesses, the Son is well pleased, and the Holy Spirit crowns."[121] The twelfth-century formula, "The servant of God N. is crowned," is inspired by the passive voice used in baptismal formulas, "The servant of God N. is baptized."[122]

Theodore the Studite taught that the church should not bless second marriages, even though they were legal, and the rite of crowning could not be repeated.[123] If the crowning at one's first marriage set passions free, a second marriage could not authentically symbolize the crowning of restraint. Thus the crowns achieved

---

[115] Schemata 221, pp. 7–8.

[116] Stefano Parenti, "The Christian Rite of Marriage in the East," in *Handbook for Liturgical Studies*, vol. 4, Sacraments and Sacramentals, ed. Anscar J. Chupungco (Collegeville, MN: Liturgical Press, 2000), 263, citing *In epistolam I ad Timotheum, Hom.* 9, PG 62:546, 51–52.

[117] Stevenson, *To Join Together*, 59.

[118] Ibid., 20.

[119] Parenti, "Christian Rite of Marriage in the East," 256.

[120] Stevenson, *To Join Together*, 21.

[121] Parenti, "Christian Rite of Marriage in the East," 263.

[122] Ibid., 263–64.

[123] Ibid., 268.

some irrepeatable consecratory function, which the Latin Rite long attributed to the nuptial blessing, as will be seen in OCM 74.

Today's Byzantine Rite notes that the crowns recall those with which the martyrs are crowned in heaven. The priest says of the bridegroom, "The servant of God, _____, is crowned unto the handmaiden of God, _____: in the name of the Father, and of the Son, and of the Holy Spirit." He proclaims a similar text as the bride receives her crown. The reader then proclaims an adaptation of Psalm 21 (20):3, which recalls the crowning of the king.[124]

In the Coptic Rite, the crowning follows an anointing of the couple. The priest offers a prayer to God who has crowned saints with imperishable crowns, that he bless the crowns to be placed on the couple. Among the requests is this: "Grant to your servants who will wear these crowns an angel of peace and the bond of love. Strengthen them against all shameful thoughts and indecent desires." The priest also prays for the faithfulness of the children to be born of this union. As he crowns the couple, the choir sings, "Crown them with honor and glory. The Father blesses, the Son crowns, the Holy Spirit sanctifies and makes perfect. Worthy, worthy, worthy are the groom and his companion."[125]

In the Armenian Rite, as the crowns are removed, the priest prays, "[I]nstead of the crowns that pass away may the angel of peace guard them holy and spotless, one in spirit and in counsel."[126] The concluding prayer in the East Syrian Rite asks "that their children may be worthy of the ornaments of this day."[127] Thus, the crowns, which have highlighted the chaste couple's victory over passions, are to inspire a new virtuous generation.

The Italian ceremony permits the crowning of the spouses where this is customary or with permission of the ordinary. It sees the crowning as "a sign of their participation in the royalty of Christ." The priest crosses his arms to place one crown on the

---

[124] Searle and Stevenson, *Documents of the Marriage Liturgy*, 69–70.

[125] Ibid., 93–95.

[126] Stevenson, *To Join Together*, 61.

[127] Ibid., 70.

groom and then the other on the bride, while saying, "N., (servant of God), receive N., (servant of God), as a crown."[128]

OCM 41 permits the crowning of the *bride* where this is customary, but it is not customary in the Latin Rite. And in the Eastern Rite, both bride and groom customarily wear crowns. The permission was included from the early drafts of the postconciliar ceremony,[129] and it found its way into paragraph 15 of the first edition. Perhaps it was another way of expressing a tradition around the veiling of the bride. Or perhaps it intends to offer pastoral care in a circumstance where an Eastern Rite bride marries a Latin Rite groom in a Latin Rite ceremony. Or the mention of the bride may have intended to forge a link with the traditional blessing of the bride. Or this could have been an oversight left uncorrected.

Regarding the sixth point on omitting the rings and the joining of hands, the study group was familiar with exceptions.

> The future Roman Ritual of matrimony should not only keep local customs intact, but also keep in view difficulties proper to any cultures different from European culture. This principle of adaptation, which is enunciated in articles 37–40 of the Constitution, was in use long ago for the liturgy of matrimony. Thus the first Ritual in Japan, in the year 1605, omitted the giving of the ring and changed the rite of the joining of hands (see F.-X. Tsuchiya, S.J., *Das älteste bekannte Missions-Rituale: [The Oldest Known Missions Ritual:] Nagasaki 1605*, Trierer Theologische Zeitschrift 1963, pp. 221–232). The same Holy Office in the year 1892 gave permission to the archbishop of Pondicherry in India of substituting for the nuptial ring a token called *tali*, dangling from the neck of the bride. (*Collectanea S. Propagandae*, 1893, pp. 573–74)[130]

The group wanted these freedoms acknowledged in the introduction, so this part of the former paragraph 15 has been repeated in OCM 41. Both editions of the OCM express considerable openness to adaptations.

---

[128] *Rito del Matrimonio* 78, http://www.liturgia.maranatha.it/Matrimonio/r1/3page.htm.

[129] Schemata 204, p. 3.

[130] Schemata 182a, p. 4.

42.

Conferences of bishops may compose their own marriage rite with the approval of the Apostolic See. The minister must ask for and receive the couple's consent, and the couple must receive the nuptial blessing.

This lightly edits paragraph 17 of the first edition, which required a priest to preside, whereas the second edition tacitly acknowledges the possible ministry of a deacon or assisting layperson. The second edition requires that its introduction be included in any adapted rite, adjusted where necessary to explain the flow of the ceremony that follows.

Traces of this paragraph can be found in the drafts, which required a priest to receive the consent of the couple.[131] The drafts had merely repeated what SC 77 had envisioned.[132] The inclusion of the nuptial blessing in such ceremonies had also come at the request of the Second Vatican Council.[133]

43.

When peoples receive the gospel for the first time, their wedding customs should be considered and preserved intact if they are honorable and do not represent superstitious errors.

This is the former paragraph 16, moved a little later in the introduction probably because it pertains to a more unusual circumstance. The paragraph still cites SC 37, the first of its paragraphs for adapting the liturgy to the cultures and traditions of peoples.

In the drafts, this was another part of the introduction reworked by Seumois, though his was a bit shorter than the final version.[134] The first version was later amplified with one of the explanatory comments that the study had made to accompany its introduction.[135] Its call for preserving customs "intact" was inserted here, where it has endured in this paragraph through the remaining drafts and both editions of the OCM.

---

[131] Schemata 204, p. 4.
[132] SC 77, noted in Schemata 221, p. 3, there as paragraph 16.
[133] SC 78, noted in Schemata 221, p. 9, there as paragraph 17.
[134] Gy, [Letter to the Consilium], Schemata 204, [i].
[135] Schemata 182a, pp. 3–4, cited above.

44.

Among peoples where the marriage ceremony customarily takes place in homes, even over several days, their conferences of bishops may determine if the Catholic sacrament can also be celebrated in homes.

This is the former paragraph 18, which likewise brought the introduction to its conclusion. It has been the final paragraph since its earliest draft.[136] In a commentary, the study group said that in this paragraph "the case is considered of those cultures among which matrimony is accustomed to be celebrated in homes, as was permitted in the Roman Ritual itself up to the 19th century."[137] Once again, the study group made its appeal to adaptation based on previous permissions.

The revised introduction greatly amplifies the one from the first edition. It includes additional resources unavailable at the time, notably the revised Code of Canon Law and John Paul II's apostolic exhortation on families. More significant, it has rearranged the material to match other introductions to liturgical books and to provide a more logical flow of its contents. Editorial corrections have also enhanced the quality of the work.

The chapters that follow show great editorial care as well: attention to titles, subtitles, rubrics, sense lines for spoken texts, the description of the entrance procession, the choice of the Mass and the readings.[138] Although it is believed that Christians held marriage ceremonies at an early date, the earliest extant complete marriage service is found in the fourteenth-century ritual from the Cistercian Abbey of Barbeau in the Diocese of Sens, France.[139] The second edition of the OCM is the latest of its descendants.

[136] Schemata 204, p. 4, there as paragraph 21.
[137] Schemata 221, p. 3.
[138] Evanou, "Commentarium," 313.
[139] Searle and Stevenson, *Documents of the Marriage Liturgy*, 156.

I. The Order of Celebrating Matrimony within Mass

The opening chapter, as in the previous edition, presents the celebration of matrimony within Mass. The Second Vatican Council declared that marriage is normally to be celebrated this way.[1] The Sacred Congregation of Rites strengthened this stance in 1965 while the council was still in session: "Unless there is some good, excusing reason, marriage shall be celebrated within Mass, after the gospel and homily."[2]

Prior to the council, the nuptial Mass followed the wedding. The Eastern Rites do not have a close link between marriage and the Eucharist.[3] The study group commented on this change in perspective.

> According to article 78 of the Constitution, matrimony *ex more*, that is, ordinarily, must be celebrated within mass. That is "without the imposition of any obligation" because the celebration of matrimony within mass sometimes cannot take place "because of practical difficulties of places or times." (Statement of Archbishop Hallinan on emendations, p. 9)[4]

Contemporary to the Council of Trent, the 1543 marriage ceremony of Metz, France, incorporated marriage within the nuptial Mass. The consent occurred at the offertory, and the giving of the

---

[1] SC 78.

[2] IO 70.

[3] Kenneth W. Stevenson, *To Join Together: The Rite of Marriage* (New York: Pueblo Publishing Company, 1987), 80.

[4] Schemata 182a, p. 5; see also Schemata 157, p. 5.

ring and marriage prayers after the post-communion.[5] When the study group set to work on implementing the council's vision, and specifically its request to have weddings within Mass, the members knew that the Metz ritual offered a precedent, "according to which matrimony is celebrated not before Mass nor immediately after the gospel, but at the time of the offertory and in connection with the procession of the offertory's bread and wine."[6]

THE INTRODUCTORY RITES

The First Form

45.

Vested for Mass, the priest goes with servers to the church door, where he receives and joyfully welcomes the bridal party.

This is most of the former paragraph 19. The first edition included two options here, one permitting the priest to greet the couple at the door, the other to greet them at the altar. Now these have been separated into two distinct descriptions of the entrance. The second option begins at OCM 48.

The first edition stated that the rite of welcome could be omitted. This has been removed from both options for a wedding within Mass, but it remains in the circumstance of marriage between a Catholic and a catechumen or a non-Christian. There, OCM 155 permits the option of omitting the welcome and starting with the Liturgy of the Word. But here it may not be omitted.

The priest may say whatever words of welcome he wishes. These are directed to the people at the door and are meant to be "off-mic": a private, not a public greeting.

Both editions of the OCM optimistically begin this paragraph with the view that the ceremony will begin "at the appointed time." Weddings rarely do. The phrase, however, is less an admonition to punctuality as a concession that the postconciliar liturgy's preferred opening words cannot be used. The Introductory Rites of the Order of Mass say that the service begins "When the people are

[5] Mark Searle and Kenneth W. Stevenson, *Documents of the Marriage Liturgy* (Collegeville, MN: Liturgical Press, 1992), 99.
[6] Schemata 157, p. 5.

gathered."[7] This replaced the preconciliar rubric that Mass begins with "The vested priest."[8] At the start of a wedding, however, the people are not yet gathered. The bride and groom have not yet made their entrance. In lieu of describing the status of the assembly, the postconciliar rubric simply notes that the ceremony gets underway at the appointed time.

The color of the vestments for the Mass is established by the criteria in OCM 34. If the priest offers the Ritual Mass for the Celebration of Marriage, then he wears white; if he celebrates the Mass of the day, then its vestment color prevails. The first draft of the postconciliar ceremony simply mentioned that the priest was vested in a chasuble.[9] It did not mention the other vestments nor the color. The next draft had him wearing a chasuble of "festive color."[10]

The Roman Ritual of 1614 had the priest wearing a surplice and white stole.[11] The preconciliar missal required white vesture for the Mass for the spouses.[12]

The servers are mentioned in this paragraph probably because the preconciliar rite said the priest should be assisted by at least a cleric wearing a surplice.[13] No vesture is mentioned for the servers because that is treated in the GIRM, which says that servers may wear an alb or "other appropriate and dignified clothing."[14]

No rubrics tell the bride and the groom what to wear. There are traditions, however. As the history of the title of the ceremony shows, the service was sometimes called the "veiling of the bride." Hence, a long tradition is widely retained that the bride wears a veil on her head.

Traditionally, the bride also wears a white gown. It is assumed that the color refers to purity, even to virginity. Isidore of Seville used to bind the newly married bride and groom with a white and purple

---

[7] Roman Missal, Order of Mass 1. Hereafter OM.

[8] *Missale Romanum, Ordo Missæ.*

[9] Schemata 182 add, p. 2, there as paragraph 1.

[10] Schemata 204, p. 4, there as paragraph 22.

[11] *Roman Ritual*, 460.

[12] *Missale Romanum,* "*Rubricæ generales,*" 121d.

[13] *Roman Ritual*, 460.

[14] GIRM 339.

cord: "white pertains to purity of life, purple to the children of their blood."[15] Later rituals, however, demand no color for her dress.

When a bishop celebrates a wedding Mass, he wears Mass vestments and uses the miter and pastoral staff.[16] If he presides but does not celebrate, "he wears an alb, pectoral cross, stole, and white cope, and uses the miter and pastoral staff."[17] In that case, a vested priest celebrates the Mass. Deacons and other ministers dress appropriately.[18]

The rubric envisions that the priest and servers go to the door to receive the couple. This innovation made up for an absence in the preconciliar liturgy, which had the bride and groom kneeling before the altar, but never explained how they got there.[19] Into this vacuum, elaborate processions stepped. The greeting at the door was not intended to circumvent the procession but to demonstrate the welcome of the local church and to help the wedding party transition from the outside world to the religious celebration.

It had historical precedents—but with a different purpose. In some places, the ceremony began at the door. For example, a twelfth-century manuscript of a seventh-century practice notes that all come to the doors of the church where the priest blessed the ring and gave it to the groom. After these prayers, the assembly entered the church.[20] The eleventh-century English Missal of Bury St. Edmunds similarly has the ring ceremony at the beginning but outside the door of the church. Still in the public square, the priest then formally asked the groom and then the bride if they consented to marriage. After the giving of the ring and the dowry,

---

[15] Korbinian Ritzer, *Formen, Riten und Religiöses Brauchtum der Eheschliessung in den Christlichen Kirchen des Ersten Jahrtausends* (Münster: Aschendorffsche Verlagsbuchhandlung, 1962), 352.

[16] CB 601.

[17] Ibid.

[18] Ibid.

[19] *Roman Ritual*, 460.

[20] Adrien Nocent, "Il matrimonio cristiano," in *La Liturgica: I Sacramenti: Teologia e storia della celebrazione*, Anamnesis 3/1 (Genova: Casa Editrice Marietti, 1989), 348, citing *De Antiquis Ecclesiae Ritibus*, 1. I, c. IX, a. V, 356–59, in A.-G. Martimort, *La documentation liturgique* . . .

all entered the church for the Mass and the nuptial blessing.[21] This tradition perhaps explains how the preconciliar wedding came to take place before the Mass instead of during it. The door of the church served as the sanctuary of the wedding.

In drafting the postconciliar marriage ceremony, the study group hoped to recover the significance of the door. In the first draft they wrote,

> *The reception of the groom and the bride may take place at the entrance of the church according to the local custom.*
>
> In this case the Roman Ritual can propose a rite of reception by way of example, with great flexibility, that the legitimate customs of peoples or regions not be unduly disturbed.[22]

The study group shared elements of the discussion in a summary of the minutes of the meeting. The relator was Gy.

> *The reception of the couple.* (1) Where? a) Why not in front of the altar and the sanctuary gates (Ansgar Dirks)? b) Or no reception, or let it happen at the entrance of the church, which now is the last vestige of matrimony celebrated at the double doors of the church (Johannes Wagner).
>
> (2) *Obligatory or no?* a) Not obligatory (Relator, Wagner). The couple will have to wait longer (Aimé-Georges Martimort); that's not true everywhere; for example, in Belgium (François Vanderbroucke). b) Let it be required so that they may cross into a religious "climate" (Cellier). c) It may at least be positively recommended in the rubrics that the entrance may become sacred; there are great benefits (Anselmo Lentini).[23]

The study group's next draft altered the wording to account for these discussions.

> *The reception of the groom and the bride may take place at the entrance of the church or, if it seems appropriate, in front of the altar.*

---

[21] Searle and Stevenson, *Documents of the Marriage Liturgy*, 149–55.

[22] Schemata 157, p. 6, there as paragraph 13.

[23] Schemata 157 adnexum, p. 1.

> *Where circumstances suggest it, or if the episcopal conference will have*
> *determined it, the celebration of matrimony may begin at once with mass,*
> *the rite of reception having been omitted.*
>
> Concerning the appropriateness and place of some rite of re-
> ception, we kept in view the fruits of Rituals already in existence,
> the diversity of situations, and the observations proposed to us in
> the committee of relators. All these things considered, some rite
> of reception generally seems to be useful so that the climate of the
> celebration may truly be religious even from the beginning, and
> the very entrance of the couple into the church may become sacred.
> Nevertheless, according to pastoral circumstances or the judg-
> ment of the conference of bishops, it may end up more appropriate
> that the reception take place in front of the altar or be completely
> omitted.[24]

Additional comments accompanied a subsequent draft. The
study group continued to work out the best way to present its
vision.

> In the rite of reception itself, the celebrant may conduct a dialogue
> with the families or with the wedding party, teaching a profound
> sense both of the endowment and the covenant that the families
> contract between themselves. Then he may conduct a dialogue with
> the couple, anticipating, if the event calls for it, the questioning of
> those being married with its invitation, concerning which, see below
> in chapter III the numbers 26–27. In the arrangement of this rite,
> there may take place some symbolic giving and receiving of gifts;
> (it would be most desirable that some quantity of money also be
> brought forth to be divided among the poor;) if the event calls for
> it, the celebrant may bless the wedding garments that the bride (or
> even the groom) is wearing, and also the rings; that blessing would
> then be considered more of a preparatory rite.
>
> Then all go up to the altar in procession.[25]

To complement this vision, the same draft added a paragraph to
the rubrics of the entrance procession.

[24] Schemata 182a, p. 6.
[25] Schemata 204, p. 3, there as paragraph 15; see also Schemata 221, pp. 8–9.

> *Among those peoples where the escorted bride is solemnly led to be handed over to the groom, she may be received in the church with the group of all the escorts, as has been said above in the chapter on adaptations, n. 14.*[26]

This rubric was one of the paragraphs that Seumois helped edit, given his experience with mission territories.[27] It refers back to paragraph 14 of the introduction of the same draft, which supplied the background.

> Wherever, according to the legitimate customs of the people, the bride is solemnly led from the home of her parents to the home of the groom, this solemn ceremony may be arranged in a certain way with the very rite of the church, and put to use. Therefore, when all these things have correctly taken place in the home of the parents, the party of those escorting the bride go to the church, where, meeting the other party pertaining to the groom, both are received at the same time by the celebrant.[28]

Bugnini summarized all this work in his reflections on the drafts:

> The welcome is meant as a sensitive human gesture that will bring the couple, their relatives, and their friends into an atmosphere of spiritual fellowship.
> The flexibility displayed in the rubric reflects the opposing views expressed during the discussions within the Consilium. There were those who saw the rite as possibly giving rise to discrimination: for the wealthy, reception at the door of the church, with a great deal of pomp and ceremony; for the poor, reception at the altar. Others disliked the idea of a procession through the church and other possible drawbacks. All agreed that room must be made for a rite of reception, precisely in order not to lose an opportunity of immediately placing the couple and the assembly in the atmosphere proper to a sacramental celebration.[29]

---

[26] Ibid., 4, there as paragraph 22.

[27] Gy, [Letter to the Consilium], Schemata 204, p. [i].

[28] Schemata 204, p. 3, there as paragraph 14.

[29] Annibale Bugnini, *The Reform of the Liturgy, 1948–1975*, trans. Matthew J. O'Connell (Collegeville, MN: Liturgical Press, 1990), 701–2.

In the final version of the ceremony, a bishop has another variation. He does not go to the door, but the parish priest (pastor) or
another presbyter does. The priest is vested with cassock, surplice
and stole, or alb and stole, unless he is celebrating or concelebrat-
ing the Mass. Then he wears the alb, stole, and chasuble. The priest
receives the bride and groom at the door or in front of the altar. He
leads them to their places. After the bishop reverences the altar, the
priest presents the bride and groom to him.[30]

Noble as all these thoughts are, few Catholic weddings begin
with a greeting at the door. Perhaps the rubric pared the discussion
too much and its intent was lost. But more likely the societal traditions behind the procession of the bride have been too powerful to
overcome. In the planning room, the study group imagined that the
priest would greet the wedding parties at the door, welcome them,
and help establish a spiritual transition. In a strong secular tradition
in the United States, however, the groom does not see the bride on
the wedding day before they meet in the sanctuary. This tradition
has become more and more artificial with the increase of cohabitation among couples, yet superstition has ruled over liturgy.

As will be seen in comments on OCM 46, the bride and the
groom were meant to follow the priest to the altar, which provides
another reason for the greeting at the door. They are the ministers
of the sacrament of marriage, and their symbolic entrance behind
the priest bears ritual significance. All this was implied in the rubrics, but they have gained little traction in practice.

The English translation says that the priest greets "the bridal
party." This expression appears only in this paragraph and its parallel in the wedding without Mass.[31] It translates the Latin word
nupturientes, which is translated elsewhere in the OCM as "the
engaged couple." The intent was for him to receive the bride and
groom, not necessarily the entire bridal party. Here, the expression
may be a concession to the practice that the engaged couple rarely
stand at the door together before the wedding. The priest is more
likely to find "the bridal party": the bride and her bridesmaids,
perhaps also the groomsmen. If the groom is not there, however,

---

[30] CB 602.
[31] OCM 80.

the priest will not be able to greet him, thwarting the original intent of OCM 45.

The rubric says that the priest greets them "warmly." This clause was added to the opening rubric in the penultimate draft, acknowledging the human elements of the priest's greeting and the couple's joy.[32] "Warmly" translates the Latin word *humaniter*, which admonishes the priest to greet the couple "like a human being." There seems to be some realization that often he does not. Weddings are stressful for everyone, even the priest. But at this moment, he should extend the warmth of the church as the couple enters matrimony. A similar concern appears in at least two other of the postconciliar liturgical books. In the Rite of Acceptance into the Order of Catechumens from the Rite of Christian Initiation of Adults (RCIA), the priest is to greet the candidates for the catechumenate *humaniter*.[33] And in the confessional he greets the penitent with *humanioribus verbis*.[34] In all these ways, the priest puts on the pleasant face of the church.

In Mexico, the priest may lead a sprinkling rite when he arrives at the door. This takes place even before the procession and the sign of the cross that begins the Mass. A precedent is found in the preconciliar Sunday Mass, when the priest could exorcise and bless water, and then sprinkle the altar, himself, the ministers, and the people—all before the Sunday Mass began.[35] At a wedding in Mexico, the priest may say in these or similar words, "Brothers and sisters, welcome to this celebration that fills us all with joy. Recalling our baptism, let us thank God for this gift of his love." After a moment of silence, he leads the people in a threefold acclamation of praise to Father, Son, and Holy Spirit for the gift of baptism. The people respond, "Blessed be God forever," after each phrase. The priest signs himself with water and then sprinkles those present,

[32] Schemata 221, p. 10.

[33] Rite of Christian Initiation of Adults 49, in *The Rites*, 54, translated there as "in a friendly manner." Hereafter RCIA.

[34] Rite of Penance 41, in *The Rites*, 545, translated there as "with kindness."

[35] *The Roman Ritual in Latin and English with Rubrics and Plainchant Notation: The Blessings*, vol. 3, trans. and ed. Philip T. Weller (Boonville, NY: Preserving Christian Publications, 2008), 12.

saying, "Sprinkle us, Lord, with the water of your mercy and purify us from all our sins." Then to begin the procession to the altar, he says, "Let us go rejoicing to meet the Lord." All answer, "Amen." If there is no sprinkling, he greets the group at the door and then says, "Brothers and sisters, let us go rejoicing to meet the Lord."[36] All then form the procession and enter the church.

The Mexican edition has three complete formularies for celebrating matrimony within Mass. Each of them presents one example of parts of the Mass where there are several options, such as the collect, the universal prayer, and the nuptial blessing. All the options are available at any time, but the editors sought and obtained the Vatican's permission for three complete versions of the wedding within Mass for the first chapter of this liturgical book.

46.

The entrance chant takes place during the customary procession to the altar. With minor variations, this is the former paragraph 20. The words "Entrance Chant" are taken from the current translation of the Roman Missal.[37]

The English translation redacted by the CDWDS surprisingly omits important details in the Latin. A fuller translation would say this:

> The procession to the altar then takes place: the ministers go first, the priest follows, and then the engaged couple, who, according to local customs, may be honorably escorted at least by the parents and two witnesses to the place prepared for them. Meanwhile, the Entrance Chant takes place.

The CDWDS's omission of this fuller description of the procession is hard to explain. Perhaps it was omitted because it means to describe a procession according to local customs. Even though the full rubric was in force between 1969 and 2016, it was rarely practiced. Perhaps the failure to adopt it in practice convinced the CDWDS that it was not the custom in English-speaking countries. The abridged

[36] *Ritual* (Mexico), 41–42.
[37] GIRM 121.

rubric appears in the editions of the OCM published in Australia, England and Wales, and in the United States of America.

The full rubric was preserved in French Canada[38] and in Mexico.[39] It also appears in Colombia[40] and, surprisingly, in the Spanish edition published by the USCCB.[41] Thus the English and Spanish translations in force in the United States do not match at this paragraph.

Ideally, there is one procession up the aisle, led by a person carrying the cross, others with candles, the reader, the deacon, and the priest. The attendants come next, followed by the groom with his parents and the bride with hers. The couple will be exchanging mutual consent; they may anticipate this by entering equally in the procession. Another version would have the bride and groom coming last, arm in arm. All of these faithfully carry out the English translation of OCM 46. Unfortunately, so would a practice of having the priest enter last.

One small change opens this paragraph in Latin. The first edition began with the word "if." It combined the options of having or omitting the greeting at the door. Without a greeting at the door, it envisioned no procession to the altar. The second edition presumes that Mass will always begin with a procession.

This heightens the difficulty created by this paragraph's omission of the description of the procession. OCM 45 has already created the circumstance in which the priest goes to the door of the church to meet the bridal party. They all have to get to the sanctuary somehow. The sequence of participants in the procession is carefully crafted in Latin, but it remains a mystery to those who read it in English.

The Catholic Church has required the presence of two witnesses at least since the Council of Trent.[42] In Hispanic and other

---

[38] *Rituel Romain*, 16.

[39] *Ritual* (Mexico), 42.

[40] *Ritual* (Colombia), 25.

[41] *Ritual del Matrimonio* 46.

[42] *Enchiridion symbolorvm definitionvm et declarationvm de rebus fidei et morum*, ed. Henricus Denzinger and Adolfus Schönmetzer (Barcelona: Herder, 1973), 1813–16.

traditions, several couples serve as *padrinos* of the wedding, helping to pay for the expenses and performing ceremonial functions at different moments. Two of them, however, serve as canonical witnesses. Their participation in the procession is welcome. By custom, however, the wedding party often swells to a great number of friends of the bride and groom who join the procession as well. OCM 46 offers no upper limit to the number of people who may enter in procession.

The assembly is expected to sing an opening hymn during the procession. This happens more easily among Hispanics than among Anglos. Traditionally, throughout most of the United States and other countries instrumental music accompanies the entire procession, and the bride enters last. Traditionally, again, she enters to the accompaniment of a solo organist playing *Treulich geführt*, or the "Bridal Chorus," from the beginning of Act III of Richard Wagner's opera *Lohengrin*, which debuted in 1850. The opera's wedding guests sing the chorus, but an instrumental version sounded at the wedding of the youngest child of Queen Victoria and Prince Albert, Victoria the Princess Royal, to Prince Frederick Wilhelm of Prussia at the Chapel Royal, St. James Palace, in 1858. A custom was born.

Many Catholic dioceses and individual parishes ban the "Bridal Chorus" from weddings on the grounds of its secular origin or that the inseparable association of the tune with the English words "Here Comes the Bride" places too much attention on her. It could, however, be argued that Lohengrin's character is a Knight of the Holy Grail, and he marries Elsa in a church, and that attention will be fixed on the bride no matter what music is played if she is last in the procession. Furthermore, organists frequently play other instrumental music from the Romantic era, making it hard to demonize one piece from an opera. Still, as OCM 30 has requested, all the music at the wedding should express the faith of the church.

The French Canadian edition added to OCM 46 a note that instrumental music may replace the entrance chant: "The organ or musical instruments may play a piece adapted to the rite and the church."[43] The Mexican edition adds even more:

---

[43] *Rituel Romain*, 16.

Meanwhile, the entrance chant takes place or the organ or another instrument plays festively. The entrance chant or the music should express the faith of the Church and be appropriate to the rite of Matrimony. All should take care that this procession have a true liturgical character and avoid the appearance of any other thing.[44]

The English editions do not make the same observation, though weddings in the United States typically begin with an instrumental. In fact, many wedding processions have two separate pieces of music, one reserved for the bride. But this is contrary to the nature of the music at the beginning of Mass and to the equality of the spouses as they enter and celebrate this ceremony.

OCM 46 is hoping people will sing. The rubric refers to the entrance antiphon of the Mass. According to OCM 34, there are occasions when the Mass for marriage yields to a Mass of importance on the liturgical calendar. In that case, the recommended antiphon comes from the Mass of that day, so a considerable variety of potential antiphons exists. When those days do not conflict, however, the wedding Mass offers its own antiphons from the Missal's Ritual Mass for the Celebration of Marriage.

There have long been other options. By the eleventh century, the Missal of Bury St. Edmunds permitted the Votive Mass for the Holy Trinity to replace Votive Mass for the Spouses.[45] The Mass of the Holy Trinity was ordinarily permitted only on Sundays, so the option of using it for weddings underscored the festive significance of these celebrations in the liturgical life of the parish. In the twelfth-century Roman Pontifical, the Votive Mass for the Holy Trinity opened with an antiphon that proclaimed, "Blessed be the Holy Trinity and undivided unity. Praise him because he has granted his mercy to us."[46] The 1570 Missal retained that antiphon and cites Tobit 12:6 as its source. (The same verse in the new Vulgate has a few differences, though the key phrases for this

---

[44] *Ritual* (Mexico), 42.

[45] Stevenson, *To Join Together*, 42.

[46] *Le Pontifical Romain au moyen-âge, Tome I: Le Pontifical Romain du XIIᵉ siècle*, ed. Michel Andrieu, Studi e Testi 86 (Vatican City: Biblioteca Apostolica Vaticana 1938), 301. Hereafter, *Le Pontifical Romain*.

antiphon are not much affected.)[47] The antiphon's first phrase honoring the Trinity obviously postdates any Old Testament book and expands the simple word for "God" from the verse in the Vulgate. The antiphon is joined to Psalm 8:2, praising how wonderful is God's name through all the earth.[48] The antiphon endured in the Missal up to the Second Vatican Council. The postconciliar Missal further expanded the address to the divinity from "the Trinity" to "Father, Son, and Holy Spirit," and retained the final phrase, "for he has shown us his merciful love." The citation to Tobit has been removed, but this antiphon derives from the same passage in the Vulgate, Tobit 12:6.

According to the Missal of Bury St. Edmunds, the wedding began at the door of the church with the arrival of the parties and the giving of the ring. As the procession entered the church, Psalm 128 (127) was sung,[49] a psalm hailing the blessings of family life. It contributed to the early repertoire of wedding music.

The entrance antiphon in the pre–Vatican II Votive Mass for Spouses varied over the centuries. The tenth-century Roman-Germanic Pontifical used Psalm 90 (89).[50] The Roman Pontifical of the twelfth century inserted an entrance antiphon from Tobit 7:15 and 8:19 (which have no equivalents in the new Vulgate). These combine Raguel's prayerful address to Tobiah and Sarah and his household's thanks to God.[51]

From among the options of these pontificals, the 1570 Missal's Mass for Spouses chose the entrance antiphon from the twelfth century.[52] Perhaps this verse held some allure to the post-Tridentine church because it upheld verses from Tobit, a book that the Reform-

---

[47] *Nova Vulgata Bibliorum Sacrorum editio* (Vatican City: Libreria Editrice Vaticana, 1979).

[48] *Missale Romanum*, p. [49].

[49] Searle and Stevenson, *Documents of the Marriage Liturgy*, 151.

[50] *Le Pontifical romano-germanique du dixième siècle: Le texte avec utilisation des collations laissées par M. Andrieu*, ed. Cyrille Vogel and Reinhard Elze, Studi e testi 226, 227, 269 (Vatican City: Biblioteca apostolica vaticana, 1963–1972), vol. 2, 415. Hereafter PRG.

[51] *Le Pontifical Romain*, 260.

[52] *Missale Romanum*, p. [75].

ers had claimed was noncanonical. Or perhaps they chose it because it was the more recent option.

The post–Vatican II Roman Missal recommends three entrance chants. The first is based on Psalm 20 (19):3, 5. In context, the people are singing to the couple: "May the Lord send you help. . . . May he grant you your hearts' desire."[53] The second is based on Psalm 90 (89):14, 17. This one seems to express the sentiments of the couple: "[F]ill us with your merciful love. . . . . Let the favor of the Lord our God be upon us."[54] The third is based on Psalm 145 (144):2, 9. It expresses the potential prayer of anyone present, even the bride or groom: "I will bless you day after day, O Lord . . . for you are kind to all."[55]

As often happens, the *Ordo cantus missæ* offers a different selection.[56] Like the lectionary, the *Ordo cantus missæ* is part of the Roman Missal, though published as a separate volume. First printed in 1970, it contains a wider selection of texts for antiphons and responsories than those appearing in the Missal. Musical accompaniment is found in the *Graduale Romanum*,[57] in which the monks of the Abbey of St. Peter in Solesmes, France, preserve the chant tradition of the Catholic Church. There is no official English translation of the *Ordo cantus missæ*, but its suggestions for the antiphons at Mass deserve consideration as part of the original vision of the complete post–Vatican II Missal.

The first suggestion from the *Ordo cantus missæ* is Psalm 68 (67):6, 7, 36, and 2. The psalm praises God, who lives in his holy place yet gives people a home where they can dwell in one heart. The second option is Psalm 90 (89):1, 2. It acclaims God as a refuge

---

[53] Roman Missal, Marriage A.

[54] Ibid., B.

[55] Ibid., C.

[56] *Ordo cantus missæ, editio typica altera* (Vatican City: Libreria Editrice Vaticana, 1987), 354.

[57] *Graduale sacrosanctæ Romanæ ecclesiæ de tempore et de Sanctis primum Sancti Pii X iussu restitutum et editum Pauli VI Pontificis Maximi cura nunc recognitum ad exemplar "Ordinis cantus missæ" dispositum et rhythmicis signis a Solesmensibus monachis diligenter ornatum* (Solesmes: Abbatia Sancti Petri de Solesmis, 1974). Hereafter, *Graduale Romanum*.

from one generation to the next. This is the same antiphon cited above in the Roman-Germanic Pontifical. The final option is Psalm 34 (33):10, 11, and 2. It offers the consoling message that those who seek the Lord lack no good. All these antiphons shine with the hopeful joy that this couple will become a family blessed by God.

The Vatican published a simpler version of chants to accompany the Missal even earlier, in 1967.[58] There is found yet another antiphon for the Mass for spouses.[59] The *Graduale simplex* offers Psalm 37 (36): 1-9 (2-10), paired with an uncredited slightly altered citation of John 2:1, the opening verse of the gospel's account of the wedding at Cana. The psalm sings the benefits of those who trust in the Lord. The study group preparing the postconciliar wedding ceremony imagined that the *Graduale simplex* would supply the necessary words for the antiphons at a wedding Mass.[60]

According to the GIRM, a completely different song may replace the entrance antiphon.[61] At a wedding Mass, if none of the entrance antiphons from the Missal are used, another antiphon or hymn replaces them. Either way, the OCM hopes that the congregation will sing a hymn of faith as the wedding gets underway.

Nonetheless, at any Mass, the GIRM also permits having the entrance chant recited. All the faithful, some of them, or a reader may recite one of the antiphons assigned for the wedding.[62] It would be odd to recite an antiphon during a wedding procession, but the rubrics permit it.

If a participation aid has been prepared for the people, it would be appropriate to put it in the hands of the groom and bride as well. All members of the wedding party may need copies of music that they are expected to sing.

Perhaps the study group was just naive, but even after the council, the traditional societal wedding procession, featuring the entrance of the bride to an instrumental solo, overpowered not only

---

[58] *Graduale simplex in usum minorum ecclesiarum, editio typica altera* (Vatican City: Typis Polyglottis Vaticanis 1975).
[59] Ibid., 379.
[60] Schemata 248, p. 16.
[61] GIRM 48.
[62] GIRM 48, 198.

the greeting between the priest and the couple at the door but also the processional hymn sung by all the people as should happen at any Mass. To realize their vision in parishes will require considerable courage.

The Mexican edition inserts two paragraphs at this point of the ritual.

> With respect to the place prepared for the couple, it is appropriate to keep in mind, if possible, that they be seated in such a way that they do not turn their backs to the assembly.
>
> When the couple arrive at the place prepared for them, if it is fitting, the parents may give them the blessing before going to their places.[63]

This honors a tradition in some places in Latin America where each of their children kneels, and the parents make the sign of the cross over them. Such a gesture is reserved to clergy in the liturgical books, but its usage by parents remains strong in some cultures.

47.

The priest approaches, bows to, and kisses the altar. Then he goes to his chair.

This paragraph is new to the second edition of the OCM, but it simply fills a gap. It should be understood that at any Mass, the priest makes his entrance in this way. The source for this is the Roman Missal.[64] If a deacon assists, he also bows and kisses the altar.[65] The revised English translation matches the pertinent vocabulary in the Missal.

This paragraph does not indicate the appropriate reverence when the tabernacle is in the sanctuary. In that case, the ministers genuflect to the tabernacle before reverencing the altar.[66]

---

[63] *Ritual* (Mexico), pp. 42–43.
[64] GIRM 49; OM 1.
[65] GIRM 49.
[66] GIRM 274.

The Second Form

The second form for the beginning of the Mass supplies the option of the priest not greeting the couple at the door.

48.

The priest, vested for Mass, goes with the servers to the place where the couple will be or to his chair.

This repeats most of the material from OCM 45. The priest goes not to the door but to the place prepared for the couple. Traditionally, this is in the sanctuary, but the OCM never specifies where. It does not mention kneelers, even though these are often provided. If so, chairs for the couple would also be required. In some ethnic traditions this is quite common; in others, not. But the couple will need to assume all the postures that the rest of the assembly takes during Mass, including sitting. Whatever furniture is provided, it delineates "the place prepared for the couple."

Or the priest may simply go to his chair, but he will soon have to leave it, according to OCM 49 and 50. Perhaps this is why the Mexican edition has removed the option of going to the chair.[67] Paragraph 19 of the first edition allowed the priest to go to the altar instead of the door, but the second edition more appropriately replaces "altar" with "chair." He does not go to the altar until OCM 50. For the sake of clarity, the second edition sets apart the alternatives of going to the door or going to the chair.

49.

The priest receives and greets the couple when they arrive at their place. This is also taken from OCM 45, adjusted for the circumstance in which the priest did not greet the couple at the door.

If the priest has gone to his chair, he apparently leaves there to approach the couple. If he is at the place prepared for the couple, he simply remains. Traditionally, the couple occupy places within the sanctuary, but this is never explicitly stated. As ministers of the sacrament of marriage, they have a place in the sanctuary. They

---

[67] *Ritual* (Mexico), 43.

could, however, sit outside the sanctuary in the nave, and in some countries, they do.

OCM 49 is totally silent about the procession of the wedding party in this second form. Even in Latin there is no description of the order of procession, as the English translation omits in OCM 46. Somehow, the wedding party have to get to the place prepared for them. This silence creates a space for the traditional wedding procession.

Often the sanctuary is furnished with places for the bride and groom, possibly for the two main witnesses, and possibly for the others in the wedding party. Or pews have been reserved for these attendants.

In one common tradition, the groom and groomsmen gather in a side sacristy before Mass. At the appointed time, they take a position in front of the pews and look down the aisle toward the door. The priest enters with servers from another sacristy, he reverences the altar, and takes his position at his chair or the place reserved for the couple. Then the bridesmaids process up the center aisle. Groomsmen step forward one by one to escort them along the final steps toward their places.

Traditionally, the bride enters last, escorted by her father. At the edge of the sanctuary, he may kiss her and give her hand to the groom. Although this ancient gesture is absent from the OCM, an important vestige and reinterpretation remains at paragraph 62. The groom escorts the bride to their places.

There are many variations on the procession. Sometimes the groom stands alone in front of the pews and all the attendants walk down the aisle as couples. This has the positive effect of drawing more people into the procession, but it makes it appear that all the attendants are really at church for the bride. Alternatively, the groom may enter the procession after the priest, escorted by both of his parents, and the bride escorted by both of hers.

The OCM makes no mention of a ring bearer or a flower girl, yet children traditionally take these roles. Justification can be sought from the final words of OCM 29, which permit the preservation of local customs.

The second form surrenders hope of the unified procession one normally expects at the start of Mass. Modern culture—and even the liturgy—stresses the equality of the married partners. Yet the traditional procession keeps alive in the culture the antiquated view that the bride is property passed from her father to another male. How richer was the original vision of the study group, where the couple arrive together at the door, the priest greets them and helps them enter the church reverently. As ministers of the sacrament, they follow the priest to the sanctuary.

But once again, the power of the traditional procession has brought the rubrics of the Roman Rite to silence.

50.

The priest reverences the altar during the entrance chant and then goes to his chair.

In this version the entrance chant follows the moment when the priest greets the couple. It almost appears that there is no procession at all. People have arrived informally, and now the wedding is getting underway. The priest chats with the couple, and then the music begins—music that may open any Mass. With that the priest goes to the altar and then to his chair.

Most of this is copied from OCM 47, adjusted for the circumstances of the second form. The Mexican edition again explicitly allows instrumental music for the procession.[68]

51.

The priest makes the sign of the cross and greets the people. This paragraph is new to the second edition but clarifies what should have been understood. Any Mass begins with the sign of the cross and a greeting.[69]

The typical edition in Latin did not include the words of the alternative greetings here, but they have been inserted from the Missal into the OCM for England and Wales, though not in Australia. The Spanish language version for the United States and the Mexican edition[70] imitate the Latin—no greetings are provided in this book. The greetings appear in the French Canadian edition,

---

[68] *Ritual* (Mexico), 43.
[69] GIRM 50; OM 1, 2.
[70] *Ritual* (Mexico), 43.

including two that call for the people to respond, "Blessed be God now and forever."[71]

If instrumental music accompanied the procession and there has been no singing of the entrance chant or an opening hymn, the words of the chant need to be accounted for. As indicated above, all the faithful, some of them, the reader, or the priest may do this. It may be done before the sign of the cross or within the introductory comments in the following two paragraphs.[72]

52.

The priest invites everyone to dispose themselves inwardly for the celebration. This paragraph and the following one offer two samples of his introduction, this one addressed to the people, the second to the couple. The priest may use other words.

At any Mass, words of introduction may be freely composed, and a priest, deacon, or another minister may deliver them.[73] Here, the priest is explicitly charged with this duty.

Both these paragraphs are new to the second edition but, even earlier, members of the preparatory commission for the Second Vatican Council wanted "a certain introduction to the rite, making the engaged couple aware of the importance and value of the sacramental consent that they are about to give."[74] Its addition to the second edition springs from the same desire that led the first edition to introduce the greeting at the door. Both seek ways to help the couple appreciate the religious nature of the ceremony from its beginning.

The first of the proposed introductions establishes a happy tone and invites the entire assembly to support the couple, listen to the Word with them, and pray humbly for God's blessing of them. The opening lines are inspired by verses of the pilgrimage song, Psalm 122 (121)—standing with the couple, who come to the home of the Lord on the day that they inaugurate a home of their own. If the priest chooses to compose or improvise his own words, these give him an idea about how to proceed.

[71] *Rituel Romain*, 17.
[72] GIRM 48, 198.
[73] GIRM 31; OM 3.
[74] Schemata 32, pp. 14–15.

The Mexican translation offers three additional alternatives, including one for second marriages that may include an acknowledgment of children: "God will welcome also the prayer of your child (children), fruit of your earlier marriage, and will help everyone to form a new home enlivened by love, which is the bond of perfect unity."[75]

53.

Or the priest addresses the couple, announcing both the spirit of joy and the meaning of the celebration. The expression "partnership of the whole of life" comes from canon law's definition of marriage.[76] This introduction concludes with words inspired by the opening verses of Psalm 20 (19), originally a prayer for God's favor before battle, used here only in the sense of God's favor. The same verses inspired one of the entrance antiphons presumed in OCM 46.

If the entrance chant has not been sung or recited before the sign of the cross in OCM 51, then the priest may adapt it into his introduction for the Mass.[77] This second option may have been written as a demonstration.

Nowhere in the introduction is there a provision for the priest to ask a question such as, "Who gives this woman to be married to this man?" Nor does the bride's father answer to such a question, "I do." The question has never been part of the Catholic wedding ceremony, but the traditional wedding procession in which the father walks his daughter down the aisle essentially puts the question into ritual form. More important than having the father put his daughter's hand into the hand of the groom is the joining of the couple's hands in OCM 62.

The penitential act is omitted. The Roman Missal observes the same point. No mention is made of the Kyrie. In a Mass for the First Sunday of Lent that includes a procession, on Palm Sunday of the Lord's Passion, and at an extended Pentecost Vigil, the Missal omits the penitential act and, "if appropriate, the Kyrie," thus mak-

---

[75] *Ritual* (Mexico), 217.
[76] Canon 1055 §1.
[77] GIRM 48.

ing a distinction between the two units. Presumably, the absence of the delimiting phrase "if appropriate" in the OCM signifies that the Kyrie is omitted at a wedding along with the penitential act.

During the Ritual Mass for the Celebration of Marriage, the Gloria is said or sung.[78] This was true of the preconciliar Mass as well.[79] The translation used in Colombia says that the Gloria is sung "when prescribed."[80] At first this seems like a deviation from the Missal but perhaps is closer to the truth. The Gloria is prescribed for the Ritual Mass for the Celebration of Marriage, but there are occasions when OCM 34 calls for another Mass to be said. If a wedding takes place during a Saturday night Mass during Advent or Lent, for example, the Gloria would be omitted. If, however, the wedding takes place earlier on Saturday afternoon during those seasons, the ritual Mass is said together with its Gloria. The Mexican edition surprisingly restricts this by removing the Gloria completely during Advent and Lent.[81] (A Mexican community will surely sing a Gloria during its celebration of Our Lady of Guadalupe, which falls during Advent. The same song could enliven a Saturday morning wedding Mass during Advent, but in Mexico it does not.) Both the French Canadian translation and the book published for England and Wales include the text of the Gloria here, making it easier for the presider to use the book. The OCM of England and Wales even includes chant notation for the sung version from the Missal.

54.

When permitted, the Ritual Mass for the Celebration of Marriage is used; otherwise it is the Mass of the day.

These paragraphs repeat information contained in the introduction, OCM 34, and at the heading of the Missal's ritual Mass. They appear here in the OCM for the first time. It is important for the priest to know which Mass to say, which will have an impact on his presidential prayers, as well as the readings to be proclaimed.

---

[78] Roman Missal, Marriage.
[79] *Missale Romanum*, p. [75].
[80] *Ritual* (Colombia), 27.
[81] *Ritual* (Mexico), 44.

The collects for the ritual Mass are found in the Missal and in OCM 223–228. The version published in England and Wales moved all the collects within paragraph 54, making them easier for the celebrant to find, and included the introduction "Let us pray," along with the usual invitation to silent prayer.[82]

THE LITURGY OF THE WORD

55.

Three readings may be proclaimed, the first from the Old Testament or, during Easter Time, from Revelation. At least one reading must explicitly speak of marriage.

This expands the first edition's paragraph 21, which simply permitted a first reading from the Old Testament. Its attention to the Old Testament seemed a little quaint, but the issue surfaced because the Second Vatican Council declared that a wedding outside Mass used "the epistle and the gospel" from the nuptial Mass.[83] At the time, there was no Old Testament reading in the Mass for the spouses. The study group took up the matter at various times. In comments on the first draft, for example, the group wrote,

> *Let permission also be given to have three readings, one of them from the Old Testament.* The group, as is evident, is not proposing a requirement for three readings, nor even a general recommendation. But we judge that there are certain cases in which a permission of this sort would be good. It hurts no one and is in favor of flexibility.[84]

A later draft put it into the rubric, "*Three readings may take place, of which the first may be from the Old Testament.*"[85] The next draft repeated this and added a footnote that the change had been accepted by the Fathers, and that a list of Scripture passages for weddings was being prepared.[86] The preparatory commission for the council had called for a greater variety of lectionary readings

---

[82] OM 9.
[83] SC 78.
[84] Schemata 157, p. 6.
[85] Schemata 204, p. 4.
[86] Schemata 221, p. 10.

for matrimony within and without Mass.[87] This hope was being fulfilled.

New to the second edition is the requirement that at least one reading make an explicit reference to marriage. This applies, of course, to the circumstances when the ritual Mass is being used. The list of readings now assigns certain ones among them an asterisk. At least one of these must be chosen.

OCM 55 notes that during Easter Time the first reading should come from the book of Revelation. The lectionary includes first readings from the Old Testament on the Easter Vigil and on the Pentecost Vigil but for none of the weekday or Sunday Masses in between. Instead, the first reading comes from the Acts of the Apostles. The wedding lectionary has no readings from Acts, though it does include one from Revelation. To keep with the spirit of Easter Time, that one is to serve as the first if three readings are to be proclaimed. This is the first of the liturgical books outside the Roman Missal to make such a request. By implication, the other ceremonies taking place during Easter Time—funerals and baptisms, for example—should ideally observe the same pattern. The rubric in OCM 55 is spare, but it does seem to forbid a first reading from the Old Testament at a wedding Mass during Easter Time. If there are only two readings, the first reading may come from any of the New Testament selections.

The Mexican edition permits a selection from Acts of the Apostles during Easter Time, as well as additional readings from Revelation,[88] as noted in the commentary on OCM 166 below.

56.

When the ritual Mass is not used, one of its readings may still be proclaimed, except on numbers 1 to 4 in the Table of Liturgical Days. The same applies when a bishop presides.[89]

This seems to be at odds with OCM 34, which appears to permit the substitution of one reading even on those days. As explained in the commentary there, however, the final section of OCM 34

[87] Schemata 32, p. 15, there as paragraph 47.
[88] *Ritual* (Mexico), 221.
[89] CB 603.

probably should have been removed from the English translation because it predates the legislation of the third edition of the Missal. At the very least, if the wedding takes place at a parish Sunday Mass during Ordinary Time (number 6 in the same Table), both OCM 34 and 56 agree that one reading from the wedding Lectionary may be used. Logically, this would be a reading with an asterisk. The Mexican edition permits only the substitution of the second reading.[90]

Sample readings from the wedding lectionary are included in full in OCM 56, to make this chapter more usable. Chapter IV offers the complete list of citations and readings, which can also be found in the Lectionary. The readings are almost too handy. Reserving them for a separate book, the Lectionary, would have discouraged the priest from reading them aloud and thus exercising a ministry that belongs to others.[91]

The first sample reading from Genesis 1:26-28, 31a tells of the biblical origins of matrimony at the creation of human beings. Psalm 128 (127) is the Bible's hymn to the happiness of family life. In Ephesians 5:2a, 25-32, Paul calls marriage a sacrament (or mystery). Two options are proposed for the verse before the gospel, one with the alleluia and the other during Lent. The first cites Psalm 134 (133):3, which asks God to bless the couple, and the second is 1 John 4:16b, 12, 11, which invites mutual love because God is love. In Matthew 19:3-6, Jesus gives his instructions on the permanence of marriage. These reappear as OCM 179, 206, 194, and 216. The two suggested gospel verses, however, appear only here and not among the selections in OCM 174–177. The sample second reading and gospel occurring here repeat the epistle and gospel from the preconciliar Mass for spouses.[92]

In Mexico, the first reading and psalm carry the heading "Outside Easter Time." During Easter Time it proposes Acts 2:42-47, about the community life of the first Christians, and Psalm 100 (99) with the refrain, "The Lord is our God, and we are his people. Alleluia." The recommended second reading and gospel remain the same.[93]

[90] *Ritual* (Mexico), 45.
[91] GIRM 91.
[92] *Missale Romanum*, p. [75].
[93] *Ritual* (Mexico), 46–50.

ICEL held some discussion about how the second reading would be introduced. In the first appendix of the Roman Missal, which supplies chant notation for parts of the Mass, the text for the reader's introduction to such passages is this: "A reading from the [first/second] Letter of the Blessed Apostle Paul to the. . . ." This differs from the translation in the Lectionary, which raised an expectation that all future liturgical books would contain this new translation for the reader's introduction. The translation from the Lectionary, however, remains in the new OCM, perhaps indicating that the introduction in the Missal is to be set aside.

During Lent, the alleluia is omitted, and the Lectionary offers eight options for an acclamation to replace it.[94] The second edition of the OCM now offers a ninth: "Sing joyfully to God our strength." The acclamation appears in the Latin original as well, but the English translation supplies a source: Psalm 81 (80):2. It is not offered as an alternative to the other eight but mildly presumes that it will be used. If sung, many people will be learning it on the spot. The Mexican edition uses one of that conference's familiar gospel acclamations, "Glory and honor to you, Lord Jesus," instead of the one unique to the OCM.[95]

57.

The homily treats Christian marriage, the dignity of conjugal love, sacramental grace, and the responsibilities of those who are married.

This is the former paragraph 22, word for word except for one letter in the Latin verb, which changes the mood. The first edition said the priest "may" do this. The second edition says he does it. Although it does not say so here, the Vatican previously stated that the homily at a wedding Mass is never omitted.[96]

As the ceremony passed through its drafts, the study group considered including a complete sample homily, similar to the one in the ordination rites.[97] Due, however, to the wide variety of cultures

[94] LM 223.
[95] *Ritual* (Mexico), 49.
[96] IO 70.
[97] Schemata 182b, p. 1.

and circumstances applying to marriage, they settled on the establishment of these basic themes. The study group explained:

> As to the liturgy of the word, three Fathers asked in the last session of the Consilium that the Roman Ritual itself offer some help in preparing a homily. This has been done in two ways: On the one hand through the rubric in number 22, following the example of the rubric of Holy Thursday of the Lord's Supper, revised in the Order of Holy Week in the year 1955, which provided themes for the homily; on the other hand, in the doctrinal and catechetical Introduction of chapter 1.
>
> There may also be provided, if you like, some little notes applied to the biblical texts of the readings. However, the writing of some outlines of preaching for matrimony with the variety of pericopes seemed less agreeable.[98]

The last draft also footnoted the council, which said that the homily should expound the sacred text and the norms of the Christian life, and that matrimony takes place within Mass "after the homily."[99] During the drafting of the liturgy constitution in 1963, Cardinal Paolo Giobbe proposed that marriage take place after the gospel, but he was perhaps not thinking of the homily.[100] About a month after the constitution passed, Pope Paul VI stated in his apostolic letter *Sacram Liturgiam* that, in accordance with SC 78, "the sacrament of Matrimony must normally be celebrated during holy Mass, after the reading of the Gospel and the sermon."[101]

THE CELEBRATION OF MARRIAGE

58.

When more than one wedding takes place in the same Mass, the questions, the consent, and its reception must be done individually.

---

[98] Schemata 221, p. 4. See also the footnote to n. 22 on page 10.

[99] Schemata 280, p. 12, citing SC 52 and 78.

[100] Giampietro, p. 98.

[101] Paul VI, *Sacram liturgiam*, V. http://w2.vatican.va/content/paul-vi/en/motu_proprio/documents/hf_p-vi_motu-proprio_19640125_sacram-liturgiam.html.

This is the former paragraph 38, which used to appear at the end of this chapter. It occupied that position in the preconciliar liturgy, which had no questions for the couple, but otherwise gave similar instructions.[102] The paragraph takes a more logical position here.

Most couples want their own ceremony. Other circumstances, however, may promote more than one wedding at a time, such as multiple marriages in the same family, a desire by couples to save on expenses, shyness, or the inaccessibility of a priest or deacon.

59.

All stand and the priest addresses the couple. He may use these or similar words. This is the former paragraph 23. New to the rubric is the reference to the witnesses. What follows is, after all, what they are there to witness. The Mexican edition notes that this takes place after the homily and a period of silence.[103]

At many weddings, the assembly sits while the wedding party stands for the sake of visibility. Even the first edition, however, asked all to stand. Perhaps this was to express their role as witnesses, as well as to demonstrate the sacredness of the action taking place before their eyes. In Mexico, only the couple stands for the questions.[104] Others stand for the consent in OCM 61.

In the preconciliar rite, the couple knelt before the priest at the altar.[105] This gave rise to the custom of placing kneelers in the sanctuary for the bride and groom, an arrangement that continues, even though this rubric has changed. Ever since the very first draft of the post–Vatican II ceremony,[106] this rubric has stated that everyone stands, "including the couple," or better "even the couple," because that had not been done in the past.

There is no rubric saying which of the two should stand on the left or right. According to the preconciliar Roman Pontifical, the

---

[102] *Roman Ritual*, 464.
[103] *Ritual* (Mexico), 50.
[104] Ibid.
[105] *Roman Ritual*, 460.
[106] Schemata 182 addendum, p. 2.

woman positioned herself to the left of the man.[107] The Sarum Missal had followed the same arrangement, "the reason being that she was formed out of a rib in the left side of Adam."[108] The Genesis account of the creation of Eve, however, does not say from which of Adam's ribs she was created.[109]

There is no clear indication where the priest should stand, as there was no clear indication in OCM 49 where the couple is located. Many priests stand on the altar side of the couple. To highlight his role as a witness, though, a priest may stand at the edge of the sanctuary or in the center aisle of the nave. In this way he stands as the head of the assembly, who also act as witnesses, and the couple turn to face them all.

No instructions govern the placement of the rest of the wedding party. If space permits, they could enter the sanctuary with the couple and the two principal witnesses. Or they could remain at their places so that all may see the most important figures clearly.

The sample introduction is virtually the same as the previous one, but where the first edition says that the couple had come for the Lord to seal and strengthen their "love," it now says they come to seal and strengthen their "intention to enter into Marriage." This is a stronger statement of the specific nature of a church wedding. Similarly, instead of saying that Christ blesses this "love," it specifies "the love that binds you." This love has a specific purpose.

The first draft of this introduction varies only slightly from the final form, but it did insert this sentence after the first: "For the intimate partnership of life and conjugal love, made by the Creator from the beginning and formed by his laws, is renewed in the marriage covenant, that the mutual consent of spouses may be

---

[107] *Pontificale Romanum Reimpressio editionis iuxta typicam anno 1962 publici iuris factae, partibus praecedentis editionis ab alla omissis, introductione et tabulis aucta*, ed. Anthony Ward and Cuthbert Johnson (Rome: CLV Edizioni Liturgiche, 1999), 360.

[108] *The Sarum Missal in English*, The Library of Liturgiology & Ecclesiology for English Readers, ed. Vernon Staley, vol. 9, pt. 2 (London: Alexander Moring Ltd., The De La More Press, 1911), 144.

[109] Gen 2:21.

strengthened with an irrevocable law."[110] It also said that the love that Christ abundantly blesses is "flowing from a divine font of charity" to be "a sign of his delight in the Church."[111] The following draft shortened it,[112] perhaps at the suggestion of the first draft, where a footnote reads,

> The subcommission judged it useful that questions not begin abruptly, but be introduced by an invitation, of which a model is proposed here. Is it too long? (The text is inspired by the constitution *Gaudium et Spes*, numbers 48–50).[113]

Indeed, a look at GS 48, 49, and 50 reveals the source behind OCM 59. This partly explains why the address is in the second person except for the middle section, which describes what Christ does for those consecrated by baptism. That thought is found in GS 48.

The address says that the couple stand before "the Church's minister and the community." ICEL had considered "the community and the minister of the Church" because in Latin the phrase "of the Church" seems to refer both to the minister and to the community. Either way, it is hard to pull out the complete sense in English.

The Spanish edition for the United States has the priest call the couple by name, even though the Latin and English do not indicate this. The priest is free to use his own words here.

Not included before this introduction is the Litany of the Saints that the USCCB had requested. Among the adaptations passed at the bishops' November meeting in 2013 was "the optional inclusion of a Litany of the Saints that highlights saints and blesseds who were married; this litany, when used, would begin the celebration of the marriage rite."[114] Apparently, this intended to show a favorable comparison between weddings and ordinations. The Italian wedding ceremony allows the inclusion of the Litany of the

---

[110] Schemata 182 addendum, p. 2.
[111] Schemata 182 addendum, p. 3.
[112] Schemata 204, p. 4.
[113] Schemata 182 addendum, p. 3.
[114] *Newsletter* XLIX (November–December 2013): 47.

Saints within the prayer of the faithful. Its version for weddings opens with an appeal to Mary under the titles of Mother of God, Mother of the Church, and Queen of the family; and to Joseph, the husband of Mary. Other saints include Joachim and Ann, Zachary and Elizabeth, and Aquila and Priscilla.[115] The same litany appears in the Mexican edition as an option after the intentions in the universal prayer, before their concluding prayer.[116] The CDWDS did not approve the adaptation for the USCCB. No reason was given.

The Questions before the Consent

60.

The priest asks the couple about freedom, fidelity, and children. Each responds separately. This is the former paragraph 24.

These questions are new to the post–Vatican II marriage ceremony. They establish the couple's canonical eligibility for matrimony in the Catholic Church, as well as their intent freely to enter marriage at this time. Prior to the council, the couple established their eligibility through the publication of banns. The insertion of questions before the exchange of consent came about in the discussions of the study group working for the Consilium.

As work was getting underway in 1964, the study group faced a specific request from the council's Preparatory Commission: "a clear admonition, in which are declared to the couple not only the strictly juridic duties, but also their moral duties, and also the ones toward God and their future children, to which they themselves are binding each other."[117] From this germinated the idea for a series of questions before the consent.

The study group first discussed the questions in April 1966, making them optional.

> *Then the questions take place, according to the judgment of the episcopal conferences.*

---

[115] See http://www.liturgia.maranatha.it/Matrimonio/r1/3page.htm.
[116] *Ritual* (Mexico), 234–35.
[117] Schemata 32, p. 15.

The questions that this concerns, or the interrogation concerning the meaning of matrimony and the duties of spouses, are nonetheless distinguished from the questions needing to be made even before the celebration, and from the very expression of consent. The questions solemnize the interrogations already made privately, prepare for the consent, and teach the whole community the character of Christian matrimony.[118]

The next draft expanded the idea and cited it as an example of "that old principle that the law of praying becomes for all the faithful the law of believing."[119] It presented three questions in the vernacular that had already been in recent use in Germany.

> N., I ask you: Have you examined your conscience before God, and have you come here freely and without force to enter marriage with this bride?
> Are you willing to love, honor and be faithful to your future wife until death parts you?
> Are you prepared to accept the children that God will send you from his hand and to bring them up according to the duty of a Christian father?[120]

The study group proposed questions such as these, inspired by a passage such as LG 41, which lists duties of married couples in their quest for holiness. It cautioned that the question about faithfulness should not reduplicate the words of the consent to follow. And it referenced GS 50 "concerning the responsibilities of parents in procreation, as well as the difficult question about the education of children who were born of mixed marriages."[121]

The questions they formulated were these:

> N., have you come here to enter into matrimony with this spouse without coercion, freely and wholeheartedly?

[118] Schemata 157, p. 7.
[119] Schemata 182a, p. 8.
[120] Ibid.
[121] Ibid., p. 9.

> Are you prepared, as you follow the path of matrimony, to love and honor your spouse for as long as you both shall live?
>
> Are you prepared to bring up the children lovingly received from God as befits a Christian parent?[122]

The expressions "as long as you both shall live" and "children lovingly received from God" are both inspired by LG 41. Still, not all the bishops were pleased.

> On the one hand, Archbishop Tulio Botero Salazar [of Medellín, Colombia] proposed that the questions be omitted because they form a more formal than real ceremony, provoking insincere and mechanical responses, and because the desired effect is better obtained through classes of premarital preparation. To explain the significance of the questions, Bishop René Boudon [of Mende, France] reminded the Fathers of the example of religious profession, in which, even if the obligations are in the future, they are distinctly recalled before making the vows.[123]

Bishop Agostino López de Moura of Portalegre-Castelo Branco, Portugal, wanted the scrutinies even for couples who were uneducated because "by means of the scrutinies, the uneducated may gain a clearer awareness of the sacrament and its obligations."[124] Bishop Otto Spülbeck of Meissen, Germany, had experience of the questions in the German vernacular and reassured the other bishops that "the responses of the couples are not only not formalistic, but are given with great responsibility and are heard in total silence." Gy, the Relator, explained: "a) the questions do not replace a pre-marriage course; b) they are not to be a formalistic matter, but rather have catechetical value: before the entire community they tell the obligations of Christian matrimony."[125] Due to the distinction between the questions and the consent, and the catechetical value of the questions, the bishops of the Consilium agreed to include them in the liturgy.

---

[122] Schemata 183, p. 3.
[123] Schemata 182b, p. 2.
[124] Ibid.
[125] Ibid.

In the next draft the questions had gone from the singular to the plural, and the expression "with this spouse" was removed from the first question. It underwent no further changes. The second question remained essentially the same, but one expression was added: "after the example of the love of Christ and the church?" which drew an image from Ephesians 5:32. The final question was changed from "as befits a Christian parent" to "according to the law of Christ?" For the first time a rubric specified that the couple were to respond separately.[126]

The following draft provided an introduction and refined the questions, hoping to make them the same in every case. There would, however, be two exceptions pertaining to the last question. Bishop Colombo, the theologian from the Secretariat of State, proposed that in the third question about the children whom the couple may receive, the words "from God" could be omitted if one of the spouses did not believe in God.[127] This pertained to marriage within Mass, and his remarks intended to address the situation of a Catholic marrying a Catholic who had lost faith in God. The entire third question could be omitted if the couple were advanced in age, a rubric that the study group copied from the recent German collection of marriage ceremonies.[128] By this time the questions took the same basic form as they did in the final edition. The reference to the church was removed from the second question and inserted into the third.

In presenting the final draft to the Consilium, the study group wrote that the ceremony that they had prepared enriched its predecessor in various ways. One example was "the questions that precede the sacrament, inspired by the German ritual, [which] affirm publicly the conditions necessary for the Church for this to be a true marriage."[129] The questions were essentially the same as the previous draft.[130]

---

[126] Schemata 204, pp. 4–5.
[127] Schemata 221, p. 4.
[128] Ibid., p. 11.
[129] Schemata 280, p. 11.
[130] Ibid., p. 7.

The Consilium agreed to include the questions in the ceremony. They objected, however, to the optional removal of the words "from God" in reference to the origins of the children. Citing Cardinal Cicognani, Ciappi wrote, "The true and objective right of the believing Catholic party should not give way to the subjective and only putative right of the non-believing Catholic."[131] They struck the option of removing the words "from God" from the third question.[132] That resulted in the final version of the questions and rubrics.

Although the second edition did not change these questions in Latin, the English translation draws out a few nuances. Instead of asking if the couple have come "freely and without reservation," they are asked if they have come "without coercion, freely and wholeheartedly." The second question now includes the expression "as you follow the path of Marriage" and eliminates the earlier translation's sexist expression "man and wife" (not "husband and wife.") The third question asks not only if the couple will bring children up but also if they are prepared to do so. The third question shares some thoughts and vocabulary with OCM 3, part of the revised Introduction. Although ICEL's translators considered having the minister ask the couple if they were prepared "to educate" their children, they settled on "to bring them up."

Some variations to these questions appear in French-speaking Canada. The minister has a brief introduction: "N. and N., you have heard the word of God who reveals the greatness of human love and marriage." Then, the questions have been rephrased: "You are about to unite yourselves to each other in marriage. Are you doing this freely and without force?" "In uniting yourselves in the vow of marriage, you promise each other mutual love and respect. Is this for your whole life?" "Are you prepared to welcome the children whom God will give you and to educate them according to the Gospel of Christ and in the faith of the Church?" They answer together or separately, "Yes," to each of these, though they may answer to the second question, "Yes, for all my life." Then the priest may add these or similar words if they seem appropriate:

[131] Schemata 280 addendum, p. 2.
[132] Ibid., p. 3.

"Are you prepared to accept together your mission as Christians in the world and in the Church?" They answer, "Yes."[133]

In a completely alternate version, the minister addresses the assembly: "With N. and N. we have heard the word of God, who reveals the greatness of human love and marriage." He makes this combined statement: "Marriage presupposes that the couple unite themselves one to the other freely and without force, that they promise mutual love and respect for their whole life, that they welcome the children that God gives them and educate them according to the Gospel of Christ and in the faith of the Church." Then he says to the couple, "N. and N., is that indeed how you wish to live in marriage?" They answer together or separately, "Yes." He may then add the question about their mission as Christians.[134]

In Mexico, the couple answer more fully: "Yes, I come freely" to the first question, and "Yes, I am prepared" to the others. Mexico also has an alternate version of the questions: "N. and N., are you coming to enter matrimony with complete freedom?" "Do you promise to love and keep mutual faithfulness with each other throughout your whole life?" "Are you prepared responsibly to receive children, the fruit of your love, and to educate them in the faith of Christ?" The couple answer "Yes" to each question.[135]

In England and Wales, civil law requires the couple to make an additional declaration, which is added to the ceremony as OCM 60a. Names and surnames must be used. The priest asks, for example, "Are you, John Smith, free lawfully to marry Mary Jones?" He responds, "I am." A similar question is asked of the bride to obtain her reply. Or the groom reads or repeats these words after the priest: for example, "I do solemnly declare that I know not of any lawful impediment why I, John Smith, may not be joined in matrimony to Mary Jones." The bride makes a similar declaration. Or the groom may say, for example, "I declare that I know of no legal reason why I, John Smith, may not be joined in marriage to Mary Jones." The bride makes a similar statement. The traditional

[133] *Rituel Romain*, 26.
[134] Ibid., 27.
[135] *Ritual* (Mexico), 51.

Catholic custom by which the couple state only their first names is insufficient for a civilly binding union in England and Wales.[136]

Through these questions the couple are declaring their freedom to marry. The responsibility to make this declaration honestly sits squarely on their own shoulders. The publication of banns of marriage, through which others in the community could raise objections, is no longer required. Nor does the Catholic ceremony include the dramatic statement, based on the early Book of Common Prayer, "If anyone can show any just cause why they may not lawfully be joined together, let him now speak, or else hereafter for ever hold his peace."[137] The couple declare their eligibility on their own.

The Consent

61.

The priest introduces the consent with a summary of the preceding questions. He says that the couple have the intent of entering matrimony, and he asks them to join their right hands and declare their consent. In the first edition, this opened paragraph 25, which also included the words of consent. Now those have been moved to a separate number. In Mexico, the rest of the community stands for this introduction, as the couple already have done.[138]

This introduction has remained virtually unchanged since it appeared in the first draft of the study group in 1966. The word order is slightly different, and the priest asked the couple to declare their "will,"[139] which was changed to "consent" in the second draft.[140] The consent is an expression of the will.

In French Canada the priest has four choices here, each with a different introduction. For example, "Because you have decided to unite yourselves in the bonds of marriage, in the presence of

[136] OCMEW, pp. 32–33.
[137] Searle and Stevenson, *Documents of the Marriage Liturgy*, 217, alt.
[138] *Ritual* (Mexico), 52.
[139] Schemata 183, p. 5.
[140] Schemata 204, p. 5.

God and of his Church, join hands and exchange your consent."[141] Or, "In order that you may be united in Christ and that your love, transformed by him, may become a visible sign of the love of God, before the Church gathered here, join your hands and exchange your consent."[142]

The French Canadian ritual does not specify the "right hand" as does the Latin and the English. The Spanish translation in force in the United States does not specify the right hand,[143] nor does the one in Mexico,[144] but the one in Colombia does.[145] The Mexican book further instructs the couple to face each other.[146]

The symbolism of the hand can be traced back to the Old Testament marriage of Sarah and Tobiah, where Sarah's father Raguel takes her by the hand and gives her to Tobiah (7:12). The Old Vulgate says more explicitly that he takes the right hand of his daughter and gives it to the right hand of Tobiah (7:15). (This is the same passage that contributed to an entrance antiphon in preconciliar ceremonies.) At many contemporary weddings, at the end of the procession, the father of the bride, who has walked her down the aisle, enacts a similar gesture when he entrusts her to the waiting groom. Instinctively, the father may set his daughter's hand into the groom's. The Mozarabic *Liber Ordinum* in use in Spain in the early Middle Ages had the priest hand the bride to the groom before the blessings.[147] The Catholic Church, however, does not retain these traditions. The rubrics make no mention of the hand of the father of the bride, or the intervention of the priest. Instead, the couple join their right hands in a symbol of expressing their will to give themselves to each other.

---

[141] *Rituel Romain*, 28.

[142] Ibid.

[143] *Ritual*, 10.

[144] *Ritual* (Mexico), 52.

[145] *Ritual* (Colombia), 32.

[146] *Ritual* (Mexico), 52.

[147] Marius Férotin, *Le* Liber Ordinum *en Usage dans l'église wisigothique et mozarabe d'Espagne du cinquième au onzième siècle*, ed. Anthony Ward and Cuthbert Johnson (Rome: CLV Edizioni Liturgiche, 1996), 299. Hereafter *Liber Ordinum*.

The symbol is quite ancient. The joining of right hands signified marriage in ancient Rome since the first century BC[148] and
extending for several hundred years, as evidenced in both pagan
and Christian iconography.[149] Roman sarcophagi showing a man
and a woman joining hands give evidence of their marriage. It
is unknown if the early Roman ceremony included a joining of
hands, though it is plausible that this led to the common artistic
representation. Gregory Nazianzen referred to the custom when he
wrote Vitalian the disappointing news that he could not take part
in the marriage of Vitalian's daughter Olympia, "to join the hands
of the two young spouses in order to join them to God's."[150] From
the thirteenth century the Syrian Oriental Orthodox Rite includes
a joining of hands as part of the ceremony.[151] The joining of hands
was omitted from the 1605 *Rituale* compiled for the missions in Nagasaki because of Japanese cultural sensitivities.[152] The 1614 Roman
Ritual had the couple join hands after the consent as the priest
pronounced that he was joining them in matrimony.[153]

As an innovation, the study group moved the gesture forward
to the words of consent, which shifted the emphasis away from
the priest's reception of the consent to the couple's giving it. When
an engaged couple today join their right hands, they partake of
a very early Roman symbol uniting them with couples over two
millennia.

62.

His right hand joined to the bride's, the groom gives his consent
to marry her, and she then consents to marry him. In the United

---

[148] Adrien Nocent, "The Christian Rite of Marriage in the West," in *Handbook
for Liturgical Studies IV: Sacraments and Sacramentals*, ed. Anscar J. Chupungco
(Collegeville, MN: Liturgical Press, 2000), 277.

[149] L. Reekmans, "*Dextrarum iunctio*," http://www.treccani.it/enciclopedia
/dextrarum-iunctio/ (Enciclopedia-dell'-Arte-Antica).

[150] Stefano Parenti, "The Christian Rite of Marriage in the East," in *Handbook
for Liturgical Studies*, vol. 4, Sacraments and Sacramentals, ed. Anscar J. Chupungco (Collegeville, MN: Liturgical Press, 2000), 256.

[151] Stevenson, *To Join Together*, 62.

[152] Ibid., 115.

[153] *Roman Ritual*, 462.

States the couple may use an alternative form, as was true in the first edition, where both versions appeared within paragraph 25. The English of both forms of consent has been slightly changed for the second edition of the OCM.

According to canon law, the consent of the parties constitutes marriage.[154] The consent is an act of the will by which the man and the woman give themselves to each other.[155] This teaching originated with Scholasticism, especially with Peter Lombard (+1164), who wrote that "the efficient cause of marriage is consent." He argued that the consent had to be verbal, not mental, and present, not future. When the man and the woman say to each other, "I take you for my spouse," they are married.[156] Prior to this time, people understood that the priest's blessing established the marriage, and this position is still widely held in the East. The Roman Rite, however, places its stress on the exchange of consent in the presence of the church's minister. The liturgy and the canons of the church do not explicitly call the spouses the ministers of the sacrament and the priest the mere witness, probably out of concern for the Eastern Rites, but these are effectively, ritually, and symbolically their roles.

The earliest record of the couple declaring their consent in the vernacular, and not simply responding affirmatively to questions about their consent, comes from the fourteenth-century French rite from the Cistercian abbey of Barbeau.[157] The fifteenth-century Sarum Missal, offering a view of English ceremony before the Reformation, included a double form of consent. The priest asked the man and the woman if they would take the other, to which they answered, "I will," and then they each declared their consent to each other while holding their right hands. The formula became popular throughout the English-speaking world: "I, N., take you, N., to be my wedded wife, to have and to hold from this day forward, for better, for worse, for richer, for poorer: in sickness and

---

[154] Canon 1057 §1.

[155] Canon 1057 §2.

[156] Searle and Stevenson, *Documents of the Marriage Liturgy*, 148–49, citing Peter Lombard, *Sentences* Lib. IV, dist. xxvii, 3.

[157] Stevenson, *To Join Together*, 43. See also Searle and Stevenson, *Documents of the Marriage Liturgy*, 156.

in health till death do us part, if holy church will ordain it; and thereto I pledge my troth." The bride said the same but added her promise to be obedient to her husband in bed and at table.[158] This formula influenced the work of the English Reformer Thomas Cranmer (+1556), and a version still appears in the *Book of Common Prayer*.[159] The second edition of the OCM retains it as the alternate form of consent in the United States, Australia, and England and Wales. The version in the United States includes the expression "to love and to cherish," absent from the first edition but making it closer to the version in use in England and Wales. There, the groom and bride have the option of saying "I take thee" instead of "I take you," showing the antiquity of the custom. They must use both their first and last names, as the civil law of England and of Wales requires it.[160]

In the 1614 Roman Ritual, the consent was obtained through the question of the priest just before the wedding Mass began. He asked the groom, "N., do you will to receive N. here present for your legitimate wife according to the rite of holy mother Church?" "I do," he responded. Then the priest asked the bride the same question concerning the groom, and she made the same response.[161] Prior to the Second Vatican Council, the Roman Rite did not permit the bride and groom to make this complete declaration to each other. They simply answered, "I do."

When the study group revised the consent, it wanted the couple to make the entire declaration, effectively taking the priest out of the consent. They wrote,

> The words of consent should be expressed not with the simple and bare affirmative response of the groom and the bride to the questioning priest, but in a formula that the groom and bride pronounce one after the other, and 'nonetheless with the firm law that the assisting priest asks for and receives the consent of those making the agreement' [SC 77]. . . .

---

[158] *Sarum Missal in English*, pt. 2, 145–46, alt. See also Searle and Stevenson, *Documents of the Marriage Liturgy*, 163–66.

[159] Stevenson, *To Join Together*, 91–95.

[160] OCMEW, 34–35.

[161] *Roman Ritual*, 460.

The proposed method, with pastoral and indeed theological respect, more clearly and more appropriately expresses the role of the groom and the bride, who are ministers of the sacramental contract.[162]

They thought that having the couple speak these complete lines "does not seem to offer a difficulty as long as the formula not be too long."[163]

The group wondered whether the rubrics should explicitly state that the priest says the words first, and then the couple repeat after him. Martimort thought that the engaged alone should say the words, but Wagner argued from ancient Roman custom and the practice of all tribunals that the priest should speak first and the couple repeat after him. Msgr. Emmanuel Bonet, a Spanish auditor of the Roman Rota, reminded the group that the Oriental Rites require the blessing of the priest for validity.[164]

In a later draft, the group turned to the popular English formula from the Sarum Missal, the York Missal, the 1948 *Our Catholic Marriage Service* from London, and the *Book of Common Prayer* as a model: "I, N., take thee, N., for my lawful wife, to have and to hold, from this day forward, for better, for worse, for richer, for poorer, in sickness and in health, till death do us part."[165] They proposed using this as a model. They affirmed the decree of Saint Pius X, *Ne temere*, which required the priest to ask for and receive the consent, but the actual consent they confidently gave to the couple.[166]

They composed the consent with these words for the groom: "I., N., take you, N., for my wife, and I promise to keep faith with you forever from this day, in good times and in bad, in poverty and in wealth, in sickness and in good health, that I may love you and honor you until death separates us." The bride stated the same

---

[162] Schemata 157, p. 8.
[163] Ibid.
[164] Schemata 157 adnexum, p. 3.
[165] Schemata 182a, p. 9.
[166] Ibid., p. 10.

with the logical adjustments addressing the groom.[167] One of the members of the subcommission wanted the formula to express the mutual gift of the partners, underscored many times in GS 48–51. He proposed, "I, N., receive you, N., for my wife, and I hand myself to you as a spouse. I promise that I will keep faith."[168]

In early 1967, Bishop Colombo's observation about the consent was reported to the group: "At first glance, he liked the English formula of consent, which he had heard at the marriage of Princess Margaret, and it seemed to him appropriate to show well how divorce is a stranger to the sense of Christian marriage."[169]

The next draft removed the words "forever from this day."[170] The final draft noted that the formula was inspired by the traditional one in English-speaking countries by both Catholics and non-Catholics.[171] The formula still included the expression "in poverty and wealth,"[172] which was eliminated before the first edition of the OCM. Bugnini explained that Pope Paul himself requested the removal of that phrase in a letter to the Sacred Congregation for the Doctrine of the Faith on December 3, 1968.[173]

The final translation of both editions does not slavishly include the meaning of the Latin word *ut*. The Latin text has each partner say, "I promise to be faithful to you . . . so that (*ut*) I may love you and honor you." The meaning of the formula is that each does not merely promise faithfulness and love but faithfulness in order to love. ICEL heard a proposal to insert the word "so" before the final lines in this way: "so to love you and honor you." But this did not carry. Instead, the revised translation turned an independent clause, "I will love you," into a phrase, "to love you." Also, instead of saying, "I promise to be true to you," each now says, "I promise to be faithful to you."

[167] Schemata 183, p. 3.
[168] Ibid.
[169] Schemata 204, p. 9.
[170] Schemata 221, p. 12.
[171] Schemata 280, p. ii.
[172] Ibid., p. 8.
[173] Bugnini, *Reform of the Liturgy*, 703.

Some who reviewed the proposed revised translation objected to the expression "in good times and in bad" because the "good times" can have an overly secular connotation. But the words had already been translated in one of the final blessings in the Missal, found also at OCM 249, so the same English words appear here.

In French Canada, there are three corresponding versions of the consent. The first is a translation of OCM 62.[174] In the second version, the groom asks, "N., do you wish to be my wife (spouse)?" She says, "Yes, (I do). And you, N., do you wish to be my husband (spouse)?" He says, "Yes, (I do)." Then he continues with a form of the consent.[175] The third form also begins with the same questions, though each gives a fuller response; for example, "Yes, I wish to be your wife (spouse)." After each has questioned and responded, the bride says, "I receive you as a spouse, and I give myself to you," and the groom says the same. Together, they say, "To love one another faithfully in good times and in bad and to support one another all our life long."[176] A fourth formula corresponds to OCM 63.

In Colombia, the second edition of the OCM offers the couple a selection of six formulas from which they may make their consent. The first is a translation of OCM 62.[177] The second corresponds to OCM 63.[178] The third resembles the second formula of French Canada, where the couple ask each other if they will to be married.[179] In the fourth, the groom begins: "I, N., give myself to you as your spouse, and I receive you as my spouse." The bride responds, "I accept you and receive you." He says, "I promise to remain faithful to you in happiness, in adversity and sorrow, in health and in sickness, in poverty and prosperity, to love you and respect you throughout all the days of my life." Then the bride begins the same sequence.[180] The fifth formula is a variation on the third, beginning

---

[174] *Rituel Romain*, 29.
[175] Ibid., 30.
[176] Ibid., 31.
[177] *Ritual* (Colombia), 32.
[178] Ibid., 32–33.
[179] Ibid., 33–34.
[180] Ibid., 34–35.

with the question, "N., do you wish to be my spouse?"[181] The sixth is an abbreviated version of the first, omitting the references to prosperity and adversity, health and sickness.[182]

The two versions of the consent in the edition for the United States exercise restraint, adopting the first directly from the OCM and the second, very similar, from a longstanding English tradition. In the Spanish edition for the United States, an alternate form of consent appears within this paragraph. The groom asks, "N., do you want to be my wife?" "Yes, I do," she says. Then she asks, "N., do you want to be my husband?" "Yes, I do," he says. The groom says, "N., I receive you as my wife, and I promise to love you faithfully throughout my whole life." She says, "N., I receive you as my husband, and I promise to love you faithfully throughout my whole life." This copies one of the additional versions in Mexico, which offers a third option: "I, N., receive you, N., as my spouse, and I pledge myself to you as a legal spouse, according to what the Holy Mother Catholic Church commands."[183]

63.

The priest may put the words of consent into question form. This material is taken from the end of the former paragraph 25, now with a number of its own. Both versions of the consent from OCM 62 are presented in full in question form in OCM 63. The second form is special to the United States. Like its counterpart in OCM 62, there is no Latin original. The original edition paired the two methods—the declaration and the question format of the first version of the consent, and then the declaration and question format of the second version. Now the methods are separated: The two declared versions are placed together in OCM 62, and the two question versions are in OCM 63.

Throughout the history of the Roman Rite, it was more common to see the consent given as a response to questions. In the Roman Pontifical of the twelfth century, for example, the bishop asked the bride's father, "Do you want to give this woman to this groom?"

[181] Ibid., 35–36.
[182] Ibid., 36.
[183] *Ritual* (Mexico), 52–53.

The father responded, "I do." Then the bishop asked the groom, "Do you want to receive her as your wife?" He responded, "I do." The bishop asked the woman, "Do you want to receive this man for your husband?" She said, "I do." Then the bishop asked the groom, "Do you receive her into your trust?" He said, "Indeed." The bishop asked the woman, "Will you heed him in your trust?" She responded, "Indeed."[184] After the Council of Trent, the question format appeared in the 1614 Ritual as the only option.

The study group tried to reverse this trend completely, eliminating the question format and promoting only the declared statement. But when the OCM was finally published in 1969, both methods appeared. Bugnini wrote that the reinsertion of the traditional questions came from the Sacred Congregation for the Doctrine of the Faith and from Pope Paul. A letter from the congregation on December 13, 1968, said that the traditional formula should "always" be an option. It was included, but as the second alternative. Some people objected that marriage would not seem like marriage if the couple did not say "I do." But the study group felt that the fuller declarations were far richer.[185]

In England and Wales, the question format is forbidden because of civil requirements. OCM 63 is completely missing from the second edition of the ceremony published there. The numeration proceeds from 62 directly to 64.

The Reception of Consent

64.

The priest receives the consent of the couple. He asks God to strengthen the consent that they have made. An alternative form has been added to the second edition; otherwise, this is the former paragraph 26.

This reception represents one of the most significant changes to the Catholic marriage ceremony after the Second Vatican Council. In the Roman Ritual of 1614, after the couple answered the question giving their consent, the priest asked them to join their hands.

---

[184] *Le Pontifical Romain*, 300.
[185] Bugnini, *Reform of the Liturgy*, 703.

Then he said, "I join you together in matrimony. In the name of the
Father, and of the Son, and of the Holy Spirit. Amen." He could use
other words according to a local rite. He then sprinkled the couple
with blessed water.[186] The priest had an active role in commanding
the joining of the couple's hands following their consent, and in
declaring that he had joined them in matrimony.

The earliest record of such words comes from fourteenth-century
Rouen in France during a time when the couple was expected to
give their consent publicly, and a priest represented the church.[187]
Although the couple effect the sacrament, the church required a
priest to be present, and his words made it sound as though he
were conferring the sacrament upon them.

When the study group first went to work after the Second
Vatican Council, its members realized that the preparatory commission had favored retaining the words "I join you."[188] This
prompted some discussion. Msgr. Joseph Pascher of the University of Munich wondered why the commission wanted to keep it.
Lentini, a Benedictine from Italy, explained that it offered a way
of thinking that the priest was a minister of the sacrament. Bonet,
a specialist in law, noted that the council fathers said that the
spouses are ministers. "We have therefore an open way." But he
continued, "Nevertheless, the question is whether the complete
intervention of the Church is enclosed within the intervention of
the couple alone." This point became difficult to resolve.[189]

By the end of 1966, aware that the formula "I join you" was
fairly recent in church history, the study group proposed the idea
that the intervention of the priest would become a kind of prayer
to God. This seemed to honor the couple's role while slightly shift-
ing the responsibility of the priest.[190] They proposed this formula:
"I in the name of the Church receive your consent, and one with

---

[186] *Roman Ritual*, 462.
[187] Stevenson, *To Join Together*, 44.
[188] Schemata 32, p. 15; Schemata 157, p. 3.
[189] Schemata 157 adnexum, p. 3.
[190] Schemata 182a, pp. 10–11.

all the witnesses present here, I give thanks to God who has joined you together. Now may the Lord fulfill his blessing in you."[191]

A footnote, however, probably from Gy, raised a concern:

> I wonder if the past tense, "who has joined you together," doesn't imply that the marriage was completed "by the intervention of the couple alone," a disputed question that we should leave open (cf. the observation of Msgr. Bonet at the meeting of the relators . . .). Would it not be better to adopt a formula carrying the words, "May God himself join you together, and may he fulfill his blessing in you," by expanding from the first part the citation from Tobit 7:15 (Old Vulgate) (cf. the entrance antiphon for the mass of marriage . . .)?[192]

This argument seems to have had an effect. By the next year the formula changed to reflect the revised tenses of the verb.[193] It remains in force through the second edition of the OCM. A footnote from another draft explained,

> The Council Fathers agreed on October 9, 1964, that the formula by which the priest received the consent of each partner be brought back in another way. The formula that is now proposed in no way intends to prescind the disputed question of whether the sacramental rite is completed only with the words of consent, or if it also includes the intervention of the priest receiving the consent (cf. Schemata 182, number 19).[194]

The final draft contained this explanation: "The words with which the celebrant receives the consent have been modified in a way that they express the specific role of the spouses in the sacrament, and, at the same time, do not seem contrary to the conception of the Oriental Churches on the role of the priest."[195]

The second edition of the OCM has added an alternative formula for the reception of the priest. It is loosely based on a prayer

[191] Schemata 183, p. 4.
[192] Ibid.
[193] Schemata 204, p. 5.
[194] Schemata 221, p. 12.
[195] Schemata 280, p. ii.

that served as part of wedding ceremonies in centuries past. For example, a manuscript from the twelfth century Ordo III includes this prayer, offered by the priest after the couple have entered the church and lie prostrate: "O God of Abraham, God of Isaac, God of Jacob, bless these adolescents, and sow the seed of eternal life in their minds, that they may desire to do whatever they have learned is for their advantage. Through your Son Jesus Christ, the recoverer of humanity, who lives with you."[196] Evanou says that this was ultimately the source for what appears in the second edition here.[197]

The prayer also appeared in the eleventh-century Pontifical of Egbert[198] and the eleventh-century Pontifical of Robert of Jumieges.[199] The same prayer appears in the twelfth-century Roman Pontifical together with this just preceding it: "May the God of Abraham, the God of Isaac, and the God of Jacob himself protect you and fulfill his blessing in you."[200] This prayer is found in the Old Vulgate of Tobit 7:15, where Raguel takes his daughter Sara's right hand and places it into the right hand of Tobiah, also the source for a much-used entrance antiphon. The 1614 Roman Ritual concluded the wedding with this blessing:

> May the God of Abraham, the God of Isaac, and the God of Jacob be with you, and may he fulfill his blessing in you, that you may see your children's children up to the third and fourth generation, and afterward may you possess eternal life without end, with the help of our Lord Jesus Christ, who with the Father and the Holy Spirit lives and reigns as God for ever and ever.[201]

The blessing of seeing the third generation of children appears in Genesis 50:23, and seeing the fourth generation is in Job 42:16.

---

[196] Ordo III: Ex ms. Pontificali monasterii Lyrensis, annorum 600, *De Antiquis Ecclesiae Ritibus*, 1. I, c. IX, a. V, II:356.

[197] Jean Evanou, "Commentarium," *Notitiae* XXVI (1990): 315.

[198] Searle and Stevenson, *Documents of the Marriage Liturgy*, 106.

[199] Ibid., 111.

[200] *Le Pontifical Romain*, 301.

[201] *Roman Ritual*, 468.

The prayerful declaration as it appears in the OCM begins with the threefold invocation of the God of Abraham, Isaac, and Jacob, which thus connects to Tobit 7:15 (Old Vulgate), and then recalls the first parents of the book of Genesis and Jesus' admonition that what God has joined no one may put asunder (Matt 19:6). This forms the biblical backdrop to the prayer of the priest that God will strengthen and bless the consent that the couple have declared before the church. The first edition of the OCM had eliminated the traditional prayer requesting a blessing from the God of Abraham, Isaac, and Jacob. This alternative reception is new, but it is well founded on biblical and euchological traditions.

The translation of the first option uses the expression "the consent you have declared." Translators considered "the consent you have given," but it was noted that in OCM 61 the priest invites the couple to "declare" their consent. Some commentators thought that the last line of both versions should retain the traditional expression that what God joins together, "no man" may put asunder but, several biblical translations having been consulted, "no one" was chosen to avoid gender-exclusive language. The same translation appears in OCM 5.

In French Canada, the priest need not, but he may, accompany either formula with a gesture. He may extend his right hand in the direction of the couple. Or he may place his right hand on the joined hands of the couple.[202] It is unclear if this gesture would bring more life to the words or if it would call more attention to the presidency of the priest, a stance the study group was trying to diminish.

65.

The priest invites the people to bless the Lord, and they all respond with an acclamation. This is new to the second edition of the OCM. The people may respond with a different acclamation in speech or song, but they are to make some response.

There are pastoral challenges with this. The people will not spontaneously know that they are to respond or with what words.

[202] *Rituel Romain*, 33.

If the couple have prepared a participation aid, the dialogue can be included there. If music is prepared for the wedding, then an acclamation can more easily be sung—even intoned once by a cantor and then repeated by the people.

Other acclamations are permitted, though none is specifically proposed. All could sing an Alleluia, or the refrain of the psalm, or another song in the liturgy. In Mexico, however, the people are given another suggested response: "Amen."[203] The Mexican edition also includes musical notation for keyboard and guitar accompaniment.

Following this acclamation, again in Mexico, the people are seated.[204] They stand only for the consent and its reception. Perhaps this throws more focus onto the sacrament itself—but at the cost of diminishing its ancillary ceremonies.

When Adrien Nocent wrote his 1986 commentary on the post–Vatican II wedding ceremony, he inserted a prophetic pastoral lament: "The participation of the faithful should be promoted much more with some acclamations; for example, during the blessing or even earlier, at the very moment of consent. In fact, in this sacrament the participation of the assembly has been almost completely forgotten."[205] Perhaps the compilers of the revised edition took note.

After all have been seated, the Mexican edition adds this paragraph: "At this moment, according to the customs of the place, the groom lifts the veil with which the bride has covered her face."[206]

The Blessing and Giving of Rings

66.

The priest blesses the rings. All answer, "Amen." Alternative formulas appear at OCM 194 and 195. The priest may sprinkle the rings with blessed water. He gives them to the couple. This is the former paragraph 27.

[203] *Ritual* (Mexico), 56.
[204] Ibid.
[205] Nocent, "Il matrimonio cristiano," 364.
[206] *Ritual* (Mexico), 56.

The optional sprinkling is new to the second edition. The first edition did not call for the sprinkling of rings with blessed water at all, though in practice many priests and deacons have done it uninterruptedly. Now they may with impunity.

In the twelfth-century Roman Pontifical, only the groom presented a ring to the bride; she did not reciprocate. The bishop made the sign of the cross over the ring and sprinkled it with blessed water.[207] In the Sarum Manual the priest sprinkled the ring after blessing it, unless it had been previously blessed.[208] For cultural purposes, the ring was omitted from the ceremony in the 1605 Nagasaki Ritual.[209]

In the 1614 Roman Ritual, the rubrics pertaining to marriage are fairly spare, but the introductory paragraph, which describes the ministers and their vesture, also says that one of them carries "a vessel of blessed water and a sprinkler."[210] The priest used these objects to sprinkle the ring after he blessed it.[211]

The prayer of blessing from the 1614 Ritual reappears in OCM 194, though the earlier version used words that pertain to one ring, and the current version changes the form of the nouns, pronouns, and verbs in order to pertain to two.

The blessing first appeared in a 1966 draft of the OCM[212] and remained unchanged through all the later drafts and editions of the Missal. Kenneth Stevenson says that it originates from a twelfth-century prayer from Rennes, Normandy.[213] A long history had the groom place a ring on the bride's finger at the door of the church at the start of the ceremony. It functioned as an engagement ring before the giving of consent. The study group opted to keep the ring ceremony after the consent, as it had been in the 1614 Ritual.[214]

[207] *Le Pontifical Romain*, 301.
[208] Searle and Stevenson, *Documents of the Marriage Liturgy*, 167.
[209] Stevenson, *To Join Together*, 115.
[210] *Roman Ritual*, 460.
[211] Ibid., 462.
[212] Schemata 183, p. 4.
[213] Stevenson, *To Join Together*, 140.
[214] Ibid., 128–29.

ICEL at first favored a translation of the blessing's last line with the words "faithfulness and love." The word order differs from the Latin, but the rhythms were thought to work better in English. Some translators also thought that "faithfulness" had a broader connotation than "fidelity," which people may associate with sexual fidelity alone. In the end, "love" was moved to the earlier position, and the translation of "faithfulness" became "fidelity." The word "your" from the first translation has no equivalent in Latin and does not appear in the revised.

If a bishop is presiding, he puts aside his pastoral staff to bless the rings. He wears his miter if he uses this version of the blessing. If he uses one of the alternatives, however, he removes his miter, because they directly address God.[215]

In Colombia, all the versions of the ring blessing are found together at this point of the book. The two from the Latin appendix have been moved forward. The same is true in French Canada, where a fourth option has also been approved, indicating the place where the priest makes the sign of the cross with his hand over the rings: "Lord our God, you who made a covenant with us through Jesus Christ, bless + now these rings [covenants]: that they may be for N. and N. the sign of their fidelity and the reminder of their love."[216]

In Mexico, the tradition of the *arras* is so strong that they are always included together with the rings. In fact, the first option is for the priest to bless both the rings and the *arras* in a single prayer. He may sprinkle both with blessed water.[217] The introduction of the Mexican edition already explained the significance of the *arras*, as noted in the comments on OCM 36.

At the conclusion of this paragraph, the OCM says that the priest gives the rings to the bride and bridegroom. Normally he does this in the reverse order. As with all the other texts shared by the couple, the groom speaks first.

67A.

First the husband, and then the wife, places a ring on the partner's finger. They may recite the noncompulsory formula. This is the former paragraph 28.

---

[215] CB 608.
[216] *Rituel Romain*, 34.
[217] *Ritual* (Mexico), 57.

In the pre–Vatican II ceremony, the groom placed the ring on the bride's finger while saying nothing. An optional spoken formula was added in the first edition in the OCM, and this has not changed. The rubric in the first translation said that each "may say" the words, but in practice they nearly always did. Now a more literal translation of the same Latin rubric reads, "saying, as the circumstances so suggest."

The words are based on a ring ceremony from the wedding of Judith, the daughter of Charles the Bald, to Ethelwulf, king of East Anglia, in 856, when Ethelwulf was returning home from a pilgrimage to Rome.

> Receive a ring, a sign of faithfulness and love, and the conjugal bond of joining together, that "no one may separate those whom God has joined together" (Mark 10:9), who lives and reigns for ever and ever. I betroth you, a virgin chaste and pure for one man, the future spouse, as the holy women—Sarah, Rebekah, Rachel, Esther, Judith, Anna and Naomi—were for their men, while our Lord Jesus Christ bestows favors as the author and sanctifier of weddings, who lives and reigns for ever and ever.[218]

The use of a ring has a time-honored history. Both Clement (+99) and Tertullian mention the engagement ring.[219] Isidore of Seville explained the significance of its placement: "Hence it is placed on the fourth finger, for in that finger, it is said, there is a vein which carries the blood to the heart."[220] Another early version of the groom's words can be found in the twelfth-century pontifical, perhaps dating from a ceremony several centuries earlier. After the bishop sprinkles the ring with blessed water, the groom places it on the finger of the bride and says, "N., with this ring I marry you, in the name of the Father [and of the Son and of the Holy Spirit]."[221] In the 1614 Ritual, the groom put

---

[218] Ritzer, *Formen, Riten und Religiöses Brauchtum*, 256, citing *Caroli Calvi . . . Capitula* (Paris 1633), 498ff; see also Stevenson, *To Join Together*, 140.

[219] Stevenson, *To Join Together*, 19.

[220] Searle and Stevenson, *Documents of the Marriage Liturgy*, 119.

[221] *Le Pontifical Romain*, 301.

the ring on the bride's finger, but the priest said, "In the name of the Father and of the Son and of the Holy Spirit."[222]

In the East, the Byzantine Rite introduced a ring ceremony in the tenth century, and two rings by the eleventh.[223] The Syrian Oriental Orthodox Rite, based on a thirteenth-century ritual, includes an engagement ring for the bride and wedding rings for the bride and groom.[224]

In the ritual from the Abbey of Barbeau, the groom moved the ring successively from the bride's right thumb to her index and middle finger while invoking the three names of the Trinity, and then placed it on her ring finger while saying, "N., with this ring I wed you, with my body I honor you, and I endow you with the dowry agreed upon by my friends and yours."[225] The Sarum Manual has the same explanation and instructions for moving the ring from finger to finger, ending with the fourth, "for in that finger there is a vein which runs to the heart."[226]

For the most part, one ring was used in the ceremony, as in the 1614 Ritual. There were exceptions, such as the local ritual in Bordeaux in 1596.[227] After the post–Vatican II ceremony called for two rings, Nocent wrote a defense in favor of the single-ring ceremony. He realized that the postconciliar ceremony greatly strove to stress the equality of the spouses, and the two rings are another sign of that value, but

> the single ring does not only mean that the wife is bound to the husband, but that he is visibly bound to her in fidelity. But up to about the eleventh century, and much later in Normandy, for example, the blessing of a single ring placed by the husband on the ring finger of his wife, far from corresponding to a conception of the husband as superior to the woman, it meant, to the contrary, the covenant that Christ confers on the Church, his spouse adorned with glory. If it is Christ who confers the covenant (ring), that does not mean that the

[222] *Roman Ritual*, 462, 464.
[223] Stevenson, *To Join Together*, 76.
[224] Ibid., 62–63.
[225] Searle and Stevenson, *Documents of the Marriage Liturgy*, 160.
[226] Ibid., 168.
[227] Stevenson, *To Join Together*, 102.

wife is inferior to her husband, but that she receives from him, as the Church receives from Christ, the covenant (ring) of unity.[228]

In the Spanish translation in force in the United States, as in the new ring prayer in French Canada,[229] the word for the wedding ring is a cognate with the word for a covenant. Other Spanish translations use the word for "ring." But in some non-English speaking parts of the United States and Canada, it is as though the partners are saying, "Receive this covenant." The ring is understood, but the double meaning is quite apparent. Because of the double-ring ceremony, its connection to the covenant that Christ bestows on the church (and not vice versa) is obscured.

From the beginning the study group faced the reality that the Fathers of the Second Vatican Council had favored retaining the custom of blessing only one ring.[230] Members of the study group preferred two rings, allowing the conferences some options: They could omit the rings if the usage presented difficulties in the local culture. Admitting the long tradition of having only the bride wear a ring, the study group judged "that the use of two rings should not only be permitted but prescribed as a sign of the mutual fidelity of both spouses." A conference could elect to omit the blessing of rings.[231]

The study group also determined the sequence of the ring ceremony within the structure of the rite. The Germans, for example, were following an older tradition of giving a ring before the giving of consent. Another proposal placed the consent between the blessing and giving of rings, in order to move from the spoken consent to the action without interruption. But the group settled on the sequence already in place in the 1614 Roman Ritual, of Norman origins, which began with the consent and then continued with the blessing and giving of rings. "We prefer the more commonly modern interpretation according to which the rings are considered as a sign of the consent just given and the promise of fidelity."[232]

[228] Nocent, "Il matrimonio cristiano," 362.
[229] *Rituel Romain*, 34.
[230] Schemata 32, p. 15; Schemata 157, p. 3.
[231] Schemata 157, pp. 6–7.
[232] Ibid., p. 7.

Some of the discussion has been preserved. Dirks preferred giving the conferences some freedom because rings could present cultural difficulties. Gy believed that they should decide on two rings "if the rite is retained . . . , that the equality of the spouses be clearly expressed according to the thought of the Council." Wagner noted that there were other ways of showing equality in the past, such as in the promise of the groom, but they had to consider the present needs of the ceremony in the Roman Rite. Pascher advised, "Pastorally, two rings should be used, lest the males think that they are not bound." Joaquím Nabuco of Brazil noted that the practice of having two rings was already spreading. Wagner thought that the use of a single ring raised the question whether the bride alone was bound to the marriage. "The one who gives the ring binds the one who receives it." Pascher even said, "It is doubtful that in the liturgy the ring is the image of the union between Christ and the Church, to which it is compared."[233]

A similar discussion took place concerning the sequence of the ritual elements. For example, Anton Hänggi of the University of Fribourg, who favored the first (German) option of putting the ring ceremony before the consent, thought that the complete consent was expressed better if the action preceded the words. Wagner offered that the second suggestion, placing the consent between the blessing and exchange of rings, was "not necessary," though Cellier held that placing the blessing between the consent and the exchange of rings "interrupts what the couple expects."[234] In the end, the third option held.

The study group knew that these three options were already in force in certain parts of the world. Germany was practicing the first, and Poland had the blessing of rings at the beginning of the entire ceremony. Canada had placed the consent between the blessing and exchange of rings.[235]

As with the custom of having the couple join hands, the Roman Rite already tolerated variations in the giving of rings. As noted above, the Holy Office in 1892 had permitted the archbishop of

---

[233] Schemata 157 adnexum, p. 2.
[234] Ibid.
[235] Schemata 182, pp. 5 and 11.

Pondicherry, India, to substitute a token called a *tali*, suspended around the bride's neck, for the ring.[236]

The study group summed up its discussions:

> Concerning the blessing and giving of rings, five matters need to be considered:
> a) the use of not only one ring but two;
> b) at what moment of the rite the rings should be blessed;
> c) which symbolism should be expressed in that blessing;
> d) whether the words that accompany the blessing of rings should be spoken by the priest or rather by the couple themselves;
> e) permission for the episcopal conferences to replace the rings with another sign of the indigenous civilization when it is more fitting.

The use of two rings is now more and more widespread. It has been introduced in all recent Rituals, and at the council it was proposed by some bishops for the future Roman Ritual. That proposal has already been approved by the fathers of the council on October 9, 1964.[237]

Concerning the sequence of the ritual elements, the study group offered this conclusion:

> In the traditional Roman order noted above, this difficulty remains, that the formula of blessing the ring interrupts in a certain way the sequence of 1) the consent, 2) the words of the priest confirming or receiving the consent, 3) the giving of the ring(s), but, as Father Martimort best put it to us, the formula of blessing may become shorter, and—I may say so—lighter, that it will not disturb but rather illustrate the rite.[238]

The group also discussed giving the couple something to say while they exchanged rings, according to the judgment of the episcopal conferences. In this way, they themselves—and not

[236] Schemata 182, p. 4.
[237] Ibid., p. 11.
[238] Ibid., p. 12.

the priest—pronounce the words that accompany the gesture. If, however, a conference permitted, the exchange could be made in silence.[239] The report explained,

> According to the modern Roman Rite, while the groom places the ring on the bride's finger, the words "In the name of the Father, etc." are said by the priest. Before the Roman Ritual of the year 1614 the words that accompanied the exchange of the ring, both in Roman usage and in particular rituals, always were said by the groom himself. These words generally better expressed the meaning of Christian matrimony than the simple formula, "In the name of the Father, etc." If it pleases all of you, we think that this should be restored in some way with a formula not long but more expressive, while always preserving the law of the conferences of bishops.[240]

That led to the composition of the formula appearing in the draft in 1966,[241] which remains in place in the OCM today. This first draft did not mention that the words were optional, but they were made so in the next draft[242] and the final one,[243] as they are today.

In 1967, Seumois managed to have an adaptation inserted into the rubrics of the ritual at this point.[244] *"In particular rituals, under the judgment of the territorial Authorities, certain ceremonies may be introduced here; e.g., the crowning or veiling of the bride, which, according to the diverse customs of peoples, may solemnly express that the marriage has been accomplished."*[245] This did not survive in this place in the next draft[246] nor in the final ritual, but it found expression in the OCM's Introduction (41).

The first English translation had the couple say to each other, "take this ring," but this has changed to "receive" this ring. Other translations were considered: "accept this ring" and even "wear this ring," but "receive" was thought the best solution. The words

---

[239] Schemata 157, p. 9.
[240] Schemata 182, p. 13.
[241] Schemata 183, p. 4.
[242] Schemata 221, p. 13.
[243] Schemata 280, p. 9.
[244] Schemata 204, p. i.
[245] Ibid., p. 5.
[246] Schemata 221, p. 13.

pertain to the specific action underway, the handing on of the ring from one partner to the other, and its acceptance. The partner does not so much "take" the ring as "receive" it.

For a similar reason, the heading of this section has changed from the "exchange" of rings to the "giving" of rings. The rings are given and then received.

In an early version of ICEL's translation, each partner asked the other to receive the ring "as a sign of my faithfulness and my love." In Latin the word "my" appears twice, but this is partly because the gender of the two nouns requires a change in the form of the pronoun. Translators probably favored ending the phrase with a strong syllable, so their proposal reversed the order of the nouns. In the end, the nouns appear in the same order as they do in Latin, and "faithfulness" was changed to "fidelity." This matches the changes made to the blessing given by the priest in OCM 66.

French Canada received permission for the priest to offer the nuptial blessing after the giving of rings. A rubric states, "The nuptial blessing is normally expected after the Lord's Prayer. For pastoral reasons, the nuptial blessing may be said here rather than after the Lord's Prayer."[247]

The Blessing and Giving of the Arras

67B.

According to custom and pastoral judgment, the priest may bless *arras* (coins) for the couple to exchange. Each partner asks the other to receive them as a sign of God's blessing. This practice comes primarily from Mexican and Filipino traditions, and it appears for the first time as an optional ceremony in the United States. Some couples already included the ceremony, but the second edition of the OCM has approved an English translation of what appeared in the Spanish edition for the United States in 2010. The bishops approved the translation for placement in an appendix,[248] but the CDWDS put it here, where it also appears in the

---

[247] *Rituel Romain*, 35.

[248] "USCCB Approves *Misal Romano, Tercera Edición*; Marriage and Confirmation Rites," *Newsletter: Committee on Divine Worship*, United States Conference of Catholic Bishops XLIX (November–December 2013): 47.

Spanish edition for the United States. Traditionally, the *arras* are a small box containing thirteen coins. The coins are usually ornamental, not currency.

According to the Instituto de Liturgia Hispana,

> *Arras* literally means pledge. During the ceremony, the spouses gave each other a wedding- or pledge-token. This token became known as the *arras*. Although it is not clear what exactly was given as a token during the first millennium, the *arras* today is a small cask containing 13 gilded or plated coins in the smallest size or denomination; the baker's dozen symbolizes prosperity.[249]

John Chrysostom mentions the use of *arras*, symbolized as a ring given at betrothal.[250] This usage has been handed down in the Byzantine tradition together with a prayer recalling the betrothal of Isaac and Rebekah.[251]

One of the first references to the word in the West comes from Spain in the eleventh-century Mozarabic *Liber Ordinum*, in a prayer which could be several centuries older:

> O Lord almighty God, who for a symbol of the holy union of Isaac and Rebekah commanded your servant Abraham to secure the exchange of pledges (*arrarum*), that by the offering of gifts the number of their children might increase, we ask your Omnipotence that by the oblation of these pledges, which your servant N. is able to offer his beloved spouse N., you the Sanctifier might draw near and kindly bless them along with their gifts. Protected in this way by your blessing and joined by the bond of love, may they rejoice that you possess them happily forever with your faithful ones. O, most Loving.[252]

The fourteenth-century Cistercian Ritual of Barbeau put the priest in charge of the distribution of thirteen coins.

---

[249] *Gift and Promise: Customs and Traditions in Hispanic Rites of Marriage* (Portland, OR: Oregon Catholic Press, 1997), 5.

[250] Stevenson, *To Join Together*, 21.

[251] Ibid., 75.

[252] *Liber Ordinum*, 298.

Then the priest asks for the rings and thirteen pieces of silver. He gives away as much of the silver as he pleases and puts the remainder, with the ring, in the palm of the woman's right hand, placing the man's hand on top of it. Holding the hands in his own, the priest says to the man,

N., say after me:
N., with this ring I wed you,
with this money I endow you,
and with my body I honor you.
To the honor of God,
and of our Lady St. Mary,
and of all holy men and women
and of Monseigneur N.,
here present.
Then the money is put in the bride's purse.[253]

The groom then places the ring on the finger of the bride. Thus the ceremony connects the ring with the gift of the groom's coins. In seventeenth-century Coutances, the ring and coins were part of the betrothal ceremony. The priest offered this prayer:

O Lord, sanctify these coins,
offered as a symbol of the settlement
which has been agreed.
As the bride has been well settled,
so instruct her also in the ways of heaven.
Through Christ our Lord.[254]

The Sarum Manual explained that "the clink of coins signifies interior love which is always to be fresh between [the couple]."[255] Coins, which are normally silent, seem to possess other abilities when they are together.

After the giving of rings and the *arras*, it may seem natural for the couple to kiss. The Catholic ceremony, however, has never promoted the practice. A kiss is implied during the sign of peace later in the nuptial Mass at OCM 75.

[253] Searle and Stevenson, *Documents of the Marriage Liturgy*, 159–60.
[254] Ibid., 195–96.
[255] Ibid., 168.

In practice, the couple planning to give the *arras* have appointed another married couple to serve as *padrinos*. These approach the couple at this time and hold the *arras* for the blessing. The rubrics make no mention of sprinkling the *arras* with blessed water, though this may be customary in some places. The OCM, however, seems intent on keeping the symbol of the rings primary. The rings may be blessed with water. The rings will ever shine publicly on the fingers of the married couple. The coins will be only a memory.

The blessing by the priest is directly taken from the second option in the Mexican ritual.[256] The first option calls for a blessing of the rings and the *arras* together, but the second is a simple blessing of the coins. It now appears in the Spanish-language ritual for the United States word for word, and an English translation is available for the first time.

The Mexican edition describes the action more fully: "The groom takes the *arras* and, holding them between his joined hands, entrusts them to the bride, who receives them with her two hands below those of the groom."[257] He lets them drop from his cupped hands into her open hands placed below his. In Mexico, she does not pour them back as she does in the United States.

The foreword to the Mexican edition, written by Bishop Jonás Guerrero Corona, states, "The sign of the *arras* demonstrates that the matrimonial union demands happily sharing everything in life, 'as a pledge of God's blessing.'"[258]

The words that the couple say to each other were composed for the 2010 Spanish translation for usage in the United States, and these have now been translated into English. These are based on a different exchange of words found in the Mexican ritual, which may be translated as follows:

> Groom: N., receive also these *arras*, as a pledge of God's blessing, and of the care that I will take that our home will never lack what is necessary.

[256] *Ritual* (Mexico), 59.
[257] Ibid., 58.
[258] Ibid., 12.

Bride: N., I receive them as a pledge of God's blessing, and a sign of the good gifts we will share.[259]

Clearly the meaning of the *arras* has been reinterpreted for the United States. Originally they were part of the gift that the groom gave to the bride in assurance of his ability to provide for her. For this reason the *arras* have origins—together with the ring—in the ceremonies of betrothal. Now they appear still yoked with the rings but as a ceremony after the giving of consent. The *arras* have become a sign of the benefits that each of them has received from God, the gifts that they now will share together. As the ring ceremony expanded from the giving of a single ring to a mutual exchange, so—in the United States—the *arras* have changed from being a sign of the groom's responsibility into another sign of equality in marriage.

The Mexican edition next adds the option of the presentation of a holy Bible. This custom is often requested in the United States, but it does not appear in either the Spanish or English translations of the OCM. The Mexican ceremony may be translated as follows:

> *According to the custom of some places, at this moment the presider may conduct the presentation of the Bible to the spouses in these or similar words:*
>
> Receive the book of the Holy Scriptures that contain the Word of God. May this Word be a font of light and life in the path you undertake as Christian spouses.[260]

In practice, *padrinos* may present the Bible to the priest. He does not bless or sprinkle it. In Mexico the priest, not the *padrinos*, presents the book to the couple.

68.

All may sing some hymn or canticle of praise. This is new to the second edition of the OCM. It attempts to engage the participation of the people in praise of God and in witnessing the order of matrimony.

---

[259] Ibid.
[260] *Ritual* (Mexico), 60.

In French Canada, this sentence has been added to the rubric: "The organ or musical instruments may play a piece adapted to the rite and to the church."[261] In Mexico, the words and music for two acclamations are given right in the ritual, together with accompaniment for keyboard and guitar. The suggested texts are "Let us sing to the Lord with joy, for he has blessed their love" and "Glory and praise to you, Lord, for you have blessed their love."[262]

This is a time in the ceremony when some couples light a unity candle. OCM 29 permits the use of local customs, and it may be judged that the unity candle qualifies as one, such as the inclusion of a ring bearer and flower girl in the procession. There are variations on how it is carried out, but frequently, before the ceremony begins, a pillar candle is set between two narrower candles on a small table—not on the altar. The parents or mothers of the couple may each light one of the smaller candles when they enter the church in the moments before the ceremony begins. Then, later, perhaps after the ring ceremony, and after the *arras* if included, the couple take the smaller candles and together light the pillar candle between them. Although it has never been included in the rubrics for a Catholic wedding, the ceremony has been adopted in countless celebrations. Some couples choose this time to have the singer perform a solo. But this is when the OCM envisions that the entire community may join in singing a hymn. The rubric does not exclude a soloist, but it clearly promotes congregational singing.

The Universal Prayer

69.

The universal prayer, or prayer of the faithful, takes place in the usual manner. This is the former paragraph 29, which said that the formulas to be used were those approved by the Conferences of Bishops. Few if any conferences ever did this. The rubric has been removed. But for the first time the OCM provides sample formulas in an appendix (216–217).

---

[261] *Rituel Romain*, 35.
[262] *Ritual* (Mexico), 60–61.

If the Mass requires the Creed, it follows the universal prayer. This comes into question whenever the Ritual Mass of marriage cannot be used because the Table of Liturgical Days requires another Mass for the wedding (OCM 34), or if it takes place on the eve of Sunday or a holy day. Not all of the days in the first four parts of the Table require a creed—for example, weekdays of Holy Week, or All Souls Day (November 2) if it falls on a weekday. But any wedding taking place during a Mass on a Saturday night, for example, will require the Creed.[263]

Unusual is that the Creed follows the universal prayer. Normally on Sundays it comes first. In this case, however, the universal prayer is still part of the rite of marriage, so it displaces the Creed. The same sequence occurs when celebrating the scrutinies of the RCIA during Lent.[264] The immediate cause for this sequence probably lies with the Second Vatican Council. It called for the marriage rite to be moved from before Mass to a position during Mass after the gospel and the homily, and before the universal prayer.[265] The study group explained,

> According to article 78 of the Constitution, the celebration of matrimony concludes in a certain manner with the prayer of the faithful. For this reason it is better, if you agree, that in this special case the creed, if it has been called for by the rubrics, be placed after the prayer of the faithful. You established the same for the catechumenate of adults (schemata 112, numbers 17, 46, 55, etc.), and it agrees with the report 113 on the mass, number 54.[266]

When a bishop presides, the Creed is said when the rubrics call for it, and the universal prayer takes place "in the usual way,"[267] according to the English translation of the Ceremonial of Bishops. This suggests a discrepancy in the sequence of these two elements in the liturgical books. The English translation, however, has

[263] See GIRM 68.
[264] RCIA 156, for example. *The Rites*, 118.
[265] SC 78.
[266] Schemata 182, p. 13.
[267] CB 609.

reversed the order of two clauses in the Latin original, which treats the universal prayer first, and then the Creed.

There was no universal prayer at Mass immediately prior to the reforms of the Second Vatican Council. The idea to include one specifically for marriage originated with the council's preparatory commission, which called for "a brief litanic prayer needing to be recited by those present together with the priest."[268] The Vatican published several sample prayers for a variety of ceremonies in 1966.[269] These included a set for the celebration of matrimony, composed in Latin and with a French translation.[270] These served as a basis for the composition of sample prayers in the second edition of the OCM (216–217).

The study group wrote, "For the text of the prayer of the faithful in the celebration of matrimony, an example has already been proposed by the competent study group in the booklet, *De Oratione communi seu fidelium* (Vatican City, 1966). Concerning others, the matter pertains to the episcopal conferences."[271] As noted above, the first edition of the OCM proposed that conferences of bishops would provide these; an official booklet of sample prayers never appeared in most vernacular languages.

A version of the pertinent rubric appeared in two drafts from 1967, where they suggested that the formulas "be approved by the territorial authority."[272] This changed back to "approved by the conference of bishops" in the final draft.[273] The reference to the conferences has been removed from the OCM. In practice, such prayers are either composed at the local parish or through a previously published service. Now the second edition of the OCM includes official samples in English for the first time.

---

[268] Schemata 32, p. 15.

[269] *De Oratione communi seu fidelium: Natura, momentum ac structura, Criteria atque specimina, Coetibus territorialibus Episcoporum proposita* (Vatican City: Libreria Editrice Vaticana, 1966).

[270] Ibid., 148–51.

[271] Schemata 182, p. 13.

[272] Schemata 204, p. 6; Schemata 221, p. 13.

[273] Schemata 280, p. 9.

In French Canada, the Creed may be moved to the start of the marriage rite, not if the rubrics call for it, but "if it seems appropriate."[274] This may be done even in a wedding outside of Mass in one of three forms.[275] The first is a renewal of baptismal promises for all present. The second is the profession of the Nicene or the Apostles' Creed. "This profession of faith may be said by the priest or the deacon with the future spouses and the whole assembly, or with some individuals, for example the witnesses and the friends of the future spouses, the members of the parish or some marriage preparation teams."[276]

Also in French Canada several samples of the universal prayer appear in an appendix. The first is a translation of the first of the two Latin samples. The priest's introduction and conclusion come earlier in the book in the order of matrimony during Mass.[277] The second set is freely composed. So is the third, which begins each petition with a quote from the words of Jesus. For example, " 'They are no longer two but one. What God has joined, let no one divide,' says the Lord. Let us pray for N. and N.: may they remain in mutual love and fidelity." Five sample responses are also provided; for example, "Remember your love, O Lord."[278] A French translation for the second sample from the second edition of the OCM appears within the body of the book together with the priest's introduction and conclusion from the first sample.[279]

In Colombia, the translation of the two samples appears within the body of the book in proper sequence, so that the priest does not have to turn to the appendix.[280] Mexico presents its own version of the universal prayer within the first chapter,[281] and nine more options in a later chapter, together with a brief litany of the saints,[282] as described in the commentary on OCM 59.

---

[274] *Rituel Romain*, 25.
[275] Ibid., 124.
[276] Ibid., 125.
[277] Ibid., 40.
[278] Ibid., 136–38.
[279] Ibid., 40.
[280] *Ritual* (Colombia), 39–42.
[281] *Ritual* (Mexico), 61–62.
[282] Ibid., 224–35.

In Mexico, after the universal prayer and the Creed, if said, "the *lazo* is placed on the spouses while they kneel, but this may be kept for the nuptial blessing."[283] In the United States, the *lazo*—if used—is recommended for the nuptial blessing in OCM 71B, but it may be placed on the couple earlier, such as at this moment.

The bishops of the United States approved "a rubric allowing for the option of praying the Nuptial Blessing after the Universal Prayer, instead of its current position after the Lord's Prayer,"[284] but the CDWDS did not consent to the change.

THE LITURGY OF THE EUCHARIST

70.

The bride and groom may bring the bread and wine to the altar. This is the former paragraph 30, though less prolix.

The study group working out the marriage ceremony knew that the study groups working on the Mass had already proposed the idea for having the faithful bring gifts to the altar in October 1965: "Then the paten—and if needed even other patens or ciboria—along with the bread and wine and water are brought to the altar. If appropriate, this may be done by the faithful. . . ."[285] The suggestion for the bride and groom to bring the bread and wine forward first appeared in a 1966 draft of the marriage ceremony.[286] It was repeated the following year[287] and in the final draft.[288]

The second edition of the OCM keeps this option in play, even though there are some practical difficulties. For example, the bread and wine are often placed on a small table near the front door before Mass, and the couple would have to walk back down the aisle to pick them up and bring them to the altar. In cases where the bride's dress finishes with a train, this could be especially awkward for her. The gifts could sit on a table closer to the place

[283] Ibid., 62.
[284] "USCCB Approves *Misal Romano*," 47.
[285] Schemata 113, p. 5.
[286] Schemata 183, p. 4.
[287] Schemata 221, p. 13.
[288] Schemata 280, p. 15.

reserved for the bride and groom. Or other members of the community could bring them up the aisle, hand them to the couple, who could then present them.

Notably, the rubric says that the couple bring the gifts "to the altar," a phrase which was ultimately removed from the Order of Mass 22, where it first appeared in a draft of 1965, and from which the rubric in the OCM directly derives.[289] The GIRM now says that the gifts are to be received "at an appropriate place,"[290] without specifying where. Nonetheless, the word "altar" has persisted in this rubric, unchanged and probably undetected. Instead of placing the gifts on the altar, the couple are probably expected to give them to the priest or deacon. The rubric, however, says that they bring them "to the altar."

As to music for the preparation of the gifts, other liturgical books make suggestions for the OCM. For example, the *Ordo cantus missæ* has two offertories,[291] which also appear in the *Graduale Romanum*.[292] One is a setting of Psalm 34 (33):8-9. "The angel of the Lord is encamped around those who fear him, to rescue them. Taste and see that the Lord is good."[293] The other is from Psalm 31 (30):15-16. "But as for me, I trust in you, O Lord; I say, 'You are my God. My lot is in your hands.' "[294] This was the chant in the 1962 *Missale Romanum*[295] and can be traced all the way back to the tenth-century Roman-Germanic Pontifical.[296] The twelfth-century Roman Pontifical had a different verse: "Blessed be the Father and the only-begotten Son of God, and the Holy Spirit, for he has had mercy on us."[297] This is a shorter version of the entrance antiphon from the same pontifical, with its concluding faint allusion to Tobit

[289] Schemata 183, p. 4.

[290] GIRM 73 and 178.

[291] *Ordo cantus missæ*, 354.

[292] *Graduale Romanum*, 645.

[293] *The Revised Grail Psalms: A Liturgical Psalter* (Chicago: GIA Publications, 2010).

[294] Ibid.

[295] *Missale Romanum*, p. [76].

[296] *Le Pontifical Romano-Germanique*, 415.

[297] *Le Pontifical Romaine*, 310.

12:6. This became the offertory antiphon for the votive Mass of the Holy Trinity,[298] which could be used for weddings before the Second Vatican Council. Perhaps these antiphons were meant to instill a sense of trust in the newlyweds.

The *Graduale simplex* proposes a completely different source, Psalm 37 (36). The four verses are not numbered, but they are 27, 28a, 29, and 40. The refrain is a slightly altered version of verse 28a: "Those who wait for the Lord will inherit the land."[299]

In French Canada, the published edition has moved the prayers over the offerings from the appendix into this first chapter where they are easier for the priest to find.[300] Two additional prayers with no Latin original have been included.[301] In Colombia, too, the prayers over the offerings appear in place, not in the appendix.[302] The Mexican edition puts one of the prayers in this chapter.[303] English-speaking conferences did not receive the same permission.

71A.

The newly married couple may be mentioned by name in the eucharistic prayer. This is the former paragraph 32, though now without a reference to the prefaces, which have been copied from the Missal into an appendix of the OCM. In Mexico, one preface has been placed in this first chapter for ease of usage.[304]

Mention of the couple's names formerly enhanced only Eucharistic Prayer I, the Roman Canon, but they may now be included in Eucharistic Prayers II and III. There is no such insertion for Eucharistic Prayer IV because it has its own preface that cannot be replaced with another one. Hence, it is presumed not to be used for weddings. The formulas are provided in OCM 202–204. These also appear in the Missal's Ritual Mass for the Celebration of Marriage.

---

[298] *Missale Romanum*, p. [50].
[299] *Graduale simplex*, 382–83.
[300] *Rituel Romain*, 42.
[301] Ibid., 43.
[302] *Ritual* (Colombia), 42–43.
[303] *Ritual* (Mexico), 63.
[304] Ibid.

In French Canada, a fourth preface composed in French has been approved and appears here as another option for the opening of the eucharistic prayer.[305] Even more astonishing, French Canada obtained permission in 1982 for a complete eucharistic prayer suitable for weddings.[306] The prayer is still in force, published by the French Canadian episcopal conference as a separate fascicle.[307] Called "The Eucharistic Prayer for Marriage," it opens with a preface praising God for the continued unfolding of love and life in the world and for Jesus' message of love, for which the couple, their parents, friends, and all present praise God, joining with the angels in the "Holy, Holy, Holy." The prayer continues its praise of God for the gift of marriage, and for Christ, who renews God's covenant with humanity. After the institution narrative, the priest prays for the church whom God wants "beautiful, young, free and faithful, like a fiancée."[308] He prays that God will preserve the couple's tenderness and help those who love and are loved to comfort others. He also prays "for those who died in their thirst for goodness and love."[309]

The Blessing and Placing of the Lazo *or the* Veil

71B.

Before the nuptial blessing, the spouses may be united with a *lazo* or under a veil. These customs, like the *arras*, derive from Hispanic and Filipino traditions. Traditionally, the engaged couple have invited a married couple to serve as the *padrinos* of the *lazo* or the veil. They bring it forward. The priest blesses it. They place the *lazo* around or hold the veil over the couple. The rubric suggests that the placing could happen earlier; as noted in the comments on OCM 69, the Mexican edition has the couple put it on just before the preparation of the gifts.[310] These customs enjoy some fluidity of execution.

[305] *Rituel Romain*, 47.

[306] *Notitiae* 18 (1982): 142.

[307] *Prière eucharistique pour le mariage* (Ottawa: Conférence des évêques catholiques du Canada, 2011).

[308] Ibid., 9.

[309] Ibid., 10.

[310] *Ritual* (Mexico), 62.

The *lazo* here is called a "wedding garland," and some of them resemble a double rosary. It is placed over the heads of the couple and unites them around the shoulder. Alternatively, the *padrinos* may hold a veil over the heads of the couple, or they may take the hem of the bride's own veil and pin it to the shoulder of the groom. Sometimes the *lazo* and veiling are both observed. In some places in Mexico *padrinos* hold candles (*velas*) instead of a veil (*vela*).

The blessing that the priest speaks is an English translation of the one from the Spanish ritual in the United States. It has no equivalent in the Mexican edition, which simply calls for the placing of the *lazo* without any prayer of blessing. The priest, however, may deliver a catechesis in these or similar words:

> N. and N., as Christian spouses you are already united for ever. At this moment in which Holy Mother Church is going to implore solemnly over you the blessing of God, the *lazo* will be placed on you, a symbol of the indissoluble unity that, through love and selfless giving, you must live all the days of your life.[311]

The veil is one of the oldest symbols of the wedding, and the oldest liturgical symbol clearly attested. It is mentioned by Pope Siricius and St. Ambrose in the fourth century.[312] As noted in the commentary on the title, one of the earliest names for a wedding was "veiling."

From Spain, the *Liber Ordinum* instructed the couple to approach the sanctuary after the celebration of the Mass. The parents of the bride presented her to the priest. He veiled the couple and placed a cord around them.[313]

In the Sarum Missal, the groom and bride lay prostrate in prayer at the step of the altar while four vested clerics held a pall over them, unless one or both had been married before.[314] Along with the nuptial blessing at the time, these symbols were reserved only for first marriages.

---

[311] Ibid., 65.

[312] Nocent, "The Christian Rite of Marriage in the West," 285–86.

[313] *Liber Ordinum*, 298.

[314] *Sarum Missal in English*, 154.

As the study group drafted the revised ceremony, they wrote in the introductory material, "During the nuptial blessing, the veil of the bride may be extended over the shoulders of the groom."[315] This eventually gave way to the more generic description in the Introduction that a crowning of the bride or the veiling of the spouses may take place (OCM 41).

The foreword to the Mexican edition offers a catechesis on the *lazo*:

> With the imposition of the *lazo*, especially if it is done in the moment of the nuptial blessing, matrimony is shown as the most direct and profound realization of the identity of the human creature, man and woman, united in a single destiny. Thus it is indicated that matrimony does not constitute a merely conventional human institution, but a sacred reality that the Lord himself placed as a foundation of humanity for its edification. It visibly expresses the unity that has begun to exist in the life of those who now are spouses.[316]

The rubrics in the United States do not tell when to remove the *lazo* or the veil, but the Mexican edition says, "When the nuptial blessing is over, the *lazo* is removed."[317] In that way, it stands as a clearer symbol of that blessing's purpose.

The Nuptial Blessing

72.

After the Lord's Prayer, the priest omits the prayer "Deliver us, Lord," and faces the bride and groom. He omits parts of the prayer if one of the spouses will not be receiving communion. He may also pass over parts referring to future children if the couple, for example, are advanced in years. But he never omits the nuptial blessing. This is the first part of the former paragraph 33 with more explanations drawn from the former paragraph 34. A similar set of rubrics appears in the Missal's Ritual Mass for the Celebration of Marriage.

---

[315] Schemata 204, p. 3.
[316] *Ritual* (Mexico), 12.
[317] Ibid., 65.

Prior to the council, the Roman Ritual of 1614 put the blessing of the bride between the Lord's Prayer and the embolism, "Deliver us, Lord, we pray."[318] Before that the Gelasian Sacramentary had given these instructions to the priest: "You complete the entire canon, and you say the Lord's Prayer, and you bless her then with these words."[319] Thus it appears that since at least the seventh century this blessing was included inside a celebration of the Eucharist, and that its original purpose served to bless the bride in anticipation of the sign of peace and the sharing of communion. As the parts of the Mass were rearranged over the centuries, this basic sequence held. Originally, however, the blessing seemed less attached to the Lord's Prayer and more closely affixed to the peace and communion. After the bread and wine were consecrated in the eucharistic prayer, the priest blessed the bride in preparation for the ritual signs of peace and unity.

The OCM's rubric specifies that the nuptial blessing is always given. This was important because there were times before the council when the nuptial blessing could not be given, as explained in the comments concerning OCM 34. The same 1964 instruction that permitted giving the blessing on any day also permitted a previously married person to receive the blessing.[320] The Roman Pontifical of 1962 still forbade the bishop to give the nuptial blessing if the woman was a widow.[321]

The *Liber Ordinum* had separate blessings for people entering a second marriage[322] or a person marrying one who was previously married.[323] But these are both a series of short prayers, each concluding with amens, and thus they do not resemble the structure of a nuptial blessing, which remained unique. One of these reappears in the Bobbio Missal.[324]

---

[318] *Roman Ritual*, 466.
[319] Gelasian 1449.
[320] IO 73.
[321] *Pontificale Romanum* 1469.
[322] *Liber Ordinum*, 301.
[323] Ibid., 300.
[324] *The Bobbio Missal: A Gallican Mass-Book*, ed. E. A. Lowe (Woodbridge, UK: The Boydell Press, 1920), p. [552].

It may seem that the rubric excluding widows implied that a woman blessed was thus consecrated for marriage and for the rites of communion as a married woman. She never lost that consecration bestowed on her in the blessing.

The Sarum Missal, however, drew another conclusion. Marriage is a sacrament of the love of Christ for the church. The nuptial blessing consecrates the bride for her permanent union with her husband, as the church is consecrated as the single bride of Christ. The Sarum Missal noted that such a marriage "has somewhat of a sacramental defect, because it has not a full signification, since it is not a union of one and one, as in the case of the marriage of Christ and his Church."[325] If a single woman married a man whose wife had died, however, then she did receive the nuptial blessing.[326] Again, the blessing pertained to what she represented.

When the study group first met to plan the changes to the marriage ceremony, they summed up the current situation:

> Everyone knows that the Roman Rite of Matrimony consists of two parts, one part that formerly took place before Mass and now happens after the homily, and another part that continues with the blessing of the bride after the Lord's Prayer. This duality, perhaps not fully logical, descends from a historical reason, since the blessing of the bride was for the first millennium the only rite of matrimony in the Roman liturgy, implicitly containing in itself an expression of consent. After the expression of consent and other rites were introduced before Mass in the eleventh and twelfth centuries, the ancient blessing of the bride was preserved and even now is kept by the Constitution with appropriate emendations, concerning which, see below, number 29.[327]

The study group received reactions to its work, to which they also responded:

> *The prayer over the bride, according to the determination of the Council and of the relator Archbishop Paul Hallinan [of Atlanta, United States]*

[325] *Sarum Missal in English*, 158.
[326] Ibid.
[327] Schemata 157, p. 4.

in the name of the conciliar commission, ought to preserve the character of blessing the bride alone; nevertheless, it has been appropriately emended to remind "both spouses of their equal obligation to remain faithful to each other" [SC 78]. Since the text of this prayer is approved, it will be considered whether it is opportune to introduce also another formula ad libitum, *and indeed of the same character.*

Here it may be noted that it was necessary for the Council to emend the text proposed by the preconciliar commission, which read thus: "The prayer over the bride should be appropriately so emended that it may be recited over each spouse." After the emendation, the text remained thus: The prayer over the bride should be appropriately so emended that the spouses remember "the equal obligation to remain faithful to each other."

To the prayer, "O God, who by your mighty power," also beautifully and faithfully emended, perhaps it will be appropriate to add another formula *ad libitum* and indeed of the same kind.[328]

Thus the concerns about emending the prayer to include the groom were running into difficulty. So was the placement of the prayer within the sequence of ceremonies in the Mass. Msgr. Pierre Jounel, a consultor from France, thought that the sequence was acceptable: "All the sacraments have a relationship to the eucharist, and it is sufficient that the blessing of the bride is placed before the offertory." Placid Bruylants, a Benedictine consultor from Belgium, agreed that it was enough that "matrimony be celebrated within mass." Martimort cited the view of St. Thomas Aquinas that a special relationship existed between matrimony and the Eucharist: "The sacrament thus will receive greater solemnity, and the couple will be better prepared for communion." Pascher added that this would be especially true if the couple could drink from the chalice. Wagner, however, said that some conversation would have to take place with those preparing the Order of Mass to see how it could be interrupted. Ligier said, "Already we may say that the blessing of the bride in no way disturbs the order of the canon itself, for the canon is completed with the doxology and the amen. Then from the doxology up to communion all the liturgies admit additions both in the East and the West." Wagner concurred. The mind of the

[328] Ibid., p. 10.

groups was, "[I]f the blessing of the bride is transferred, the rite will lose much and be impoverished." On a related matter, Wagner and Hänggi believed that the "Deliver us" prayer should not be omitted because "it has its own importance."[329]

Later the group reconsidered the "Deliver us" prayer, also called the embolism, because it seemed that the sequence of prayers was too heavy. The Gelasian Sacramentary placed the greeting of peace right after the blessing of the bride,[330] as did the Gregorian,[331] which convinced the study group that the blessing therefore followed the embolism, though that is not clear from the evidence. They weighed this practice against the "modern" sequence in the Missal that put the blessing between the Lord's Prayer and the embolism.[332] Then they proposed another solution:

> It seems fitting both to alleviate the order of prayers and to express better the completely traditional reason and the reason of any theological weight for which the nuptial blessing takes place in this part of the Mass.
>
> As to the order of prayers, although the embolism "Deliver us" has its own importance, and as such in this case two members of our group thought it should be retained, after considering the matter again, the study group of Rituals gathered at Verona unanimously decided in this special case of the Mass for Spouses, the nuptial blessing with its introduction could take the place of the embolism "Deliver us," if the Fathers agree.[333]

The drafts, however, were developed with the "Deliver us" in place right after the Lord's Prayer, with the nuptial blessing to follow.[334] Only in the final draft was the embolism omitted.[335] The group explained its thinking.

[329] Schemata 157 adnexum, p. 4.
[330] Gelasian 1453.
[331] Gregorian 838b.
[332] Schemata 182a, p. 14.
[333] Ibid., p. 15.
[334] Schemata 183, p. 5; Schemata 204, p. 6; Schemata 221, p. 13.
[335] Schemata 280, p. 9.

It is proposed, besides, that in the Mass of the spouses, the embolism of the Lord's Prayer (the "Deliver us") be omitted. Its text, rendered in a living language and pronounced out loud, sounds less pleasing because of its immediate proximity to the blessing of the bride ("Deliver us from every evil"). And the succession of the liturgical action would proceed more orderly by placing the "prayer over the bride" immediately after the "Our Father." It would be done this way: the Lord's Prayer, the prayer over the bride, the "peace of the Lord."[336]

In the end, then, the decision to remove the embolism from a wedding Mass had to do with avoiding the heaviness of too many prayers in succession, along with the concern that the prayer for delivering from evil would sit unhappily adjacent to a prayer for the bride.

In French Canada, the nuptial blessing may take place earlier in the ceremony, after the blessing and exchange of rings.[337] In that case, the priest does recite the embolism after the Lord's Prayer.[338]

The rubric says that the priest gives the blessing "standing and facing the bride and bridegroom." These words are holdovers from the preconciliar rubric, which instructed the priest to say the prayer "standing on the epistle side of the altar facing the groom and the bride kneeling before the altar."[339] A bishop had to genuflect to the Blessed Sacrament before turning to face the couple.[340] At the time, the priest celebrated most of the Mass with his back to the people. He turned to face the people when addressing them. The nuptial blessing has always been addressed to God, but the priest said it facing the groom and bride. Today the priest most commonly faces the couple throughout the celebration of the Mass, so there is no need for him to "stand" anywhere else, nor to "face" them. If, however, he is presiding at an altar that does not allow that possibility, he turns to the couple at this time. Although the preconciliar prayer concerned the bride, the priest faced "the groom and the bride,"

[336] Ibid., ii.
[337] *Rituel Romain*, 35.
[338] Ibid., 49.
[339] *Roman Ritual*, 466.
[340] *Pontificale Romanum*, 362.

and although the postconciliar prayer concerns the couple, they are mentioned in reverse order, the bride first.

73.

The couple take their positions for the prayer. Either they approach the altar or they remain at their place and kneel. The priest invites all present to pray, which they do in silence. This is the first part of the former paragraph 33. It also appears in the Missal's Ritual Mass for the Celebration of Marriage.

The rubric concerning the couple's posture is new. As sometimes happens with new rubrics, it is not completely clear, even in Latin. Is the couple to kneel whether approaching the altar or remaining at their place, or only if they remain in their place? Apparently the couple could approach the altar and stand there to receive the blessing, or kneel down where they have been standing. The Mexican edition has added a rubric at the end of the blessing instructing the couple to stand, thus eliminating the doubt.[341] In Mexico, the couple kneel for either option.

In the past, couples have taken other postures. In the English Missal of Bury St. Edmunds, the couple lie prostrate to receive a blessing just before the peace dialogue.[342] The Ritual from Barbeau says that the couple are covered with a veil. In the Roman Ritual of 1614, they kneel.[343]

The priest's words in OCM 73 are addressed to the congregation. This departs from a long tradition in which he said a short prayer, the *Propitiare*, before the nuptial blessing: "Be favorable, O Lord, to our supplications, and kindly assist your foundations that you commanded for the increase of the human race, that what is joined at your authorship may be preserved by your help. Through Christ our Lord."[344] The Gelasian has a different prayer in this place,[345] which seems to replace the one found in the Verona

---

[341] *Ritual* (Mexico), 71.
[342] Searle and Stevenson, *Documents of the Marriage Liturgy*, 154.
[343] *Roman Ritual*, 466.
[344] Ibid.
[345] Gelasian 1450.

Sacramentary.[346] Yet the Verona's prayer is the one that endured throughout the life of the Roman Ritual of 1614,[347] probably because it was restored after the Gelasian in the Gregorian Sacramentary.[348] The post–Vatican II ceremony breaks this tradition by removing the *Propitiare*. It does so for the pastoral concern of having the priest enlist the participation of the people instead. He does this not only by addressing some words to them but also by inviting their silent prayer before he begins the nuptial blessing.

The study group considered the sequence of these prayers in 1966.

> *Concerning the order and the parts and prayers of the Mass for Spouses from the end of the Canon to communion:*
> On the one hand, this complete order is burdened with a certain irregular succession, even if the blessing of the bride is retained in its own place, that is after the embolism "Deliver us." For these happen in succession:
> 1) the Lord's Prayer,
> 2) the embolism "Deliver us;"
> 3) the prayer "*Propitiare,*"
> 4) the blessing of the bride.
> On the other hand, the place of the blessing of the bride in the part of the Mass that immediately precedes communion seems to have theological significance, namely, expressing the connection between the two sacraments of matrimony and the eucharist: Almost immediately after that blessing, the spouses receive the sacrament of unity.[349]

The study group made three proposals to lighten the order of the prayers and to underscore the connection between matrimony and Eucharist.

> *An invitation or direction by the priest to introduce the blessing may be substituted for the prayer "*Propitiare*", which up to now introduced the blessing of the bride (and perhaps needs to be preserved among the prayers of the mass* ad libitum*).*

---

[346] Verona 1109.
[347] *Roman Ritual*, 466.
[348] Gregorian 837.
[349] Schemata 157, p. 9.

The prayer *"Propitiare"* is certainly not of the same importance as the blessing of the bride itself, nor does it seem to matter to the structure of the rite, which was rather burdened up to now. On the other hand a brief direction seems necessary so that those participating understand that the order of Mass on this day has been changed for the blessing of the bride.

Must the embolism after the Lord's Prayer be retained in this special case, or may the prayer over the bride with its own invitation substitute for it?

This is a hard question, nor is the answer evident. Therefore by common agreement the members of our study group ask the relators that they please open their heart in a special way on this matter.

It seems that the connection between matrimony and the eucharist should be underlined both in the invitation before the blessing and in the very text of the blessing.[350]

The group made another formal request for this change later that year.[351] The members sent two versions of the introduction, one by Lécuyer and another by Mazzarello. Both still indicated that the imminent prayer was for the bride. They both included a reference to the Eucharist as a way of linking the nuptial blessing with the upcoming communion. The phrase, "that . . . he may mercifully pour out the blessing of his grace," was taken from a blessing of deacons in the Verona Sacramentary.[352] Mazzarello had proposed it.[353]

Apparently the Vatican had heard several requests to move the nuptial blessing to another position in the Mass, but this link between blessing and communion, which the study group tried to demonstrate in the introduction to the prayer, remained important. As Evanou noted in his commentary on the second edition of the OCM, "Christian marriage finds in some way its seal in the communion at the eucharistic sacrifice."[354]

[350] Ibid., 10.
[351] Schemata 182a, p. 15.
[352] Verona 949.
[353] Schemata 182 addenda, p. 8.
[354] Evanou, "Commentarium," 317.

The next draft combined the two suggestions into one introduction, which is the one that appears in the OCM, except that this draft still referred only to the bride and her marriage. A footnote explained that "another invitation must be used *ad libitum* if the spouses do not receive communion."[355] Presumably this covered the situation when a Catholic was marrying a non-Catholic outside the celebration of Mass. This became explicit in the final draft: "In the invitation, if the spouses or one of the spouses do not receive communion, the words 'by the sacrament of Christ's Body and Blood' may be omitted."[356] The pertinent words were enclosed in brackets to alert the celebrant.[357] This same final draft included one more justification for changing the nature of the words from a prayer to God into an invitation to the people: "It has been done this way for Ordinations."[358]

The revised translation of this invitation supplies an example of how ICEL distinguished the verbs "may" and "will" with respect to an invitation to prayer. Here the priest says, "let us humbly pray to the Lord that . . . he may mercifully pour out." The first translation used the word "will," not "may," in this sentence, and ICEL preferred that approach. To pray that God "may" be able to do something sounds incorrectly as though there is some possibility that God may not be able to do it. The community is praying that God "will" do something. The final translation, however, came back from the CDWDS with the word "may." The translation of this invitation has been copied over from the Ritual Mass for the Celebration of Marriage in the Roman Missal.

At the conclusion of the introduction, all pray in silence. The translation says that they do this "for a while." This is the same expression that appears in the Order of Mass for the silence that follows the words "Let us pray" at the collect.[359]

[355] Schemata 221, p. 13.
[356] Schemata 280, p. 11.
[357] Ibid., p. 9.
[358] Ibid.
[359] OM 9.

The Mexican edition gives the priest five different samples of this introduction to the nuptial blessing.[360] The CDWDS apparently believed that the introduction could be given in these or similar words.

74.

The priest extends his hands over the bride and groom and offers the nuptial blessing. Musical settings and alternate blessings appear later in the OCM at 205, 207, and 209. This is the conclusion to the former paragraph 33 with some material from 34. The second edition created a place in Latin for the priest to say aloud the name of the bride. The first English translation permitted adding the names of the bride and the groom, which were absent in the Latin first edition. Now the English translation includes the obligatory mention of the bride's name but not the name of the groom. In many ways, this prayer still shows its origins as a blessing of the bride. The Spanish translation in force for the United States also includes the name of the groom.

The translation in the OCM comes directly from the Missal's Ritual Mass for the Celebration of Marriage. Both in the Missal and in the OCM the prayer now comes with a new title: "Nuptial Blessing." The first Latin edition carried no title for it, but the English translation assigned the title "Nuptial Blessing" both to the invitation and to the prayer. Now even in Latin the new title more officially replaces the preconciliar title, the "Blessing of the Bride."

Paragraph 34 of the first edition permitted the priest to abbreviate the prayer by reading only one of the first three paragraphs and selecting one that corresponded to the readings of the Mass. The prayer may no longer be abbreviated.

The second edition has added an epiclesis to each of these prayers for the first time in the history of the Latin Rite. The nuptial blessing in the Eastern Rites typically includes an epiclesis, and the sacrament takes effect by the priest's blessing, not by the couple's exchange of consent. The epiclesis enriches the prayers and provides a point of unity among the churches East and West. As

---

[360] *Ritual* (Mexico), 242–43.

Evanou notes, the action of the Holy Spirit is implicit in the word
"blessing."[361]

The chant setting of the prayers is new to the second edition of
the OCM both in Latin and in English. It demonstrates the importance of the nuptial blessing, of singing, and of chant as a musical
style for Roman worship. Other musical settings may be used, or
the prayer may be recited. The settings imitate the Missal's formula
for prefaces, in keeping with an old tradition.[362] This helps make
the connection between the two sacraments of the Eucharist and
matrimony.

As mentioned in the commentary on OCM 23, a bishop may
wear choir dress and serve as the presider for a wedding while a
priest celebrates the Mass. In this case, the priest who celebrates
gives the introduction to the nuptial blessing. But the bishop bestows the blessing.[363] Similarly, in the unusual circumstance when
a deacon witnesses the marriage during a Mass, it naturally falls
to the priest to give the nuptial blessing. The circumstance will be
explained in the commentary under the heading of Chapter II.

In 1964, before the revisions to the OCM, the Vatican recommended that the same priest celebrate the Mass and assist at the
marriage, but it allowed the division of these roles. In that case,
the assisting priest did not concelebrate; he vested in alb and stole
and perhaps a cope. He also preached the homily. The celebrating
priest was not to continue with the Mass until the assisting priest
had finished the marriage ceremony. The celebrating priest gave
the blessing of the bride.[364] These distinctions fell out of usage with
the revision of the OCM.

The blessing has a long history. The second- or third-century
Syrian Acts of Thomas relates an episode where the apostle is
asked to bless a couple. He prays that God will give them what
God knows to be beneficial for them, and then the apostle imposes
hands on them.[365] The words are quite brief, but they demonstrate

[361] Evanou, "Commentarium," 315.
[362] Ibid., 316.
[363] CB 611.
[364] IO 72.
[365] Stevenson, *To Join Together*, 18–19.

the instinct even from the earliest days of the church for a minister to impose hands and pray over a newly married couple.

The Jewish wedding ceremony is based on texts from the third-century Talmud and includes a sevenfold blessing. The minister blesses (praises) God, not the couple. God is praised for creating the fruit of the vine, creating all things for his glory, creating humanity, making humanity in his own image, for making the barren city of Zion joyful with children, for making this couple rejoice, and for the possibility of their rejoicing with children.[366] The ideas contained in this blessing may have inspired the development of the nuptial blessing in medieval sacramentaries.

The Verona Sacramentary places the texts for marriage at the end of its collection of prayers for the month of September, the same chapter that presents the prayers for ordination. The location may have less to do with a preferred month for ceremonies as a way of remembering where to find them. Many theological and biblical themes are present in this early nuptial blessing.

> Father, creator of the world,[367] progenitor of those being born, beginner of the origin of increase,[368] who brought forth by your hands a companion to Adam,[369] from whose bones grew bones that signified an equal form of admirable diversity, therefore, because you have commanded the sharing of the marriage bed to which people bind themselves in every age for the increase of an entire multitude, the covenants of the human race are united.[370]
>
> For in this way it was necessarily pleasing to you that one be made from two,[371] the weaker sex having been brought forth to the stronger, because she, whom you made similar to man and to you, O God, is by far weaker. By an equal pledge it pleased you that different offspring come forth while posterity flows diversely in an orderly way, and things coming later follow those that are first, that,

[366] Searle and Stevenson, *Documents of the Marriage Liturgy*, 25–28.

[367] Scriptural allusions are supplied by Nocent, "The Christian Rite of Marriage in the West," 288. Here, Gen 1:24.

[368] Gen 1:28; 9:1-7 (*sic*, but more likely verses 1 and 7).

[369] Gen 2:18-24.

[370] Gen 1:28; 9:1-7.

[371] Matt 19:5; Mark 10:7-9; Eph 5:28-33.

even if posterity should fail within one rather short lifetime, there be no end to it.

Therefore, Father, sanctify the beginnings of these things coming to this your servant, that she may keep the commands of the eternal law associated with a good and prosperous relationship. May she remember, O Lord, not only marital freedom, but also the respect for God that is commissioned in the keeping of holy covenants. Faithful and chaste may she marry in Christ and remain an imitator of the holy women. May she be lovable to a man as Rachel was, wise as Rebekah, long-lived and faithful as Sarah. May that author of transgression seize nothing of her supplies; may she remain firm in faith and trustworthiness. May she support her weakness by the strength of discipline. United to one bed may she flee the stimulations of life. May she be serious in modesty, venerable in chastity, knowledgeable of heavenly teachings. May she be prosperous in childbearing; may she be proven and innocent. And may she come to the rest of the blessed and to heavenly kingdoms. Through Christ our Lord.[372]

The Gelasian Sacramentary repeated this prayer with some textual variations.[373] It is, however, essentially the same prayer. The Gregorian, however, edited it considerably. It became the source for the nuptial blessing that survived in the Roman Ritual of 1614 and as the first of the options in the post–Vatican II OCM. For ease of comparison, this translation of the Gregorian prayer imitates the vocabulary from ICEL's current translation where the Latin words are the same:

O God, who by your mighty power created all things out of nothing, and, when you had set in place the beginnings of the universe, formed a man in the image of God, making the woman an inseparable helpmate, as you brought a beginning to the female body from the flesh of the male, and taught that what you were pleased to make one must never be divided; O God, who consecrated the bond of marriage by so great a mystery that in the wedding covenant you foreshadowed the Sacrament of Christ and his Church; O God, by whom woman is joined to man and the companionship they had

---

[372] Verona 1110.
[373] Gelasian 1452.

in the beginning is endowed with the one blessing not forfeited by original sin nor washed away by the flood.[374]

Look now with favor on this your female servant, about to be joined together in Marriage, who asks to be strengthened by your blessing. May the yoke of love and peace abide in her, may she marry faithful and chaste in Christ. Let her always follow the example of the holy women; may she be lovable as Rachel, wise as Rebekah, long-lived and faithful as Sarah. May that author of transgressions seize nothing in her by his actions; may she be firm in faith and trustworthiness, united to one bed; may she flee illicit contacts; may she support her weakness by the strength of discipline. May she be serious in modesty, venerable in chastity, knowledgeable of heavenly teachings. May she be prosperous in childbearing; may she be proven and innocent. And may they [*sic*] come to the rest granted the blessed and to heavenly kingdoms, and may they see their children's children up to the third and fourth generation, and may they reach the fullness of years for which they hope. Through our Lord Jesus Christ.[375]

The Gregorian's new introductory paragraph relies on Ephesians 5:32 to show that the marital covenant imitates the covenant between God and the church, and the biblical allusions show that neither sin nor the flood eliminated the blessings that come from married life. The conclusion shifts to the plural. The priest prays that both the bride and groom may grow together for many years. The blessing of the bride alone contributed to the length of happiness for the couple.

The tenth-century Fulda Sacramentary repeated the Gelasian nuptial blessing and offered another one as an alternative.[376] The *Liber Ordinum* has other prayers not identical but inspired by these, showing the diversity of the traditions.[377] The Roman-Germanic Pontifical took its nuptial blessing from the Gregorian,[378] as did

---

[374] Gregorian 838a.

[375] Gregorian 838b.

[376] *Sacramentarium Fuldense Saeculi X*, ed. Gregor Richter and Albert Schönfelder (Fulda: Fuldaer Actiendruckerei, 1912); 2613.

[377] *Liber Ordinum*, 298–99.

[378] PRG II:416.

the Pontifical from the twelfth century[379] and the Roman Ritual of 1614.[380] This blessing was also found in the Missal of 1570, the only one in force for the Roman Rite through 1962.[381]

This was the situation that the Second Vatican Council addressed in its constitution on the liturgy. Overturning the entire history of the purpose of this prayer, the council amplified the intent of the blessing, asking for the prayer over the bride to be "duly amended to remind both spouses of their equal obligation to remain faithful to each other." It also permitted the priest to give the blessing in the vernacular.[382]

Even while the constitution was under development, this decision did not come easily. At the meeting on April 27, 1963, just a few months before the council approved the finished version of SC, Joseph Jungmann objected to the idea of changing the text to bless both spouses. "It was important to explain the meaning and value of this prayer which should be considered in its entirety." The abbot of the community at Rome's St. Paul Outside the Walls, Cesare D'Amato, agreed.[383] But the suggestion went forward, meeting more confusion, opposition and hard work along the way.

Members of the study group remarked on these difficulties at the beginning of their work.

> As to the emendation of the prayer over the bride addressed in article 78, the things that Bishop Hallinan said in the name of the conciliar commission must be kept in view; namely, "without a radical change in the nature of the most ancient blessing of the bride alone, at least the part of this blessing that speaks of preserving marital fidelity" must refer to "both spouses."[384]

As noted in the commentary on OCM 72, Hallinan's concerns were reviewed in the emendations made in 1966, along with

[379] *Le Pontifical Romain* I: 261–262; incipit also at 302.
[380] *Roman Ritual*, 466–68.
[381] *Missale Romanum*, p. [76].
[382] SC 78.
[383] Giampietro, p. 98.
[384] Schemata 32, p. 15.

the idea of composing new alternative blessings.[385] A discussion ensued.

The prayer over the bride.

1) The first open question: What was the intent of the Council itself?

a) The Fathers of the conciliar commission were not so much in favor of the blessing of the bride herself, but for the equality between man and woman, against a stricter interpretation of the words of St. Paul (Bonet).

b) Indeed, they wanted to underscore the equality of the spouses. But an article written by De Jong concerning the "consecration" of the woman for marriage came to light. Then, although the subcommission changed nothing in the text, squaring the circle became a problem (Wagner).

c) There was a double intention of the Fathers: the venerable antiquity of that blessing, which needs to be preserved in some way; and the "consecration" of the woman for matrimony. But this last idea may be assuaged with the declaration of responsibilities of each partner. (Martimort).

2) *Hesitations about the formula in force*: These proceed both from the number of women in the Old Testament who appear, and from the difficulty of rendering it in the vernacular language. There are versions that soften it (Wagner).

- Equality is not sufficiently apparent. The biblical themes overpower modern human understanding. Today the mission and qualities of women are understood and signified otherwise (Cellier).

- It dwells exceedingly on fecundity, about which women today are wondering (Nabuco).

- Therefore perhaps to uncover another consecration of a woman, or perhaps to return to the ancient texts, but there are not many (Wagner).

3) Nevertheless, not only is it said that that theology of the consecration of the woman had its value, and that the women of the Old Testament are a beautiful example (Burkhard Neunheuser), but it has been encouraged in methodically reading the blessing now in force. Its first part does not concern the woman alone but her union with the man; therefore, it creates no difficulty. The second

---

[385] Schemata 157, p. 10.

part, however, "Look now," utters prayers that indeed look to the woman. But this can be reshaped by adding the reciprocal duties (Lengeling).

Therefore, two questions were proposed:

a) Do you agree that the blessing of the bride, preserving the current character of the blessing of the woman herself, should be profoundly adapted?

b) Do you agree that another blessing may be created and used *ad libitum*?

The second question was easily agreed upon.

But the first became a major consideration. It should not be proposed too precisely—it will come to light by reviewing and revising. Whatever it may be, the character of blessing the woman will be preserved because of the words of the report of Bishop Hallinan. Otherwise a profound revision is required for pastoral reasons (Relator). Bishop Bonet and Dr. McManus spoke in favor of greater freedom and of some "compromise." Dr. McManus recalled the word of the response, "at least" ("at least the part of this blessing that speaks of preserving marital fidelity.") The investigation of a "compromise" pertains to that which he proposed, namely Dr. McManus (Relator).[386]

Even members of the study group faced internal challenges. Members saw the contemporary difficulties with the text of the blessing, especially when it would appear in the vernacular, yet they stood at the edge of a long history of the prayer.

Later that year, Lécuyer and Mazzarello went to work on revising the nuptial blessing from the Gregorian Sacramentary. Instead of "making the woman an inseparable helpmate," they proposed "giving the woman to the man as an inseparable helpmate." They proposed deleting the words, "as you brought a beginning to the female body from the flesh of the male" in order to avoid exegetical difficulties concerning the formation of the woman's body from the man's bones. They changed the following words for the same reason; instead of speaking of the unity that came from the same origin (Eve from Adam), they alluded to the words of Christ concerning the unity of matrimony in Matthew 19:5-6. They noted that such changes had already happened in the eleventh-century

---

[386] Schemata 157 adnexum, pp. 5–6.

Spanish Sacramentary of Vich. They also changed the form of the verb at the start of the second half of the prayer from "about to be joined" to "joined," eliminating a potential question concerning whether or not the couple were married at this point of the service. They changed the expression "the yoke of love and peace" to "the grace of love and peace." They changed the order of some of the words pertaining to the holy women of the Old Testament, in keeping with ancient sources.

Then they added a section pertaining to the groom, Lécuyer proposed this: "May her man put his trust in her (cf. Proverbs 31:11), he who loves her with a faithful and chaste love, as Christ loved the Church, and may he bring the sweetest honor to his wife as a joint heir to the life of grace (cf. 1 Peter 3:7)." Mazzarello's alternative for this section about the groom in the same schemata is the one that the OCM ultimately adopted.

Concerning the threats of the devil, the revised prayer changed the words, "May that author of transgressions seize nothing in her by his actions," to "May that author of transgressions seize nothing of these your rules."

The revisers changed more of the concluding phrases into the plural. Both bride and groom are to be firm in faith and trustworthiness, both united to the same bed, and both fleeing illicit loves (although Mazzarello thought it was an awful expression). Both were to be strengthened by discipline. Both were to possess virtues, though these changed to "harmony in their life, perpetual charity, and restrained with modesty," drawn from an eleventh-century book of blessings from Canterbury, England. Mazzarello proposed "may they remain serious in mutual devotion, venerable in things pious and fitting, instructed in heavenly teachings, proven in the confession of faith." He was alluding to Ephesians 5:3, noting the virtues that are "fitting" among the holy ones. He drew the word "devotion" from oration 1172 in the Gelasian Sacramentary, which prayed that God would accept the grateful devotion of the people on an occasion of fasting. Concerning the final phrase, he wrote, "I have tried to condense in this expression the renewed appeal to the Christian witness of married couples, of which the Council has made an echo in its documents, especially *Lumen gentium* 35c, 41e."

The blessing concluded with a prayer that both be prosperous in children. One alternative version made a reference to Psalm 128 (127), which prays that children may flourish like olive plants around the table.[387]

Further commentary appeared in an adjoining report.

> Therefore this blessing on the one hand should keep the character of the blessing of the bride alone, and on the other hand be so appropriately emended that it instills the mutual responsibilities of the fidelity of each spouse.
>
> We have already worked up much sweat to fulfill this faithfully, but much work still has to be done in order that the text submitted to your judgment be worthy.
>
> But now we think it would be useful, in addition to proposing the traditional formula, namely the prayer "O God, who by your mighty power," fittingly adapted, that another formula be created, and indeed of the same fundamental characteristic.[388]

The response to all this work shed additional light on the difficulties it was encountering.

The Blessing of the Bride Alone

A. Bishop George Patrick Dwyer [of Birmingham, England] and Cardinal William Conway [of Armagh, Ireland] introduced a doubt concerning the interpretation of the Constitution given in the report of Bishop Hallinan. The Relator explained that this was officially, juridically clear: if before the vote the conciliar commission as such said, "this is the mind of the proposal and the emendation," then the votes of the Fathers had to be interpreted according to that explanation.

a) Cardinal Conway objected: Most certainly the mind of the commission may be illustrated in the sense reported, but such an explanation was not introduced in the text of the Council. The Council itself said nothing pertaining to the blessing of the bride *alone*. To me, it is dangerous to state as principle that the matter mentioned in the report and about which nothing was said in the text of the Council is obligatory.

---

[387] Schemata 183, pp. 6–7.
[388] Schemata 182a, p. 16.

b) For his part, Bishop Dwyer showed an internal contradiction of the text of the conciliar report; on the one hand, "without radical change in the nature of the most ancient blessing of the bride alone," and on the other hand, "part of this blessing . . . should refer to both spouses." What is valid for the part is valid also for the whole!

B. But Bishop Juan Hervàs y Benet [of Ciudad Real, Spain] did not agree with having a new formula *ad libitum*. He proposed that the ancient blessing be revised in the following way: a) that it be abbreviated and emended; b) that with the briefest words it have a purpose to "pray for divine grace for both partners, to keep fidelity and to fulfill matrimonial duties faithfully."[389]

In the end, the group voted in favor of a prayer for both bride and groom. They forwarded the discussion about the intent of the council fathers to the canonists of the council.[390]

As to the gesture of the priest, the drafts first said simply that he "extended his hands."[391] This was eventually clarified to an extension of hands over the couple.

In a later draft, the concerns about the length of the blessing met this conclusion: "if appropriate, two of the [first] three paragraphs may be omitted, . . . and the paragraph that relates to the reading of the Mass may be retained."[392] This permission endured through the first edition of the OCM but has been removed from the second. The original permission indicated the centrifugal power of the readings at Mass even in 1967 before the publication of the lectionary. The same draft also allowed removing references to future children if, for example, the couple were advanced in age.[393]

The following draft put the prayer into the form it held up to the first edition of the OCM with only minor changes.[394] The final draft included a brief explanation: "As the Constitution on the Sacred Liturgy prescribed, the text of the 'prayer over the bride' has

---

[389] Schemata 182b, pp. 3–4.
[390] Ibid., p. 4.
[391] Schemata 183, p. 5.
[392] Schemata 204, p. 7.
[393] Ibid.
[394] Schemata 204, p. 14.

been revised so that it expresses the equality of the duties of both spouses."[395]

Pope Paul VI used the final draft when he attended the Eucharistic Congress in Bogotá, Colombia, in 1968.[396]

Reflecting on the revisions, Nocent at first objected to the changes to the nuptial blessing. "The blessing of the bride was an honor rendered to her and it consecrated her for her role. . . . In an age when the woman is often an object, the solicitude of the church to consecrate her would have been a witness."[397] But he later conceded, "In this day and age the Church could not afford to offer a catechesis that would have no impact."[398] Once the blessing of the couple came into common practice, the objections largely disappeared.

In working out the translation, ICEL faced a question of inclusive language in the very first paragraph, which describes whom God formed in his own image. The Latin word *homine*, refers to either sex. Although ICEL tried such solutions as "the human person" or "the human being," the final translation of the single Latin word more happily has "man and woman."

Another difficulty was the length of the original sentence in Latin. At one point ICEL favored changing the first three paragraphs into independent clauses, but in the end they retained their original structure as relative clauses. The French Canadian translation does have the first three paragraphs as independent clauses, abandoning the structure, "O God, who," in favor of "O God, you."[399] The French Canadian edition also has an additional nuptial blessing, locally composed, that appears immediately after this one as an alternative.[400] Ireland had an extra blessing in its first edition from 1980.[401]

---

[395] Schemata 280, p. II.
[396] Stevenson, *To Join Together*, 131.
[397] Nocent, "Il matrimonio cristiano," 363.
[398] Nocent, "The Christian Rite of Marriage in the West," 300.
[399] *Rituel Romain*, 50.
[400] Ibid., 52.
[401] Stevenson, *To Join Together*, 153.

A particularly difficult phrase is the one the revised translation renders "made one in flesh." The Latin more literally says, "united to one bed." The study group had already seen the problem with this expression in materials that ultimately became OCM 41. The original phrase is an expression of sexual fidelity, but the explicit reference to a bed seemed appropriate, even necessary, in some cultures and embarrassing and unacceptable in others. ICEL had proposed "faithful to the bed they share" as a way of rendering the phrase in keeping with its original meaning. The phrase was subject to much discussion, and many proposals came forward: "sharing one matrimonial home," "faithful to each other," "faithful to their love," and so on. ICEL's final version is a circumlocution that refers to the couple's sexual relationship but not to their fidelity—and not to their bed.

In the second half of the prayer, the phrase "joined together in Marriage" translates a phrase that includes the Latin word *consortio.* ICEL at first translated it as "joined in the partnership of Marriage," but the word "partnership" was thought to imply nonmarital unions. The Latin word meant something more than *societas,* and something less than *communio.* Other words were considered, such as "bond," "intimacy" and "companionship," but in the end the less slavish phrase, "joined together in Marriage" seemed to express it best. In other places, including the very first paragraph of the OCM, the word "partnership" survives.

When the blessing refers to the name of the bride, the English translation calls her God's "daughter." The Latin word here, *famula,* literally means "servant." ICEL at first tried the word "handmaid," but it was another case where a literal translation seemed infelicitous to the culture. Hence, "daughter" was chosen.

Because of the length of the nuptial blessings, especially when coupled with the chant settings, the options remain in an appendix in English. Even the publication in England and Wales, which gathered most of the options in the body of the section on celebrating marriage during Mass, kept the blessings in an appendix because of length.[402]

402 OCMEW, 120–27.

In Mexico, as indicated in the commentary on OCM 73, a rubric here states that the couple stand after the nuptial blessing.[403] Also in Mexico, this is when the *lazo* is removed.[404]

75.

The priest omits the prayer "Lord, Jesus Christ" and proceeds to the greeting of peace. All exchange a sign of peace.

This is the former paragraph 35 but with more detail. For example, the omission of the prayer "Lord, Jesus Christ" was presumed, but now it is made clear. In the preconciliar Mass for the spouses, the priest recited both the embolism and the prayer for peace.[405] Both these are now omitted. The connection between the nuptial blessing and the greeting of peace now follows the examples from the Gelasian and Gregorian Sacramentaries.

Also, the sign of peace had been optional in the first edition of the OCM, as it is at a typical Mass,[406] but its elective nature is removed for a wedding. Instead of giving the sign "if appropriate," now "all present offer one another a sign that expresses peace and charity." Apparently the sign of peace is always appropriate—and obligatory—at a wedding Mass.

The sign of peace at a wedding has gone through several historical variants. For example, in the twelfth-century Roman Pontifical, the subdeacon shared peace with the groom but told him "he may not share peace further in the church with the bride."[407] Apparently some liturgists of the day thought that the grooms were giving too secular a kiss to their bride. In the Ritual of Barbeau the groom received the kiss from the priest and then gave it to the people.[408] In the Sarum Missal the priest kissed the groom, who kissed the bride, but neither the groom nor the bride could kiss anyone else.[409] Stevenson believes that the Roman Ritual of

---

[403] *Ritual* (Mexico), 71.

[404] Ibid., 65.

[405] *Missale Romanum*, p. [77].

[406] OM 128.

[407] *Le Pontifical Romain*, 302.

[408] Searle and Stevenson, *Documents of the Marriage Liturgy*, 161.

[409] *Sarum Missal in English*, 158.

1614 may have moved the nuptial blessing away from the kiss of peace and ahead of the embolism precisely to avoid a wedding kiss.[410]

The study group considered the question in 1966.

> *It seems that the connection* [between matrimony and the Eucharist] *must be stressed.* For this purpose, the practice of the "kiss of peace" may be restored for the liturgy of matrimony. For in the ancient Roman Rite, the blessing of the bride was joined to the "kiss of peace." A certain explanation from the twelfth century made note that it was the only day on which a husband was able to kiss his wife in church (Jounel). It is said that the Asians are not in favor of this (Vanderbroucke). I am not in favor of it (Lentini). The topic, which we have not yet debated, will have to be considered (Relator).[411]

In spite of these disagreements, the study group included the sign of peace in their drafts of the ceremony. "Both the couple and all, in an appropriate way, show a sign of peace and charity to each other."[412] The final draft changed the words to make it optional: "[T]he couple and all, in an appropriate way, may show a sign of peace and charity to one other."[413]

The liturgy has come a long way from restricting the nuptial kiss to requiring everyone to give a sign of peace and charity before communion. Still, by placing the sign here, and not immediately after the couple's consent, the liturgy interprets the meaning of the kiss not as a celebration of matrimony but as a preparation for eucharistic communion. The words describing this moment are sufficiently vague that a less emotional sign may be given especially in cultures that restrict kissing and touching in public.

The rubric in the Missal's ritual Mass is slightly different: "Then the bride and bridegroom and all present offer one another a sign, in keeping with local customs, that expresses peace, communion

---

[410] Stevenson, *To Join Together*, 101.
[411] Schemata 157 adnexum, p. 4.
[412] Schemata 183, p. 5; Schemata 204, p. 7.
[413] Schemata 280, p. 11.

and charity."[414] The Missal still considers the sign obligatory for all, but it specifies that it is given in keeping with local customs, and that in addition to peace and charity, it should also express communion.

Some couples give flowers to their parents during the sign of peace. The custom probably does not exceed the freedoms allowed at weddings (OCM 29) and within the sign of peace.

76.

Both the Body and the Blood of Christ may be offered to the bride and groom, their parents, witnesses, and relatives. This presumes, of course, that they are eligible for communion in the Catholic Church. This is the former paragraph 36, expanded, because the first edition gave this permission only to the couple. The OCM's list of those potentially receiving communion under both kinds now matches the list that has already been in force in the Ceremonial of Bishops.[415]

The permission will strike some people curious because it is widely thought that the priest may offer communion under both kinds to all communicants at any Mass. Effectively this is true in most dioceses; however, the bishop has the authority to determine the circumstances when communion under both kinds may be offered.[416] He may have delegated this to pastors. This rubric offers a more global encouragement for communion under both kinds at weddings in those places where the custom is not broadly practiced.

The preconciliar missal had the priest give communion to the couple after he finished drinking the Blood of Christ.[417] At the time, the faithful were not being offered the cup at all, and this applied to weddings as well. The priest drank the contents of the cup and then shared the Body of Christ with the groom and bride.

In preparing the draft of the postconciliar marriage ceremony, the study group expanded that rubric: "After the priest drinks Blood, he gives communion under both kinds to the couple, if circumstances suggest; then, he may give communion to others as

---

[414] Roman Missal, Marriage.
[415] CB 612.
[416] GIRM 283.
[417] *Missale Romanum*, p. [77].

usual."[418] This was simplified in the final draft: "The couple may receive communion under both kinds."[419] This is essentially the form of the rubric today.

The Missal assigns communion antiphons to the wedding Mass.[420] The OCM makes no mention of them, but they belong more properly to the Missal. The first antiphon is inspired by Ephesians 5:25, 27, about marriage as a sacrament of Christ and the church. The second is John 13:34, in which Jesus gives his disciples a new commandment to love one another. The third is Psalm 34 (33):2, 9, where the psalmist blesses the Lord at all times and invites others to taste and see that the Lord is good.

The *Ordo cantus missæ* adds two more antiphons,[421] which appear with musical notation in the *Graduale Romanum*. The first comes from the Beatitudes, where Jesus blesses the pure of heart, peacemakers, and those who suffer persecution for the sake of justice (Matt 5:8, 9, 10). It is paired with Psalm 34 (33), which also supplies the third communion antiphon from the Missal. Or, alternatively, it uses Psalm 37 (36):1, 3, 16, 18, 19, 23 and 27, which promotes confidence in the Lord, the superiority of justice over possessions, the lasting heritage of those who are blameless, among other themes. In general, it endorses virtues over materialism.

The second antiphon also comes from the Sermon on the Mount, where Jesus challenges his disciples to seek first the kingdom of heaven and promises that they will receive everything else (Matt 6:33). This is paired with the same verses of Psalm 37 (36) as the previous antiphon, while adding verses 28, 29, and 34ab. As noted in the commentary on OCM 70, the *Graduale simplex* recommends the opening verses of this psalm to alternate with the antiphon for the offertory chant. Both these seem aimed to help the couple overlook the materialistic concerns that threaten every family and to pursue the more stable virtues of the spiritual life.

---

[418] Schemata 183, p. 5; Schemata 204, p. 7; Schemata 221, p. 15.

[419] Schemata 280, p. 11.

[420] Roman Missal, Marriage.

[421] *Ordo cantus missæ* 354, 130.

The *Graduale simplex* recommends singing Psalm 128 (127) with an uncredited refrain that seems based on its fourth verse: "Behold, thus blessed is the one who fears the Lord." In a late draft from 1967, the study group recommended that the texts for the psalms and antiphons be taken from the *Graduale simplex*,[422] probably because it thought these would be more singable for the general public.

The Missal in use prior to the Second Vatican Council proffered only one communion antiphon, a longer version of the one that now remains only in the *Graduale simplex*: "Behold, thus blessed is the one who fears the Lord, and may you see your children's children. Peace upon Israel."[423] This comes from Psalm 128 (127), verses 4 and 6. This is also the antiphon from the twelfth-century Roman Pontifical.[424]

Earlier, the diversity of communion antiphons was extensive. The Roman-Germanic Pontifical used the opening verse of Psalm 4, "When I called,"[425] a psalm of trust in times of distress. The twelfth-century pontifical used a refrain from Tobit:[426] "Let us bless the God of heaven and confess him in the presence of all living beings, for he has had mercy on us."[427] This verse inspired the antiphon from the votive Mass of the Holy Trinity, which was also used for some weddings in the long life of the 1570 Roman Missal.[428] The Missal of Bury St. Edmunds had "Lord, I will be mindful,"[429] possibly from Psalm 71 (70):16, 17 and 18 ("Lord, I will be mindful of your justice alone. O God, you have taught me from my youth, and you will not abandon me even when I am old and gray.")

The prayers after communion appear much later in the book (OCM 210–212). In French Canada, however, they come here where

---

[422] Schemata 248, p. 16.

[423] *Missale Romanum*, p. [77].

[424] *Le Pontifical Romain*, I:262.

[425] PRG II:415.

[426] Tobit 12:6 in the Old Vulgate.

[427] *Le Pontifical Romain* I:302.

[428] *Missale Romanum*, p. [50].

[429] Searle and Stevenson, *Documents of the Marriage Liturgy*, 154.

the presider would expect them, along with two more prayers composed for usage in Canada.[430] The Mexican edition has one sample prayer placed in this first chapter.[431]

Among the local customs popular in the United States is for the bride to take flowers to an image of the Blessed Virgin Mary. The ceremony has never appeared in the Catholic order for matrimony, yet it has gained popularity to the point that some brides and parents expect that it must be done. Because there is no universal governing source for the custom, it may take place at various parts of the ceremony. As a devotional exercise, it could happen either before or after the prayer after communion. More recently, the groom commonly accompanies the bride if she elects to include this.

Also customary is for a soloist to sing "Ave Maria" at this time. Two settings are extremely popular. In 1825 Franz Schubert composed *Ellens Dritter Gesang*, a prayer that Ellen Douglas, the Lady of the Lake in Walter Scott's epic poem, sang while in exile with her father. The original lyric began with the words *Ave Maria*, but only later did others replace Scott's very different prayer translated into German with the traditional Catholic prayer to Mary in Latin. The Bach-Gounod version—music by Johann Sebastian Bach (+1750) with the Latin words sung to an instrumental melody first improvised by Charles Gounod (+1893)—may also be performed. The OCM does not envision solos during a wedding Mass, though they are not forbidden. Its view of music steers consistently toward congregational song.

The Mexican edition has included this practice as an option within the liturgical book.

> *Delivering the Bouquet*
> Where it is customary, after the prayer after communion and before the final blessing, the bride, accompanied by her groom, approaches to place a bouquet before the Blessed Sacrament or before the image of the Virgin Mary. This is the appropriate time for a Marian hymn.[432]

[430] *Rituel Romain*, 54–55.
[431] *Ritual* (Mexico), 72.
[432] *Ritual* (Mexico), 72.

The ceremony for honoring an image of the Blessed Virgin Mary is a good example of the kind of local custom that OCM 29 permits in Catholic weddings. The official liturgical text cannot possibly address all these situations, but it does make room for persistent customs to breathe life from one wedding to the next and from one generation to another.

Near the end of any Eucharist certain announcements may be made. In the preconciliar Missal, the rubric made this clear: "The priest should admonish [the couple] with a serious speech that, remaining in the fear of God and loving one another, they should preserve mutual faith and marital chastity, and they should diligently instruct children in the Catholic religion."[433] This did not carry over to either edition of the postconciliar OCM. Other brief announcements could be made, if necessary.[434]

THE CONCLUSION OF THE CELEBRATION

77.

The priest gives a solemn blessing, extending his hands over the couple. He then blesses all present. This is the former paragraph 37, and it reappears as 213 in this edition. Other formulas are at OCM 214 and 215. These are the same solemn blessings in the Missal's ritual Mass. A lengthy blessing that the first edition had included for use in the United States has been removed. As will be seen, the structure of that blessing, which included a series of prayers after each of which the people answered "Amen," comes from the Mozarabic tradition, and is still represented in a shorter way in the solemn blessings.

The solemn blessing, which is optional at any other Mass, even at Easter, is obligatory here. Perhaps because the priest is primarily a witness to the couple's exchange of consent, the liturgy has strengthened his role as the one who blesses.

The heading of this section, signaling the conclusion of the celebration, is new even in Latin. One of several new headings throughout the book, it guides the presider through the parts of

---

[433] *Missale Romanum*, p. [77].
[434] OM 140.

the ceremony and helps him find his place more easily. It matches similar headings in OCM 116 and 141.

In the first edition, all these blessings were placed in the final chapter, but now the first of them can be found more easily with the other texts pertinent to a wedding Mass. The final rubric is new, making it clear that the final blessing is not over the couple but over all those present. In Mexico, the priest begins the solemn blessing by calling the couple by name.[435] This clarifies the contrast between the three short blessings over the couple and the final blessing over all.

A bishop wears his miter and extends his hands for the greeting. A deacon may then command the people to bow for the blessing. The bishop extends his hands for the threefold solemn blessing but holds his pastoral staff as usual while making the sign of the cross over the people.[436] Alternatively, he may use one of the usual forms of episcopal blessing.[437] The first is based on a passage from St. Paul,[438] and the second includes the traditional dialogue, which begins "Blessed be the name of the Lord."[439]

Even if a priest presides, he should greet the people with "The Lord be with you," and then he or the assisting deacon should give the command, "Bow down for the blessing."[440] Then the priest gives the threefold solemn blessing. This dialogue does not appear in the OCM, but it carries over from the Missal. It can be found in the blessing of a married couple on their anniversary (OCM 251).

In the preconciliar Missal, the priest sprinkled the couple with blessed water before giving the final blessing.[441] This custom disappeared with the first edition of the postconciliar OCM.

The twelfth-century pontifical included a threefold blessing after Mass that does not appear in the OCM.

---

[435] *Ritual* (Mexico), 72.

[436] CB 613.

[437] CB 1120–1121.

[438] Phil 4:7.

[439] OM 143.

[440] Roman Missal, "Blessings at the End of Mass and Prayers over the People."

[441] *Missale Romanum*, p. [77].

> May you be filled with the blessings of almighty God and of
> our Lord Jesus Christ, by whose precious blood you have been
> redeemed.
> *Response*: Amen.
> May the one whose ineffable power created you unfailingly fill you
> with his grace.
> *Response*: Amen.
> And may he who provided you the circumstances for being born in
> this world grant you in the future a dwelling place for living hap-
> pily without end. *Response*: Amen.[442]

As noted in the commentary on OCM 64, the same pontifical
included another blessing after the consent, calling on the God of
Abraham, Isaac, and Jacob. Yet another blessing followed that one:

> May the Lord God bless you, may Jesus Christ protect you, and may
> the Lord show his face to you and look at you and give you peace
> and health of body and soul, and may Christ fill you with every
> heavenly blessing for the forgiveness of sins, that you may have
> eternal life. Amen.[443]

This brought to a close the wedding ceremonies prior to the
Mass, which then concluded with another blessing.

> Be pleased, O Lord, we pray, to bless in your name this your servant
> N. [the groom] and this your servant N. [the bride], and may they
> grow and keep chaste, and may they serve you all the days of their
> life, so that, when the end of the world has been accomplished, they
> may cling to you without stain. Through Christ our Lord.
>   May the Father and the Son and the Holy Spirit, who is three in
> number and one in name, bless you.[444]

The Gelasian Sacramentary, which includes a version of the
nuptial blessing, also has a unique blessing placed after the couple

---

[442] *Le Pontifical Romain*, 262.
[443] Ibid., 301.
[444] Ibid., 302.

have received communion and before the communion prayer. The minister prays for both the bride and the groom.

> O Lord, holy Father, almighty eternal God, we humbly raise repeated prayers to you on behalf of those who are before you. Christ is our intercessor. Be pleased to favor the joining of your servants, that they may be able to receive your blessings, that they may be fertile with a series of children; be pleased to strengthen their marriage as that of the first human being; may all snares of the enemy be turned away from them, that in this marriage also they may imitate the holiness of their ancestors, who by your providence, O Lord, were able to be joined. Through Christ our Lord.[445]

Other liturgical books have no equivalent to this prayer in its placement within the ceremony, its embrace of both partners, and in its style.

As the study group went to work on the blessings, they were familiar with this history, and they proposed a threefold blessing similar to those being developed for the Order of Mass. These were inspired by the threefold blessing that God taught to Moses.[446] They also have antecedents in the marriage ceremony of the *Liber ordinum*, where one blessing contains ten phrases, each concluding with the peoples' "Amen."[447] As will be seen in the commentary on OCM 215, a translation of this has been preserved as one option for the final blessing in the episcopal conference of Mexico.[448]

Stevenson says that Lécuyer put forward the idea that the study group eventually adopted.[449]

> *At the end of the Mass, for the blessings that now take place, namely both the special blessing of the couple and the blessing of the whole community, there may be substituted a blessing of the Mozarabic-Gallican type, that is, with three phrases.*

---

[445] Gelasian 1454.
[446] Num 6:24-26.
[447] *Liber Ordinum*, 299–300.
[448] *Ritual* (Mexico), pp. 247–56.
[449] Stevenson, *To Join Together*, 130.

Today these elements take place in sequence: 1) "Go in peace;" 2) the blessing, "May the God of Abraham;" 3) the *Placeat*; 4) the usual blessing. Having kept those things that have already been proposed to the Fathers of the Council concerning the Order of Mass and approved by them, a single blessing of the solemn type would be most appropriate for the mass of matrimony, enfolding both the blessing of the couple and the blessing of the whole community.[450]

A summary of the study group's discussion of the blessings has been recorded.

"The blessings at the end of mass." 1) Proposition: a) that "May the God of Abraham" be removed; b) that a Mozarabic-Visigothic blessing not be restricted to three phrases, that it even admit five; that it not necessarily be joined with the dismissal blessing of the faithful: these are different themes. Between them both: "Go in peace" (Wagner).

2) Perhaps there is some confusion. Does this not speak of episcopal blessings? This concerns the solemn form of the final blessing (Fischer).

3) It does not matter whether the blessing has three or five phrases. We will see the text later (Martimort). Yes—however, as long as "May the God of Abraham" is omitted, and nothing is predetermined concerning the number of elements (Wagner). The mind of the study group was that the blessings not be multiplied in order to achieve greater simplification (Relator).[451]

These points were summarized in a later report, while the Order of Mass was still being finalized. Then appeared this conclusion.

The priest blesses the people saying the usual blessing or another blessing, as has been established for the season or the day.

For the Mass of Matrimony, a blessing of the solemn type with several phrases would be most appropriate, with the interpolation of the response "Amen" (as once was done in the Mozarabic and Gallican mass and still is retained in the pontifical mass of Lyons

---

[450] Schemata 157, p. 11.
[451] Schemata 157 adnexum, p. 6.

and in the mass for spouses in Germany), so that nevertheless the final phrase of the blessing is directed to all the gathered people.[452]

At the time, it was still envisioned that the blessing would follow the dismissal, as had been the custom prior to the liturgical reforms.[453] This changed with the post–Vatican II revisions to the Order of Mass.

A later draft shows the influence of Seumois, brought in for a wider view of cultural variations. After the instructions concerning the blessing, this rubric was inserted: "Particular rituals of the concluding rite should be so ordered and arranged that they also include the legitimate traditions of the peoples and that they sanctify them with the rites of the Church."[454] This did not survive in this place, although OCM 39–44 makes other provisions for local customs.

In the next draft, the text of the blessings had still not been developed, but the study group had posed the principles to the Consilium:

> Do the Fathers agree that a solemn blessing with several phrases substitute for the formula "May the God of Abraham;" do the Fathers also agree that the final phrase of the blessing be directed to the people and take the place of the usual blessing, "May almighty God bless you?"[455]

Proposed texts for the blessings finally appeared in late 1967. The third of these is the one that eventually became OCM 77, with minor grammatical improvements. It is based on a prayer from the eleventh-century Spanish Sacramentary of Vich, as found in the German collection of rites.[456] It was probably moved into the first position of the three blessings because of its antiquity. The first of the blessings presented in 1967 was a new composition invoking

---

[452] Schemata 182a, p. 17.

[453] Schemata 183, p. 5.

[454] Schemata 204, p. 7. See also the cover letter of the same schemata, acknowledging Seumois's contributions.

[455] Schemata 221, p. 15.

[456] Schemata 248, p. 16.

the Trinity in the three phrases. This is now the second option, found at OCM 214. It came with this footnote:

> Concerning the three formulas of blessing at the end of Mass that are suggested here, let these points be noted:
>
> (1) Each blessing is addressed first to the couple, and then to all present.
>
> (2) It seemed appropriate to suggest some diversity. In the first blessing the invocations are addressed to the three persons of the Trinity, as in the blessings before the readings at matins according to the Roman custom. The second blessing is directed to Christ. The third is taken from the Mozarabic and Germanic tradition.[457]

The second blessing from this draft is now the third blessing, found in OCM 215.

The final draft included the rubric that appeared in the first edition of the OCM. It instructed the priest to bless the couple before blessing the people, using one of the formulas.[458] In the second edition of the OCM, however, this rubric has been simplified to say that the priest blesses the couple and the people. The entire blessing is considered a unit.

The English translation of the second edition specifies that the priest says the first three elements of the solemn blessing with hands extended over the couple. Then he blesses all the people. This instruction is not in the original Latin of the OCM, but it comes from the Missal. In Latin, the third edition of the Missal is a few years newer than the second edition of the OCM, so the rubric in the OCM has been updated. In the blessing of a married couple on their anniversary, the rubrics for the solemn blessing also match those in the Missal (OCM 251).

In French Canada, all the blessings are found in place at this point of the ritual, not in a later chapter.[459] Three additional solemn blessings have been approved. The first two are lengthier. The first is a variation of the one that appeared in the first edition in

---

[457] Schemata 248, p. 15.

[458] Schemata 280, p. 17.

[459] *Rituel Romain*, 56–61.

the United States. Following this blessing, the priest may offer the couple a gift from the community, "a bible, or a crucifix, or an icon, or a rosary that will be a reminder in their new home of the celebration of their marriage in the church."[460] Texts for blessing such items are found in the appendix.[461]

Each blessing concludes with the priest saying a slightly different formula from the one used at Mass. He addresses "all of you who are gathered here" because the final blessing is over the whole assembly. Individual petitions may be for the couple, but the final blessing pertains to all.

Some couples like to hear their married names announced at the end of the ceremony. In practice, after the dismissal, the priest may say something like, "Congratulations, Mr. and Mrs. John and Mary Smith," eliciting the favorable applause of the assembly. There is no rubric for this. In fact, announcements are generally made after the prayer after communion. It may fall, however, under the local customs that the Introduction to the OCM tolerates.

There is no description of the procession out of the church. Presumably, the ministers walk out as they walked in, ahead of the couple. In practice, however, the couple are usually the first ones down the aisle because of their logistical proximity to it, the opportunity for a photograph, and their desire to relax after the tension of the wedding.

Frequently the couple request instrumental music for the recessional, which is totally in keeping with the Order of Mass. The Missal does not call for singing at the end of any Mass, even though the practice is quite widespread. At weddings the most popular piece is the "Wedding March" by Felix Mendelssohn, which he composed in 1842 as part of his incidental music for a performance of Shakespeare's *A Midsummer Night's Dream* at the request of King Frederick William IV of Prussia. When the king's nephew Prince Frederick William of Prussia married Victoria, the Princess Royal, in 1858, Mendelssohn's march was performed at the wedding, and its popularity spread. In spite of its secular origins, many churches have assimilated its usage into the sacred celebrations

[460] Ibid., 61.
[461] Ibid., 139–40.

of weddings. Still, given the OCM's general treatment of music, it would be fitting for the assembly to sing a final hymn instead.

78.

After the Mass, the priest and witnesses sign the marriage record in the sacristy or in the presence of the people, but not on the altar. This is new to the second edition of the OCM. The USCCB's Spanish edition surprisingly permits a deacon to sign it. See the commentary on a deacon presiding for a wedding at Mass under the heading of Chapter II.

This refers to the record kept in the parish office, rather than the civil record, of which the Roman liturgy shows little concern.[462] The same advice, however, is prudent. If the priest is signing the civil record with the witnesses after the wedding, he should not do so on the top of the altar. The altar top is reserved for items that pertain to the Eucharist.[463] In some countries, the priest and the witnesses—and even the couple—sign the parish record, though in the United States it is more common for the parish secretary to do this in the office on the first business day after the wedding.

The document should be signed after the Mass. Some priests have had it signed at the rehearsal for the sake of convenience, but it should never be signed until the celebration has taken place.

The Roman Ritual of 1614 had also instructed the priest to fill out the parish register with the pertinent information.[464] The prohibition for doing this on the altar is not there, probably because it never occurred to people that someone might do it that way. The rubric here uncovers the existence of an errant contemporary pastoral practice.

[462] Evanou, "Commentarium," 317.
[463] GIRM 73.
[464] *Roman Ritual*, 466.

II. The Order of Celebrating Matrimony without Mass

T he first edition of the OCM put the title of this section ahead of paragraph 39. The title carried a footnote both in the Latin and the English translation, explaining that marriage should normally be celebrated within Mass, in keeping with *Inter œcumenici*,[1] but circumstances may influence another decision. This note was important at the time because several aspects of the Catholic marriage ceremony were changing. Formerly, the wedding took place just before Mass, and the nuptial blessing came during Mass. Now the church was recommending that weddings take place within the course of the Mass. While promoting this new direction, the OCM still made accommodations for celebrating matrimony without Mass. The footnote has been removed from the second edition of the OCM, probably because the explanation is no longer necessary. In its place is the brief OCM 79, which merely explains the permission.

The explanation points out that a priest or a deacon may celebrate this order of matrimony without Mass. Overall, the second edition of the OCM gives a more ample explanation of the role of deacons in the liturgy. This is true also of the third edition of the Roman Missal.

The OCM presumes that if a deacon is to preside for a wedding, then the wedding is taking place without Mass. In practice, some deacons have presided for a wedding at a Mass over which a priest always presides. The Congregation for the Clergy, however, wrote in 1998, "Where deacons have been duly delegated by the parish priest or the local ordinary, they may assist at the celebration of

---

[1] IO 70.

marriages *extra Missam* and pronounce the nuptial blessing in the name of the Church."[2] Canonist John Huels has argued that a deacon who witnesses a wedding during Mass does so validly, but not licitly, and that it is not clear if the bishop can permit otherwise. Since a doubt exists, however, "the bishop may be presumed to have the necessary dispensing power."[3] Furthermore, an undocumented private reply in 2007 from the CDWDS argued that a change in presider is not admissible.[4] This has no force of law, but it does indicate the mind of the Congregation, just as the permission for a second priest to preside for a wedding, first allowed in 1964,[5] disappeared from the OCM. Normally when a deacon presides for a wedding, it is without Mass. If he wishes to do so for some exceptional reason, he would be wise to seek permission from the diocesan bishop.

This ceremony was newly devised after the Second Vatican Council, though there was in Paris in 1839 a special form of the rite for the marriage of a Catholic and a non-Catholic.[6] As the number of such weddings grew, the Vatican had to address the situation. A papal indult in 1914 permitted Catholics to marry non-Catholics without the nuptial Mass.[7] A typical Catholic considered such weddings to have lower value, but now they are more generally accepted. When the council opened the door to full, conscious, active participation at the Mass, it unwittingly made participation at weddings difficult, especially if a Catholic is marrying a non-Catholic. Many of those attending such a service would not be eligible for communion or know the responses to make and postures to take. The wedding without Mass works better in such

---

[2] Congregation for the Clergy, "Directory for the Ministry and Life of Permanent Deacons," *Diaconatus origem*, 22 February 1998, AAS 90, no. 33.

[3] John M. Huels, "The Significance of the 1991 *Ordo celebrandi matrimonium* for the Canon Law of Marriage," *Studia canonica* 43 (2009): 107.

[4] Edward McNamara, "Follow-Up: Weddings in Lent," https://www.ewtn .com/library/Liturgy/zlitur309.htm.

[5] IO 72.

[6] Kenneth W. Stevenson, *To Join Together: The Rite of Marriage* (New York: Pueblo Publishing Company, 1987), 103.

[7] Ibid., 114.

situations because it reduces the need for participation that the Eucharist demands.

As SC was being developed, some consideration for the problem came to light. The earliest drafts of what became paragraph 78 allowed for the order of matrimony "without mass but in church."[8] It had been common for weddings between a Catholic and a non-Catholic to take place outside the sanctuary or even in the rectory. All weddings now could be celebrated inside the church. The phrase "but in church" was removed from the later drafts, probably because the location was understood. Ironically today, some Catholics want a marriage outdoors or in some other venue apart from the church, whereas in the past, a wedding in church was more generally perceived as a great honor.

In the same drafts another small change took place. Instead of treating matrimony "outside of Mass" (*extra Missam*), they spoke of matrimony "without Mass" (*sine Missa*).[9] No explanation is given, but perhaps the first left open the possibility that the wedding would still take place before Mass, hence "outside" of it, whereas the intention was to create a ceremony for a wedding without Mass. These changes were incorporated into the final version of SC. ICEL, perhaps unaware of this change, proposed that *sine Missa* be translated "Outside of Mass," in keeping with the first translation, which had called this chapter the "Rite of Celebrating Marriage Outside Mass." The final version, however, of the revised translation came back with the words "without Mass," which is more faithful to the development of this particular order of worship. The same is true of the Order of Confirmation. The first translation had a chapter for celebrating confirmation "outside Mass,"[10] and now the same ceremony is called "without Mass."[11]

---

[8] Francisco Gil Hellín, *Concilii Vaticani II synopsis in ordinem redigens schemata cum relationibus necnon Patrum orationes atque animadversiones: Constitutio de Sacra Liturgica Sacrosanctum concilium* (Vatican City: Libreria Editrice Vaticana, 2003), 236.

[9] Ibid., 236–37.

[10] *The Rites*, 495.

[11] *Ritual Para la Confirmación, The Order of Confirmation* (Washington, DC: United States Conference of Catholic Bishops, 2016), 41.

Reviewing SC, the study group made these remarks about the paragraphs pertaining to weddings between a Catholic and a non-Catholic:

> 47. As to the sacrament of matrimony celebrated without mass, the possibility of a variation in the readings ought to be researched, according to the mind of article 35 §1 (which also pertains to marriage within mass), and concerning a richer form of the blessing (now found in certain particular ritual books.) For meanwhile already, on the strength of the Letters of the *Motu Proprio* given on January 25, 1964, and of the Instruction, in all matrimonies of Catholics celebrated outside of mass the blessing is given.
>
> 48. The Council did not delay the neuralgic question concerning the rite of mixed marriages, especially because then "it was in the schema produced On Marriage." Because this schema has not yet been submitted to the Fathers, it seems fitting, if the Fathers of the Council agree, to convene a committee composed from members of our group and others who have an interest. . . .
>
> Do the Fathers agree that a mixed committee on the rite of mixed marriages be convened as soon as possible?[12]

Thus the group was looking very early for advice on how to proceed. Within a couple of years, there was already some progress, though some expressed concern about a growing practice of having two ministers assist when the couple came from two distinct Christian communities. The Sacred Congregation for the Doctrine of the Faith issued these directives in 1966:

> IV. As to the liturgical form, derogating from canon 1102, § 3 and 4, as well as 1109, § 3, it is granted to the Ordinaries of places to permit also the celebration of mixed marriages, using the sacred rites with appropriate blessings and a sermon.
>
> V. Any celebration of matrimony in the presence of a Catholic priest and a non-Catholic minister who perform their own rite at the same time must be completely avoided. Nevertheless there is no objection if, after the religious ceremony has been completed, the non-Catholic minister offers some words of congratulation and exhortation, and certain prayers may be recited together with the

---

[12] Schemata 32, pp. 15–16.

non-Catholics. All these things are permitted to be done with the approval of the Ordinary of the place, while using appropriate cautions to avoid the danger of scandal.[13]

As the group set to work, it made these observations on the development of matrimony without Mass:

> The structure of matrimony outside of mass, already outlined by the Constitution, may be more readily determined from number 74 of the Instruction. This is the same structure also for matrimony within mass up to the prayer of the faithful inclusively. Then, since the sacrifice of the eucharist may not be celebrated, immediately comes the blessing of the bride, and thus the rite concludes.
> Concerning the communion of the presanctified, as I may thus say, if a deacon assists the matrimony in place of the priest, number 32 below applies.[14]

As work continued, simplicity ruled. For example, in the draft from early 1967, this rubric appeared: "The rite described above may be used also in celebrating mixed marriages between a Catholic party and a baptized non-Catholic party if circumstances suggest and by consent of the Ordinary of the place."[15] A full ceremony resembling the one in the first edition of the OCM, however, was first developed later that year.[16] The footnote that accompanied the title in the first edition was also elaborated in this draft. It also made room for "a deacon who receives delegation to assist and bless in the name of the Church those celebrating matrimony."[17] It reaffirmed this point in concluding remarks to the ceremony, citing the *Motu Proprio* on deacons from earlier that year,[18] and this appeared in the first edition's paragraph 53.

---

[13] http://www.vatican.va/roman_curia/congregations/cfaith/documents/rc_con_cfaith_doc_19660318_matrimonii-sacramentum_lt.html; cited in Schemata 157, p. 3.

[14] Schemata 157, p. 5.

[15] Schemata 204, p. 7.

[16] Schemata 248, pp. 3–6.

[17] Ibid., 3.

[18] Ibid., 6, citing *Sacrum Diaconatus Ordinem*, 18 June 1967, number 22, 4.

When the final draft was completed, an opening letter explained its preparation.

> The rite of matrimony outside of mass uses the same texts of matrimony *within mass*, organizing them according to the structure determined by the Motu Proprio *Sacram Liturgiam*, and by the Instruction *Inter œcumenici*, harmonizing the prayer of the faithful with the prayer over the bride, which immediately follows it.[19]

The same explanatory footnote prepared for the previous draft is repeated in this final one,[20] though it was simplified in the first edition of the OCM and eliminated in the second.

79.

A priest or a deacon may celebrate a wedding without Mass, if the circumstances require or advise it. This brief explanation is new to the second edition of the OCM, but it refers back to the Introduction (24). It moves some material from paragraph 53 of the first edition, which appeared after the description of the ceremony, to this position before the description. It had appeared in the later position in the study group's last drafts.[21]

THE INTRODUCTORY RITES

The First Form

80.

For vesture, a priest or deacon wears an alb or surplice with a white stole or one of a festive color. A priest may wear a matching cope. A deacon may wear a dalmatic of the same color. He goes to the door for the greeting. This is the first part of the former paragraph 39. The second part allowed the minister to omit this initial greeting, but that permission has been removed. Some greeting does take place.

---

[19] Schemata 280, p. ii.
[20] Schemata 280, p. 12.
[21] Schemata 248, p. 6; Schemata 280, p. 15.

When a bishop presides, he wears an alb, and then a pectoral cross and stole or cope. He uses the miter and pastoral staff.[22] If a priest assists the bishop, the priest wears a stole over a cassock and surplice, or over an alb. Deacons wear the appropriate stole and dalmatic.[23]

In the first drafts of this paragraph, descriptions for the vesture do not appear, and the minister was instructed to greet the wedding party "warmly."[24] In the first edition, the directives for vesture were included, and the word "warmly" had disappeared.

Now the word "warmly" has been reinserted here. Coupled with the removal of the permission to omit the greeting altogether, it aims to set a positive tone for the opening of the celebration.

When celebrating matrimony without Mass, the same two options exist for the start of the ceremony. This paragraph opens the first option. Most of this, including that adverb, is taken from the parallel place when celebrating marriage within Mass (OCM 45).

The Mexican ritual permits the usage of blessed water,[25] as explained in the commentary on OCM 45.

81.

The entrance chant accompanies the procession. This is the first part of the former paragraph 40. The first edition, however, admitted the possibility that the procession may not take place. The word "if" has been removed, but the alternative is still present in OCM 83.

The word "priest" from the first edition has changed to "minister" because a deacon may be the presider. In Latin the word for the couple has changed from words that can mean "husband and wife" to a word that means "those about to be married." The English translation, which in the first edition called them "the bride and bridegroom," now calls them "the bridal party." That expression, however, may imply more than the bride and groom, and its adjective implies that those involved with the procession are here for the bride, not for the couple.

---

[22] CB 176.
[23] CB 614.
[24] Schemata 248, p. 3; Schemata 280, p. 12.
[25] *Ritual* (Mexico), 139–40.

Most of this is taken over from the order of celebrating matrimony within Mass (OCM 46).

In French Canada, an organ solo may replace the entrance chant,[26] as it may in the celebration of matrimony within Mass. The Mexican edition also permits an instrumental, while making a plea for sacred music,[27] as explained in the commentary on OCM 46. It repeats its concerns that the couple not be seated with their backs to the people, as well as its permission for the parents of the couple to bless them.[28]

Normally the entrance chant is associated with the celebration of Mass, but it does appear here and in some other non-eucharistic liturgical celebrations. Presumably the rules for the entrance chant at Mass also apply to a song in this situation.[29] In that case, the chants recommended by the Missal or some other appropriate song may be sung.

82.

The minister bows to and kisses the altar and then goes to the chair. This rubric is new to the second edition. The rubrics of this chapter now use the word "minister" nearly consistently because the presider may be either a priest or a deacon. The French Canadian translation more regularly uses the words "priest or deacon" to make this explicit.[30] The translation of this entire paragraph is largely taken from similar rubrics in the Missal[31] and earlier in the OCM (47).

No mention is made of the proper reverence to a tabernacle. At Mass, if the tabernacle is in the sanctuary, the ministers genuflect before reverencing the altar.[32] If the tabernacle is not in the sanctuary, then the reverences to the altar suffice. Even though this is not Mass, the minister still kisses the altar when approaching the sanctuary after the procession.

[26] *Rituel Romain*, 64.
[27] *Ritual* (Mexico), 140.
[28] Ibid., 141.
[29] GIRM 48.
[30] *Rituel Romain*, 64.
[31] OM 1.
[32] GIRM 274.

Even if a deacon is presiding, he goes to "the chair"—not to "his" chair. Presumably, this is the presider's chair. When a deacon presides for a Sunday celebration in the absence of a priest, he uses a different chair to show that the community is awaiting the presence of a priest.[33] That legislation applies, however, to a specific circumstance and ceremony in the United States. When a deacon presides for a wedding without Mass, it does not always mean that the parish has no priest. Furthermore, when presiding over the Liturgy of the Hours, a priest or a deacon presides from "the" chair.[34] Logically, then, "the chair" in OCM 82 refers to the presider's chair, whether the minister is a priest or a deacon.

The Second Form

83.

Vested for the celebration, the priest or deacon goes to the place reserved for the couple. This is based on material from the former paragraph 39, but it details more exactly the second of the options that the first edition permitted.

In the second form, there is no description of a procession. Nor does the rubric call for an entrance chant, except in the USCCB's Spanish language edition, which mentions the chant in OCM 84. The rubrics imply a more informal opening, where the priest enters from the sacristy and goes to the place where the couple are or will be. It could, however, be interpreted to allow a procession of the wedding party without the priest, accompanied by an organ solo without singing. The rubric is imprecise in this regard, but it developed from the first edition's option of not having a procession.

The options in the drafts entered the first edition: The minister either goes to the door of the church or to the "altar."[35] Now, the second form says more precisely that if he does not go to the door of the church, then he goes to the place prepared for the couple. The translation of this paragraph largely borrows from OCM 48.

---

[33] *Sunday Celebrations in the Absence of a Priest* (Washington, DC: United States Conference of Catholic Bishops, 2012), introduction 24, p. 14.

[34] *General Instruction on the Liturgy of the Hours* 256.

[35] Schemata 248, p. 3; Schemata 280, p. 12.

84.

The minister warmly greets the couple when they arrive at their place. This draws material from the former paragraph 39, and it borrows language from OCM 80. Again, the word "warmly" has been inserted into the second edition's description of the minister's greeting.

The couple arrive at their place, but the rubrics never say how. Some may assume that they still process, but this paragraph derived from the option implied in the first edition that a procession may not happen. In this case, the couple enter the church as anyone does on a typical day, and once the minister has entered the sanctuary, they take their place. That place may be inside or outside the sanctuary; the rubrics give no preference. Wherever they are to be for the ceremony, the minister goes there for the personal warm greeting.

The translation borrows largely from OCM 49.

85.

The minister bows to the altar, kisses it, and goes to the chair. This is the same as OCM 82, without the phrase "approaches the altar," presumably because he has already entered the sanctuary and thereby approached the altar.

In Latin, this paragraph makes no mention of the minister kissing the altar. It only says that he bows to it. This created a discrepancy in the first and second forms in celebrating matrimony without Mass. When the English translation came back from the CDWDS, the kiss was inserted into the second form. The same change happened with the Spanish translation in use in the United States and in Mexico,[36] as well as in French Canada.[37] The kiss, however, remains absent in the Spanish translation in force in Colombia.[38]

Most of this translation comes from OCM 50.

86.

The minister makes the sign of the cross and greets the people. Even though this is not Mass, the sign of the cross opens the ser-

---

[36] *Ritual* (Mexico), 141.
[37] *Rituel Romain*, 65.
[38] *Ritual* (Colombia), 56.

vice. This clarification is new to the second edition, as is the insertion of the greeting.

In Latin, the second edition supplied the greeting that appears in the English translation, and then it permitted the minister to use "other appropriate words taken especially from Sacred Scripture." All English translations change this to say that the minister may use a different greeting from the Roman Missal. This is more restrictive, though it lends consistency to liturgical greetings. Nonetheless, this ceremony is not Mass, so a broader selection of greetings would have been defensible. From the practical point of view, it is better to use a greeting that people recognize. Permission to draw a greeting from the Bible instead of from the Mass still appears in the translations of other language groups.[39]

Unfortunately, the greeting that the OCM suggests is not much used at Sunday Mass. This particular greeting is taken from the New Testament, where it appears nine times.[40] It is the most biblically rich of the greetings from the Missal, but it has not been used sufficiently to elicit the usual response from the people. The OCM's English translation comes directly from the Roman Missal.[41]

In Latin the people had an alternate response: "Blessed be God forever," which appeared as an option through the second edition of the Missal, though removed from the third. Further, the Latin gave the people permission to respond "in another way." This alternate response and the freedom of choosing some other one have also been removed from the English translation of the OCM's second edition. The only response the people may give is, "And with your spirit," the typical one made to a liturgical greeting from a priest or a deacon. The alternate response can still be found in the Spanish translation of this paragraph for use in the United States, as well as in Mexico,[42] though not in the one for Colombia.[43]

---

[39] *Rituel Romain*, 65; *Ritual* (Mexico), 141.

[40] Rom 1:7; 1 Cor 1:3; 2 Cor 1:2; Gal 1:3; Eph 1:2; Phil 1:2; 2 Thess 1:2; and Phil 3, as well as Rev 1:4.

[41] OM 2.

[42] *Ritual* (Mexico), 141.

[43] *Ritual* (Colombia), 56.

French-speaking Canada offers four different options for the greeting and two for the response.[44]

87.

The minister introduces the celebration with words addressed to the couple or to all those present. This is new to the second edition of the OCM. It borrows from the translation of OCM 57. This first example is addressed to the gathered assembly.

The idea came from a postconciliar instruction that called for a brief introduction, not a homily, to explain the celebration when it is celebrated without Mass.[45]

The Latin original gives only the first two lines, but the translation has repeated everything from OCM 57. The minister may use these or similar words.

88.

A second example of the introduction is addressed to the couple. Again the Latin only gives the opening lines, but the English translation copies everything from OCM 58. The minister may use these or similar words.

89.

The minister extends his hands and says a prayer. Technically, this is not called a "collect" because this is not a Mass. The Mexican book calls it an opening prayer.[46] Even its ending is briefer than one expects from a collect, though not in Mexico, where the longer ending appears. Actually, the minister may pray any of the collects from the Missal's ritual Mass; this is one of them, found at OCM 225 with the longer ending.

Because this is not Mass, the ceremony does not include the Gloria.

In the drafts for this ceremony, the study group wrote into the rubric: "[T]hen the Prayer takes place, unless out of pastoral concerns some brief instruction seems more fitting (See *Inter œcumenici*

---

[44] *Rituel Romain*, 65.

[45] IO 74a.

[46] *Ritual* (Mexico), 142.

74.)"[47] The study group saw the introduction as a replacement for the prayer. This became part of the rubric in the first edition's paragraph 40. It has been removed. The prayer is expected to take place.

In the English translation for the United States, all the optional prayers are found in the appendix. In Colombia all six options for a wedding within Mass appear again here where the presider can easily find them.[48] The first two prayers appear in reverse order because the second of the collects serves as the first suggestion for this ceremony. In French Canada the nine options for the collect reappear for this prayer in the same order.[49]

THE LITURGY OF THE WORD

90.

Readings are proclaimed as usual. The passages are taken from OCM 56 or 144–187. At least one reading with an asterisk must be selected. This updates the rubric in the first edition's paragraph 41, which called for three readings. Now the total number of readings is not specified, though the expression "in the usual manner" implies two or three readings, plus a responsorial psalm.

Even before the liturgical use of languages other than Latin became widespread, the Vatican recommended that the readings at a wedding be done in the vernacular. If the Vatican had not yet approved a translation of the desired reading, the local ordinary could do so.[50]

As noted above, the council's preparatory commission had recommended a greater variety of readings at weddings.[51] The first edition specified that one reading may come from the Old Testament, as was suggested in the drafts.[52] As mentioned in the commentary on OCM 55, however, the inclusion of the words "Old Testament" was important for the first edition because SC had mentioned only the epistle and the gospel, which were the

---

[47] Schemata 248, p. 3; Schemata 280, p. 12.
[48] *Ritual del Matrimonio*, 57–59.
[49] *Rituel Romain*, 67–70.
[50] IO 74b.
[51] Schemata 32, p. 15.
[52] Schemata 248, p. 3; Schemata 280, p. 12.

customary readings at the time. With the revised lectionary well in hand, the reference to the Old Testament reading is no longer necessary. Furthermore, it is customary that New Testament readings be proclaimed throughout Easter Time. The rubric in the French Canadian edition makes this clear, saying that the first reading in Easter Time should be the one from Revelation.[53]

The translation of this paragraph is largely carried over from OCM 55.

The Mexican edition again offers additional selections from Revelation and from Acts of the Apostles during Easter Time and puts within the second chapter a suite of suggested readings.[54]

91.

The minister gives a homily appropriate to the circumstances, based on the readings. This is basically the same as the former paragraph 42.

This is largely taken over from *Inter œcumenici* 74a, which called for a homily based on the sacred text, citing SC 52 for its source, which explains the purpose and value of the homily at a celebration of the Eucharist. Virtually the same rubric appeared in both drafts prepared by the study group.[55] The rubric is very similar to the one in OCM 57, and the translation is carried over from there. The earlier paragraph says that the homily comes after the gospel, but the word "gospel" does not appear here probably because other readings may be proclaimed when there is no Mass.

THE CELEBRATION OF MATRIMONY

92.

If more than one couple is getting married in this ceremony, some parts of the service may take place once, but the questions before the consent, the consent, and the reception of the consent must be handled individually. This is the former paragraph 52. It

[53] *Rituel Romain*, 71.
[54] *Ritual* (Mexico), 143–48.
[55] Schemata 248, p. 3; Schemata 280, p. 12.

repeats material from OCM 58 above, and the translation is the same.

This rubric was developed in the two drafts prepared by the study group.[56] There, as in the first edition of the OCM, it appeared among the comments that followed the presentation of the liturgy. Now it comes before. In this position it alerts the minister about the changes to make before the wedding proceeds.

93.

All stand, and the minister addresses the couple. An address is provided. He may use these or similar words. This is the former paragraph 43, but it now says that not only the couple but also the two witnesses positioned near them should stand along with everyone. The witnesses fulfill a canonical responsibility, so the liturgy ensures that they are nearby for the exchange of consent.

This paragraph duplicates the material from OCM 59. The same translation is used. Once again the Mexican edition asks for only the couple to stand for the questions.[57]

This rubric appeared in the two drafts prepared by the study group.[58] The witnesses were not mentioned in these either, though their presence was implied. The revised OCM acknowledges their presence and responsibility.

The two principal witnesses are to stand next to the bride and groom. Sometimes other members of the wedding party join them, though this is not necessary. Although the image is striking, it may obscure the centrality of the four main people. The two principal witnesses are present not just for visual appeal but for a canonical purpose.

ICEL had some conversation about changing the phrase from "Through a special sacrament" to "Through this special sacrament," in order to draw attention to the sacrament being celebrated at this moment. The final version, however, stayed closer to the Latin. Still, the minister may use these or similar words.

---

[56] Schemata 248, p. 6; Schemata 280, p. 15.
[57] *Ritual* (Mexico), 149.
[58] Schemata 248, p. 4; Schemata 280, p. 13.

The Questions before the Consent

94.

The minister asks the couple about the readiness for matrimony. This is the former paragraph 44. The heading to this section is new to the second edition. Also new to the second edition is the clarification that each partner responds separately to the questions, as in OCM 60.

The two drafts from the study group show the rubrics and questions that entered the first edition.[59] The translation of all the rubrics and dialogues in this paragraph are copied over from OCM 60. The French Canadian translation presents the same options added to its section on matrimony within Mass,[60] as does the Mexican edition.[61]

In England and Wales, the adjustments required by civil law appear here as they do in the section on matrimony within Mass.

The Consent

95.

The minister asks the couple to declare their consent, and they join their right hands. This is copied over from OCM 61. It is the first part of the former paragraph 45. The two drafts of the study group contained the same information that went into the first edition.[62]

In French Canada, the same variations permitted for inviting the consent within Mass are offered here as well.[63] In Mexico, the community stands before the minister gives this introduction.[64]

96.

The groom and then the bride give their consent. This carries over the same information from OCM 62, complete with the optional formula in English for the United States. This is the second

---

[59] Schemata 248, p. 4; Schemata 280, p. 13.
[60] *Rituel Romain*, 72–74.
[61] *Ritual* (Mexico), 151.
[62] Schemata 248, p. 4; Schemata 280, p. 13.
[63] *Rituel Romain*, 75.
[64] *Ritual* (Mexico), 150.

part of the former paragraph 45. The two drafts present the same material that entered the first edition.[65]

In Colombia, the six options for the consent are the same as those that appear in the section for a wedding within Mass.[66] In the United States, the Spanish translation offers an option that also appears in the ceremony for weddings within Mass. The Mexican edition does as well.[67] The version available in other English-speaking countries is copied over from OCM 63.

97.

The minister may obtain the consent of the couple through questions. This paragraph copies the material from OCM 63, which offers two sets of questions based on the consent in the previous paragraph. This is the last part of the former paragraph 45, given here with more detail. This number does not appear in the translation in use in England and Wales because it is not legal to receive consent through questions in those countries.

98.

The minister receives the couple's consent. This carries over everything from OCM 64, including the new alternate version of these words.

This is the former paragraph 46, which faithfully copied the words prepared in the study group's two drafts.[68]

The French Canadian translation allows the priest to raise his right hand or place it over the joined hands of the spouse, as it does in the version of celebrating matrimony within Mass.[69]

99.

The minister introduces an acclamation, and the people respond. This is new to the second edition, though it copies the words and rubrics from OCM 65. Another acclamation may be used. This expands the people's "Amen" that was to conclude the reception of consent in the first edition. The Mexican edition has

---

[65] Schemata 248, p. 4; Schemata 280, p. 13.
[66] *Ritual* (Colombia), 62–66.
[67] *Ritual* (Mexico), 151–52.
[68] Schemata 248, p. 5; Schemata 280, p. 14.
[69] *Rituel Romain*, 80.

placed musical notation for two possibilities within the text, introduced by the minister or the cantor.[70]

Also in Mexico, the community is seated after this acclamation, and if it is customary, the groom may then lift the veil that covers the face of the bride.[71]

The Blessing and Giving of Rings

100.

The minister blesses the rings with one of the formulas. He may sprinkle them with blessed water. This is the former paragraph 47 with the addition of the optional sprinkling. The translation of this paragraph is the same as in OCM 66.

In other countries, the same options for weddings within Mass apply here as well. French Canada, for example, has an additional form of the blessing.[72]

The study group prepared its drafts with one version of the blessing.[73] The first edition added a reference to the other versions, which still appear in the OCM today. These are in the appendix in the United States; England and Wales received permission to place all the options for this blessing as a group within this paragraph.

The Blessing and Giving of the Arras

101A.

101B.

The couple exchange their rings, reciting a formula. In the United States, this may be followed by the blessing and giving of *arras*. This copies material from OCM 67A and B. In Mexico the minister may give one blessing over both the rings and the *arras*.[74]

This is the former paragraph 48, which did not include the option for *arras*. The first edition replicated the material from the study group's two drafts.[75]

---

[70] *Ritual* (Mexico), 153–54.
[71] Ibid., 154.
[72] Ibid., 81.
[73] Schemata 248, p. 5; Schemata 280, p. 14.
[74] *Ritual* (Mexico), 155.
[75] Schemata 248, p. 5; Schemata 280, p. 48.

102.

All may sing a hymn of praise. This is new to the second edition and copies the option from OCM 68 during Mass. In French Canada, however, the song is placed after the nuptial blessing.[76]

The Universal Prayer

103A.

The universal prayer happens as usual, except that its closing prayer is omitted. The invocations should not duplicate intentions from the nuptial blessing. This is the former paragraph 49, but it has been considerably rewritten in order to account for the option of distributing communion. The sequence of events changes depending on this choice. Also, the first edition's heading included both this prayer and the nuptial blessing. Now these are separated into distinct units. In general, the second edition gives a more thorough treatment of the universal prayer.

If there is no distribution of Holy Communion, the universal prayer concludes with the Lord's Prayer, and then the minister gives the nuptial blessing. This order differs from that in the first edition of the OCM, which put the nuptial blessing after the petitions. The first edition's paragraph 51 made the Lord's Prayer optional in this case. Now it is always included. A preconciliar practice omitted the Lord's Prayer in weddings without Mass, as explained in the commentary on OCM 109.

The study group first noted the use of the universal prayer in the ceremony without Mass as a permission, not a requirement: "Before the blessing that according to the norm in article 78 of the Constitution must always be imparted, the faculty of having the prayer of the faithful is given, according to the recommendation made in the Instruction *Inter œcumenici* number 74."[77] The universal prayer by its nature assumes that those who pray it are among the baptized faithful, who exercise the office of their baptismal priesthood.[78] Perhaps this ceremony includes it because it

---

[76] *Rituel Romain*, 86.
[77] Schemata 248, p. 3.
[78] GIRM 69.

presumes that both the bride and the groom have been baptized, or because a litany of prayers seemed appropriate.

The first edition gave permission in 49b that the introduction be followed by silence instead of petitions. That option does not appear in the second edition. At a typical Mass, however, the people may respond to each petition in silence instead of making a response.[79] The spoken response is usually the more effective choice.

The instructions in this paragraph in the first edition are essentially identical to those that appeared in both drafts prepared by the study group.[80]

Parts of this translation are copied from OCM 69, which describes the universal prayer at a wedding within Mass.

In French Canada, the nuptial blessing precedes the universal prayer in a wedding without Mass, which is not the order that the second edition prefers. A sample formula for the universal prayer appears in the book at this point. The minister may use it or consult others in the appendix.[81]

Also in French Canada, the ritual gives the presider a suggested introduction to the Lord's Prayer that does not exist in the original Latin: "United in the same Spirit, let us address our prayer to the God of the Covenant, to the Father of Jesus Christ, who is also our Father."[82]

The Blessing and Placing of the Lazo or the Veil

103B.

According to cultural preferences, the minister may bless the *lazo* or veil, and *padrinos* may place them on or over the groom and bride. This repeats material in OCM 71B. It appears in both the Spanish and English editions of the OCM in the United States, though not, for example, in Colombia, where the tradition is not as strong as it is in Mexico. The Mexican edition presents the same material for the placing of the *lazo* within Mass.[83]

---

[79] GIRM 71.
[80] Schemata 248, p. 5; Schemata 280, p. 14.
[81] *Rituel Romain*, 89–90.
[82] Ibid., 91.
[83] *Ritual* (Mexico), 195.

The Nuptial Blessing

104.

The couple kneel at their place, and the priest invites all to pray for them. All do so in silence. This is the former paragraph 50 with more explanation. The translation copies material from OCM 73 and from the third option in the Missal's ritual Mass for marriage. OCM 104, however, adds one word to the minister's introduction in the Missal: "Now." And the Missal's words "by our prayers" do not appear in the OCM. The discrepancy suggests an attempt to ease the transition for people familiar with the slightly different sequence of ceremonies that takes place during Mass.

The couple are asked to kneel at their place. They have the option of approaching the altar only when the blessing is given at Mass (OCM 73). Perhaps this is because the altar does not play so central a role in the wedding without Mass.

A musical setting of the nuptial blessings is available later in the English translation. Even the Latin original provides sung notation for them. The original, however, does not give the minister's complete text at OCM 104, only the first words of his introduction. The English translation makes the more practical decision by putting in place the complete words of one of the suggested introductions.

For many centuries in the past, the nuptial blessing was not given outside of Mass. In 1914, however, the Sacred Congregation of Rites allowed the practice if the priest had obtained an indult from the Holy See. In that case, he turned toward the couple, even though he was offering prayers to God. He recited Psalm 128 (127). Then he recited the "Glory Be to the Father," and a short version of the Kyrie. He prayed the Lord's Prayer silently until the end, and led a brief dialogue. Then he gave a much shorter nuptial blessing:

> O Lord, bless + and look down from heaven upon this couple. And as you sent your holy peacemaking Angel Raphael to Tobiah and Sarah, the daughter of Raguel, so be pleased, O Lord, to send your blessing upon this couple, so that they may remain in your blessing, continue in your will, and live in your love. Through Christ our Lord. Amen.[84]

---

[84] *Roman Ritual*, 470–72.

Then the priest extended his hands over the heads of the couple while a minister held his book. He said,

> May the Lord almighty God bless you and fulfill his blessing within you, and may you see your children's children to the third and fourth generation, and their progeny, and may you reach the fullness of years for which you hope. Through Christ our Lord.[85]

Where no indult had been obtained, and the couple could not receive the nuptial blessing outside of Mass, the priest still recited Psalm 128 (127) and the prayers following it, but in place of the two parts of the nuptial blessing cited above, he concluded with this prayer:

> O Lord, we pray, stretch forth the right hand of heavenly aid to your faithful ones, so that they may seek you with all their heart, and obtain the things they worthily request. Through Christ our Lord. Amen.[86]

The priest did not move his hand in the sign of the cross while saying this prayer, as he did in the first of the prayers permitted with the indult.

This was replaced after the Second Vatican Council. The same nuptial blessings given at Mass are permitted and expected in a celebration of matrimony without Mass. No indult is required. This had been the desire from the preparatory commission working on SC.[87] The study group took up the question at the earliest opportunity.

> *"The prayer over the bride that appears in the missal may also be used in matrimony outside of mass."* Nevertheless the blessing within Mass and the blessing outside of Mass seem to pertain to the literary genres so diverse that the first may not be used in place of the second. For it ought to be taught that in the first instance it appears to follow the consecration and the Lord's Prayer and to precede

---

[85] Ibid., 472.
[86] Ibid., 472–74.
[87] Schemata 32, p. 15.

communion (Martimort). The study group thought the same thing (Relator).

Nevertheless, it may happen that the connection with the sacred eucharist may be made with an introduction; then the introduction may be omitted when the blessing is used without Mass (Lengeling). I do not want to decide the matter right now (Relator).[88]

Nonetheless, the work continued with the blessing in both instances. Both drafts prepared by the study group allowed the usage of any of the three nuptial blessings without Mass,[89] as did the first edition. The purpose, however, of the blessing changed with this decision, eliminating its connection to the Eucharist and leaving it as a blessing of the couple. This makes harder to defend the decision to keep its placement after the Lord's Prayer within Mass.

When ICEL worked on the translation of this introduction, there was some concern that people would think that some words referred not to God but to the groom: "that in his kindness he may favor with his help." But in context, it seemed not to be an issue.

In Mexico one of the optional introductions copied from the ones for celebrating matrimony within Mass contains an optional phrase referring to the couple's "participation in the Body and Blood of Christ,"[90] but if communion is distributed in this ceremony without Mass, it will be only under the form of bread.

105.

The minister extends his hands over the couple and prays a nuptial blessing. This paragraph is copied from OCM 74. The first edition's paragraph 50 did not include a text here, only the references to other paragraph numbers. Now a sample text appears in the book.

Other blessings may be used; however, OCM 207 concludes with a reference to the couple's intent to share communion together. This would not be an appropriate prayer to use at the celebration of matrimony between a Catholic and a non-Catholic who

---

[88] Schemata 157 adnexum, p. 6.
[89] Schemata 248, p. 5; Schemata 280, p. 14.
[90] *Ritual* (Mexico), 163.

will not be receiving communion. ICEL had raised the issue, but the CDWDS let it pass. OCM 207 is permitted in place of OCM 105 but is not appropriate.

All the nuptial blessings of the second edition include an epiclesis. The addition intended to create a bridge to the nuptial blessings of the Eastern Rites. In this particular ceremony, however, a deacon, not just a priest, may call down the Holy Spirit upon the couple. This would never happen in the East. Indeed, presiding at weddings in the East is reserved to priests and bishops. Deacons do not preside.

The Mexican edition states that the *lazo* is removed after the nuptial blessing.[91]

In the French Canadian edition, the song that may precede the universal prayer follows the nuptial blessing instead. Then the couple may recite their own prayer, as they may do during a wedding within Mass.[92]

106.

If communion is not distributed, the minister blesses the people immediately after the nuptial blessing. This changes the sequence suggested by the drafts[93] and is found in the first edition's paragraph 51, which put the Lord's Prayer after the nuptial blessing and before the final blessing. This version keeps the eucharistic sequence of the Lord's Prayer followed by the nuptial blessing, and it joins the two blessings at the end of the service in a way that does not happen during Mass.

The translation comes directly from the Missal's ritual Mass for marriage and from all the blessings in the OCM.

107.

The ceremony may end with a song. The most praiseworthy way is for all to sing, rather than a soloist, so that all may give praise to God.

---

[91] Ibid., 162.

[92] *Rituel Romain*, 86.

[93] Schemata 248, p. 6; Schemata 280, p. 15.

Holy Communion

108.

If communion is to be distributed, the nuptial blessing concludes the prayer of the faithful. The Lord's Prayer follows. This reverses the order of these two elements as they occur at a wedding within Mass and at a wedding without Mass and without communion. It puts the nuptial blessing, however, closer to the exchange of consent and keeps the communion rite as a separate unit. This is the former paragraph 54, with more precision. In fact, the paragraphs that follow did not appear in the first edition at all. The liturgical book now gives a more complete description of how communion takes place without Mass.

The minister goes to the place of reservation, picks up the vessel of consecrated bread, sets it on the altar, and genuflects there. He does not genuflect at the tabernacle but makes a single genuflection at the altar where the communion rite will take place. There is no mention of a corporal, which is a cloth used for the celebration of Mass. During Mass the corporal has a specific function relating to the sacrifice being offered. Outside Mass there is no sacrifice and no corporal. Mexico, however, has inserted the corporal into this rubric, blurring the distinction.[94] If a bishop presides, then an assisting deacon places the vessel on the altar, and both he and the bishop genuflect.[95]

No guidelines are given for making the decision to include communion. Under normal circumstances, the reasons for not celebrating Mass are reasons for not offering communion: One of the partners is not Catholic and would not be receiving communion, and many members of the assembly are not Catholic and would be unfamiliar with the responses, postures and gestures expected of them, and they would not be receiving communion. An argument in favor of including communion without Mass would be the celebration of a wedding in a place where Mass was not possible; for example, if no priest were available for an extended period of time, and a deacon presides for the service. In that case, Catholics who

[94] *Ritual* (Mexico), 168.
[95] CB 619.

are not able to receive communion at Mass could at least receive communion at the wedding. The original paragraph permitted distributing communion if Mass "cannot" be celebrated. The revised paragraph admits the possibility that Mass could take place but does not; for example, if the celebrant of the service without Mass is a priest.

A rubric approved for French Canada makes the case even stronger:

> Since there is no celebration of mass, normally there is no communion. If, however, communion must be distributed (which remains exceptional, for example because the priest was not able to be present to preside for the eucharist), the deacon will carry it out as indicated in the *Ritual for the Eucharist Outside of Mass*, numbers 30–38.[96]

To distribute communion, the minister in French Canada has to use this other book. The details are not copied into the marriage book, perhaps to discourage its practice.

The same paragraph in the first edition of the OCM envisioned a possible ceremony in which the couple receive communion but others do not. This has been removed from the second edition probably because all who are eligible to receive communion should be welcome if communion is being offered.

The study group's two drafts for this paragraph are identical and vary only slightly from the version that appeared in the first edition.[97]

109.

The minister introduces the Lord's Prayer, and all recite it together. This was explained in the first edition's paragraph 54, but now the words and rubrics are more helpfully put in place.

In the preconciliar wedding without mass, the priest recited the Lord's Prayer inaudibly, except for the last line,[98] which was the

---

[96] *Rituel Romain*, 91.
[97] Schemata 248, p. 6; Schemata 280, p. 15.
[98] *Roman Ritual*, 470.

custom in force for the celebration of the Mass. At a wedding, however, this could only be done if the couple had received permission from the Vatican to have the nuptial blessing at a wedding without Mass. Without that permission, there was no Lord's Prayer.

In the Latin original of the second edition, the minister introduces the Lord's Prayer "in these or similar words," but that phrase has been removed in the English translation perhaps because they never appeared in Latin in the Missal. In 1973, however, the Vatican explained that the introduction to the Lord's Prayer at Mass did not have to be given word for word.[99] As mentioned above, the French Canadian translation gives a different introduction to the Lord's Prayer, which may be given "in these or similar words,"[100] and the Mexican ritual book concurs.[101] The translation that appears in the OCM has been carried over from the Missal.[102] Of course, this is not Mass, so not all the rules governing Mass apply.

110.

The minister may invite all to give the sign of peace. He does this "if appropriate," a phrase that does not appear in the celebration of a wedding within Mass.

As mentioned in the comments on OCM 75, the second edition has removed the optional nature of the sign of peace for a wedding within Mass. It remains here. On one hand, this could be an oversight. It could, however, also reflect the nature of the ceremony. Without Mass, the parts that pertain to the people's participation in the sacrifice of the Eucharist are not included—such as the preparation of the gifts and the Lamb of God. The sign of peace can be viewed within this range. It forms part of the communion rite, expressing the unity of the baptized before they share the fruits of the sacrifice they have just offered. In general, when Holy Communion

---

[99] Congregation for Divine Worship, "Concerning the Eucharistic Prayers," *Eucharistiæ participationem,* 27 April 1973, https://www.ewtn.com/library/CURIA/CDWMISSA.HTM.

[100] *Rituel Romain,* 91.

[101] *Ritual* (Mexico), 168.

[102] OM 124.

is distributed without Mass, the sign of peace is optional.[103] The same option exists here.

The translation for the invitation comes from the Missal,[104] and the rubrics pertaining to the exchange of peace by the couple and all present come from OCM 75.

111.

The minister genuflects, lifts a host, and gives the invitation to communion. Those who are to receive make the usual response to the dialogue. The OCM has largely copied this paragraph from the rite for distributing communion outside of Mass.

This is the second genuflection the minister makes. Only those receiving communion respond to the dialogue. There is no presumption that the minister himself will receive communion. Especially if he is participating in Mass on the same day, he may simply be distributing communion to those who will receive. In the event that the minister is a deacon in a place where priests are scarce and Mass is rare, it may be more appropriate for him to receive; otherwise, probably not. When a bishop presides for a wedding without Mass, there is no indication that he receives communion.[105]

The translation for these spoken parts has been taken from the Missal.[106]

112.

The minister distributes communion with the usual formula. Consecrated wine is not to be reserved in the tabernacle, except temporarily for bringing communion to the sick,[107] so the communicants receive only under the form of bread.

The translation for the rubric and dialogue is taken from the Missal.[108]

---

[103] *The Rites*, 651.
[104] OM 128.
[105] CB 619.
[106] OM 132.
[107] Rite of Pastoral Care and Anointing of the Sick 74, in *The Rites*, 802.
[108] OM 134.

113.

A suitable song may be sung during communion, but this is optional. The choice for such a song could be inspired by the Missal's options for the communion antiphon at a wedding within Mass. But this is not required. The rubric does not specify who sings the chant, so one could argue for a soloist. The nature of communion, however, and of the people's participation, would encourage a congregational song—if one is offered at all.

114.

Communion may be followed by silence or a psalm or canticle of praise. This was part of the former paragraph 54 and appeared in the two drafts of the study group.[109]

At this point, the first edition and its drafts cited the 1967 Instruction from the Sacred Congregation for Rites that called for silence or a song of praise after communion at Mass.[110] But the second edition of the OCM has removed the citation. Post-communion silence or song is now mentioned in the Missal,[111] which provides a better source and eliminates the need to cite a 1967 instruction. Also, this is not taking place at Mass.

The translation of this rubric is taken from the Missal.[112]

115.

The minister says a prayer. This ceremony does not call it a Prayer after Communion as the Missal does. The Missal's prayer presumes that all have participated at Mass, including the sharing of communion. This is a prayer that follows the distribution of communion to those who are receiving. It has a slightly different function.

The first edition published the recommendation of the two drafts that this prayer be the second of the options from the Missal's ritual Mass for celebrating marriage. It appears here and again in OCM

[109] Schemata 248, p. 6; Schemata 280, p. 15.

[110] Sacred Congregation of Rites, *Tres abhinc annos* 15, http://www.adoremus.org/TresAbhinc.html.

[111] OM 138.

[112] OM 137 and 138.

211. It prays for the bride and groom who have been united in the sacrament of marriage, and it is offered by those who have partaken of the "table" of communion.

Besides this prayer, there are now no other alternatives. The first edition permitted other prayers to be used, and it specifically recommended the collect for the Solemnity of the Most Holy Body and Blood of Christ (Corpus Christi), which is also used at the conclusion of the Rite of Eucharistic Exposition and Benediction.[113] That prayer presumes that the community is adoring the Blessed Sacrament, which is not happening in this service.

The first edition recommended the first of the Missal's prayers if the couple alone were receiving communion. That idea has been removed. This liturgy presumes that others may also be receiving, and the prayer that follows communion bears this out. Consequently, there is only one possible prayer after communion.

The translation for this prayer comes from the Missal's second choice for the ritual Mass for marriage.

THE CONCLUSION OF THE CELEBRATION

116.

The ceremony concludes with a blessing of the couple and all who are gathered. This is the former paragraph 51. Either the simple or solemn form may be used. As noted above, for weddings within Mass, the solemn blessing is the only form given.

In French Canada, the same two blessings added to the ceremony of weddings within Mass are optional here as well.[114] Also, as in the ceremony within Mass, the minister may present a gift to the couple.[115]

In Mexico, the custom of taking a bouquet of flowers to the Blessed Virgin Mary may be performed before this blessing.[116]

There is no formula for dismissal. This probably reflects the difficulty of having the priest or deacon say a translation of "*Ite,*

---

[113] *The Rites,* 676.
[114] *Rituel Romain,* 96–97.
[115] Ibid., 97.
[116] *Ritual,* 170.

missa est." This is not a Mass. When a bishop presides for marriage without Mass, however, the deacon says, "Go in peace." All reply, "Thanks be to God," and depart.[117] Such a conclusion seems fitting when a priest or deacon presides as well.

117.
The signing of the marriage document should take place but not on the altar. This is the same rubric that appeared in OCM 78.

---

[117] CB 620.

Editio typica altera
III. *The Order of Celebrating Matrimony in the Presence of an Assisting Layperson*

The second edition of the OCM in Latin includes a chapter detailing how a layperson presides in the absence of a priest or a deacon in keeping with the circumstances of canon 1112. A conference of bishops must petition the Holy See for this permission, and the Holy See must grant it before this may be used. The layperson needs to be qualified to give instruction and lead the ceremony.

This chapter has been completely removed from the English edition in force in the United States. In some parts of the world priests and deacons are so scarce that it would be unfair to engaged couples to place on undue delay on their wedding. Canon 1112 was written for them. The bishops of the United States approved a complementary norm on this canon in 1989, promulgated the following year:

> In accord with canon 1112, the National Conference of Catholic Bishops recommends to the Holy See that it favorably entertain the requests of those individual diocesan bishops who, in view of the severe shortage of ordained ministers in certain vast territories of the United States, seek the faculty to delegate lay persons to assist at marriages.[1]

Any bishop in the United States who wishes to petition the Holy See for permission may do so in accordance with this norm, but

---

[1] See http://www.usccb.org/beliefs-and-teachings/what-we-believe/canon -law/complementary-norms/canon-1112-lay-witnesses-for-marriage.cfm.

there is no approved English translation for such a delegated lay-person to use.

The occasion for a lay presider may not only exist in circum-stances of chronic need. It could also result from some tragedy. One hopes that no calamity ever befalls the priests of a diocese when they gather for some spiritual or educational purpose, but dreaded factors could produce a need for this celebration. If so, a bishop would then have to seek permission, the Vatican would have to grant it, and an English translation would then require ap-proval. It would probably be based on the ones that have already been approved for Australia and for England and Wales.

A Spanish translation of this chapter does not appear in the edition in force in the United States, though it does in Mexico and Colombia. There is no French translation in Canada.

The word "assisting" in the title seems to indicate the presiding role of the layperson without using the same verb in place for a priest or a deacon. The rubrics never call the person a "minister." That word is reserved for priests and deacons in the previous chapter. The person is called "an assisting layperson" throughout.

When the study group began its work in 1966, the members were aware of the possibility. Their conversation took up issues given them from the preparatory commission.

> 1) "*If a priest is lacking . . . a deacon may assist for the matrimony.*" This refers to the reform of the Code (Martimort). It is sufficient that we use the rubrics that may suffice with new laws; for example, the sen-tence, "when a deacon may assist, he will do thus and so." (Bonet). 2) But it pertains to us that the Ritual foresees the possibility of giv-ing communion. In this case, is it not appropriate to invoke the law that gives the faculty of contracting matrimony before lay people when there is no possibility of a priest being present, according to the norm of canon 1098? Then a deacon, if he is present, will also give communion (Martimort). Perhaps it would be better not to in-voke this law (Bonet). But the rubrics ought to allude to the presence of a deacon (Jounel).[2]

---

[2] Schemata 157 adnexum, p. 6.

Even before the revision of the Code of Canon Law in 1983, then, the law acknowledged circumstances that permitted a valid marriage before lay witnesses. Only with the second edition of the OCM, however, did the church develop a separate ritual for a layperson to lead.

Here follows a commentary on the pertinent paragraphs from the second edition of the OCM, the *editio typica altera* (ETA).

ETA 118.

When matrimony takes place in the presence of an assisting layperson in accord with OCM 25, this order of service is followed.

ETA 119.

The layperson must receive the faculty from the diocesan bishop, prepare catechetical instruction, conduct spiritual preparation, and assist at the celebration correctly.

ETA 120.

The ceremony ordinarily takes place in a church, and the layperson wears appropriate attire approved by the bishop.[3]

THE INTRODUCTORY RITES

ETA 121.

When the people have gathered, the assisting layperson and the servers receive the couple and greet them warmly.

A procession is not described, nor any greeting at the door. These are not excluded by the rubrics, but the bare concern is that a warm greeting take place when everyone has arrived. The initial phrase is the same that opens the Order of Mass in the Missal: *Populo congregato.*[4]

ETA 122.

With hands joined, the assisting layperson says, "Blessed be God, the Father of all consolation, who has shown us his mercy."

[3] GIRM 339.
[4] OM 1.

All answer, "Amen." Or they may say, "Blessed be God forever," or some other suitable response. The greeting is based on 2 Corinthians 1:3. The layperson says it with hands joined, a small but important indication that he or she is not a priest or deacon. In a similar way, the layperson does not use the clerical greeting "The Lord be with you."

ETA 123.

The layperson gives an introduction. This is copied from OCM 52.

ETA 124.

An alternate introduction is copied from OCM 53.

THE LITURGY OF THE WORD

ETA 125.

A reader, another person present, or the assisting layperson proclaims the readings selected from the usual place in the lectionary. One or two readings may be used, but one must speak of marriage, as indicated by an asterisk. Similar instructions appear at OCM 55 and 90.

The layperson introduces the gospel, saying, "Listen, brothers and sisters, to the words of the holy Gospel according to N." The person does not use the greeting and introduction assigned to a priest or deacon at Mass.

The layperson may then give an exhortation or read a homily prepared by the bishop or the pastor.

THE CELEBRATION OF MARRIAGE

ETA 126.

The conditions for celebrating more than one marriage at the same time are repeated from OCM 58 and 92.

ETA 127.

All stand, and the assisting layperson addresses the couple. The rubric is similar to those in OCM 59 and 93. In Mexico, only the couple stand.

The assisting layperson reads a text resembling the ones found at OCM 59 and 93 but is not given the option of using similar

words. The address opens with information about who the layperson is: "Dearly beloved (or. N. and N.), you have come together
here before me, the delegate of our Bishop to assist at this celebration, and in the presence of the community of the Church, so that
your intention to enter into Marriage may be strengthened by the
Lord with a sacred seal."

The Questions before the Consent

ETA 128.

The assisting layperson questions the couple in preparation of
receiving their consent. The rubrics and questions are based on
those in OCM 60 and 94.

A unique introduction appears at this point, however: "N. and
N., the word of God has revealed to us the mystery of Marriage
and the dignity of conjugal love. So now, in the presence of the
Church, make clear your intentions in this regard." This duplicates
some of the material from ETA 127 but perhaps was thought important to strengthen the importance of the questions that follow.

In England and Wales, the couple also make The Civil Declaration of Freedom, which appears as OCM 128a. Both first and last
names are used.

The Consent

ETA 129.

The assisting layperson invites the couple to declare their consent. They join their right hands. The words and rubrics are based
on OCM 61 and 95. In Mexico, the community stands.[5]

ETA 130.

The groom and the bride give their consent as in OCM 62 and
96. In the edition for Colombia, all six versions of the consent again
appear in this place.

ETA 131.

The assisting layperson may obtain the consent through questions, as is done in OCM 63 and 97. This is not permitted by the

---

[5] *Ritual* (Mexico), 178.

civil government in England and Wales, so this paragraph is missing from the liturgical book.

The Reception of the Consent

ETA 132.

The assisting layperson declares the reception of the consent. The words are taken from OCM 64 and 98.

ETA 133.

The assisting layperson invites those present to praise God. The dialogue is taken from OCM 65 and 99. Another acclamation may be used. In Mexico, the community sits after the acclamation, and if it is customary, the groom lifts the veil that covers the face of the bride.[6]

The Blessing and Giving of Rings

ETA 134.

With hands joined, the assisting layperson prays a blessing of the rings without making the sign of the cross over them. The text of the prayer is from OCM 66 and 100. The layperson is not given the option to use alternative prayers for the blessing of the rings.

Only a priest or a deacon may extend his hands for a blessing and make the sign of the cross with his hand. These adjustments to the gestures in this ceremony are consistent with those found in the *Book of Blessings*.

If circumstances suggest, the layperson sprinkles the rings with blessed water, and then gives the rings to the couple.

ETA 135.

The couple each place a ring on the other's finger while declaring, if appropriate, a text taken from OCM 67 and 101.

In Mexico, the layperson may pray a blessing over the *arras*, again with hands joined and without the gesture of blessing and without sprinkling blessed water. The couple perform the *arras* ceremony as indicated in ceremonies where a priest or deacon presides.[7]

---

[6] Ibid., 181.
[7] Ibid., 182.

ETA 136.

All may sing a hymn of praise. This is copied from OCM 68 and 102.

The Universal Prayer

ETA 137.

The universal prayer follows. Samples appear later in the book. This is copied from OCM 69 and 103.

In Mexico, the *lazo* may be placed over the shoulders of the couple. A layperson gives the same explanation that a priest or deacon gives in the other versions of the ceremony.[8]

ETA 138.

If communion is to be distributed, the nuptial blessing comes next. If not, then the assisting layperson introduces the Lord's Prayer. This is similar to the instruction at OCM 106.

Other similar words may be used, but this introduction is scripted: "God the Father wills that his children be of one heart in charity; let us call upon him in the prayer of God's family, which our Lord Jesus Christ has taught us."

The text of the Lord's Prayer, of course, matches the one from the Missal.[9]

The Nuptial Blessing

ETA 139.

With hands joined, the assisting layperson asks all to join in prayer, and all pray in silence. This is based on OCM 73 and 104.

ETA 140.

The couple kneel while the assisting layperson recites a prayer of blessing with hands joined. The gesture distinguishes this person from a priest or deacon, who says the prayer with hands extended.

---

[8] Ibid., 185.
[9] OM 9.

The prayer was newly composed for the second edition of the OCM, so it does not reproduce the nuptial blessings given by a priest or deacon. The prayer is trinitarian. Each of the three sections blesses the Father, Son, and Spirit in turn. The people respond, "Blessed be God forever," to each section of the prayer. (The Latin original has "Blessed be God," but the English translation in force for Australia and for England and Wales includes an extra word to resemble the acclamation the people say during the preparation of the gifts at Mass. Then the assisting layperson concludes with an oration to which all respond, "Amen." The layperson may choose one of two alternatives for this closing prayer.

The structure of this nuptial blessing was based on the blessing and invocation of God over water, as found in the rites of baptism.[10] Some of the first part of the blessing is based on lines from the Missal's third preface for marriage, found also in OCM 201. The second part draws from Saint Paul's description of marriage.[11] The third part has elements that resemble the Missal's preface for the Mass for the Unity of Christians and from another citation from Saint Paul.[12] The first option for the concluding prayer has elements from the blessing in OCM 77, repeated at OCM 213; from a prayer over the offerings in OCM 197; and from a nuptial blessing in OCM 139 and 209.

In Mexico, the *lazo* is removed after this prayer, and the couple stand.[13]

If communion is not distributed, then the ceremony concludes with ETA 150.

Holy Communion

ETA 141.

If communion is distributed, the assisting layperson goes to the place of reservation, takes the vessel from there, sets it on the altar,

---

[10] Jean Evanou, "Commentarium," *Notitiae* XXVI (1990): 319, citing The Rite of Baptism for Children 223 and the Rite of Christian Initiation of Adults 389, which is RCIA 222 B, C, and D in the edition for the United States.

[11] Eph 5:14.

[12] Eph 4:3.

[13] *Ritual* (Mexico), 187.

and genuflects. This borrows material from OCM 108. Once again, the Mexican edition has added the use of the corporal,[14] which is normally to be used only for Mass.

Communion should probably not be included if one of the partners is not Catholic and if many of the people in attendance would not be receiving communion. If this is a part of the world where priests are few and the celebration of the Eucharist is scarce, however, then it may be a good opportunity for faithful Catholics to receive.

ETA 142.

The assisting layperson introduces the Lord's Prayer. The Latin original and the Spanish translation in Mexico allow the minister to do this "in these or similar words,"[15] but that has been removed from the English translation approved for Australia and in England and Wales. The texts for the introduction and the prayer come from the Missal.[16]

ETA 143.

The assisting layperson may invite the faithful to exchange a sign of peace, and all may do so. This borrows words and rubrics from OCM 143, which in turn are based on the texts in the Missal.[17] This is done "if appropriate." It probably would be for the sake of building a sense of community.

ETA 144.

The assisting layperson genuflects, holds a host above the vessel, and initiates the usual dialogue before communion.[18] This paragraph copies material from weddings without Mass, OCM 111.

ETA 145.

If the assisting layperson receives communion, he or she recites the private prayer of the priest from the Missal: "May the Body

[14] Ibid.
[15] Ibid.
[16] OM 109.
[17] OM 110.
[18] OM 132.

of Christ keep me safe for eternal life."[19] Then the layperson consumes the host. In Mexico, the minister consumes the host "reverently," a word that does not appear in the OCM but is in the Order
of Mass to describe the priest's communion.[20]

Unlike the wedding without Mass, this version does envision
that the layperson will receive communion. The same is true of
Sunday Celebrations in the Absence of a Priest.[21] This implies that
other factors have caused a deacon or priest to lead a wedding
without Mass, and he probably would have access to communion
at a different time of the day.

ETA 146.

The assisting layperson distributes communion to the faithful
with the usual dialogue. This resembles OCM 112. The rubrics and
dialogue come from the Missal.[22]

ETA 147.

During communion a song may be sung. This is not required,
but it may help unite the communicants in one heart and voice.
This is the same rubric as OCM 113.

ETA 148.

After communion, all may observe silence or sing a song of
praise. Similar rubrics are found in the Missal.[23] This also appears
in OCM 114.

ETA 149.

The assisting layperson offers the prayer that is also found at
OCM 115. Again in this case, it is not called a Prayer after Communion as in the Missal, and no other options are listed.

---

[19] OM 133.
[20] Ibid.
[21] *Sunday Celebrations in the Absence of a Priest* (Collegeville, MN: Liturgical
Press, 1997), 146.
[22] OM 134.
[23] OM 137 and 138.

In Mexico, if the bride and groom are taking a bouquet of flowers to the tabernacle or to an image of the Virgin Mary, they may do so at this time.[24]

THE CONCLUSION OF THE CELEBRATION

ETA 150.

The assisting layperson signs himself or herself with the cross while saying a concluding trinitarian formula: "May God fill us with joy and hope in believing. May the peace of Christ reign in our hearts. May the Holy Spirit pour out his gifts upon us." All answer, "Amen." These three elements are all inspired by passages from the letters of Saint Paul.[25]

ETA 151.

The celebration may end with a suitable song. This copies the rubric from OCM 107, which concerns weddings without Mass and without communion. It reappears in the blessing for an engaged couple at OCM 236. Especially if there has been no communion or no communion song, it would be fitting for all to sing something at the conclusion.

The marriage document is to be signed, but not on the altar, as explained in OCM 78 and 117.

---

[24] *Ritual* (Mexico), 193.
[25] Rom 15:13; Col 3:15; and 1 Cor 12:4-11, but especially 11.

III. The Order of Celebrating Matrimony between a Catholic and a Catechumen or a Non-Christian

This ceremony existed in the first edition of the OCM, but under the title of a marriage between a Catholic and "an unbaptized person." The second edition has changed this to two categories of unbaptized persons: catechumens and non-Christians. In actuality, there is a third group. Some people grew up in faithful Christian households but have never been baptized. They believe in God, they believe that Jesus is the Son of God, they pray, they go to church, but they have never been baptized. A pastoral judgment may be needed in the case of a Catholic marrying such a person. Possibly the ceremony in the second chapter is more appropriate in that situation because the person is neither a catechumen nor a non-Christian. It is understood, however, that the marriage between a Catholic and a non-Christian may not take place during Mass.

The change in title reflects a passage from St. Augustine's commentary on the account from John's gospel of the man born blind.

> Inquire of this man, "Are you a Christian?" "No," he will respond. "Are you a pagan then? Or a Jew?" "No longer." Ask him again, "Are you a catechumen or faithful?" If he answers you, "Catechumen," it is because he has received the anointing but has not yet been plunged in the water. By the very fact that he is a catechumen, he says, "I believe in Christ." But the anointing is not enough. He should hasten to the bath if he wants light.[1]

---

[1] Augustine, *Tractate on John* 44, cited by Jean Evanou in "Commentarium," *Notitiae* XXVI (1990): 320–21.

These distinctions found their way into the expanded title of the OCM's third chapter. The new title makes official what the French translation had already considered in 1969, where the introduction took special note of the situation of a catechumen.[2]

When the drafts of SC were being prepared in 1963, Bishop Benedict Tomizawa made a plea for the Second Vatican Council to include in its liturgy constitution one article calling for the revised ritual book to include a ceremony for the occasion when a Catholic married a non-Christian.

> *Before all, I would like to say: I am not the bishop whom the President nominated, but I am Bishop Benedict Tomizawa of Japan.*
>
> I ask that you look at page 182, article VI, on matrimony. In this chapter of the schema on the sacred liturgy, the only topic is matrimony between the faithful. But in Japan, where Catholics are a small minority, most of the marriages that are celebrated in church are marriages between a Christian and a non-Christian. Therefore it is desired that in the schema there also be the topic of the liturgical celebration of this matrimony.
>
> When the Church orders that a matrimony of this kind be celebrated before the pastor, it seems fitting that it permit for such a matrimony not only the ceremony prescribed for the matrimony of Christians, but some appropriate liturgical ceremony. This is particularly requested in Japan and, I think, also in some mission lands, where according to the customs of the people matrimony is usually celebrated with great ceremony. Although according to canon law the Ordinary of the place may permit some ecclesiastical ceremony and de facto does permit it, any celebration of Mass is always prohibited for such a ceremony. This therefore causes great sadness on the part of the Christian, and easily scandal and even offense on the part of the non-Christian. It seems that this should be completely avoided. Humbly, therefore, I would like to propose that the commission on the sacred liturgy prepare an article from the outset concerning the liturgical celebration of matrimony between a Christian and a non-Christian, in which is also contained the celebration of Mass.

---

[2] *Rituel pour la célébration du mariage* (Paris: Brepols, 1969), cited in Kenneth W. Stevenson, *To Join Together: The Rite of Marriage* (New York: Pueblo Publishing Company, 1987), 152.

Indeed the deeper reason for this proposal is that to spread the kingdom of God in mission lands we ought first to show sincere appreciation toward the Christians of goodwill, as the recent popes have often taught us. Nevertheless, in the current ecclesiastical legislation this spirit of appreciation generally does not sufficiently appear, and instead a certain severity contrary to this spirit is found. However this spirit of appreciation toward non-Christians is a genuine spirit of the Church, which already St. Peter, the prince of the apostles, expressed, going into the house of Cornelius the centurion with the following words before the foreigners: "You know that it is unlawful for a Jewish man to associate with, or visit, a Gentile, but God has shown me that I should not call any person profane or unclean. And that is why I came without objection when sent for" (Acts of the Apostles 10:28). I have spoken.[3]

Bishop Tomizawa's request failed. SC did not include the topic of a marriage with a non-Christian. The OCM eventually did, however, but without authorizing the ceremony within Mass. According to Stevenson, McManus wrote a letter to Gy in April 1966, expressing the need for a distinct rite for this circumstance.[4] The study group included the idea in its drafts, and Ciappi especially worked to make this form of the rite theologically correct.[5]

It is commonly presumed that the valid marriage between a Catholic and an unbaptized person does not result in a sacrament because of the unbaptized party, and that if that party ever becomes baptized, the marriage is sacramentalized at the same time. The study group drafting this ceremony, however, composed this note:

> Among Catholic theologians for a long time now has been debated whether or not the matrimony between a Catholic party and an unbaptized party is a sacrament for the Catholic. But a negative response to this question seems to be implied in this, that in more

---

[3] Francisco Gil Hellín, *Concilii Vaticani II synopsis in ordinem redigens schemata cum relationibus necnon Patrum orationes atque animadversiones: Constitutio de Sacra Liturgica Sacrosanctum concilium* (Vatican City: Libreria Editrice Vaticana, 2003), 699–700.

[4] Stevenson, *To Join Together*, 129.

[5] Ibid., 131.

recent times marriages of this kind had to be dissolved by the Apostolic See. Since this matter is of great importance for the preparation of the Rite, the secretary of our committee has proposed a *dubium* concerning the sacramentality of these marriages to the Sacred Congregation on the Doctrine of the Faith.[6]

The response, dated November 7, 1966, from the Eminent Pro-Prefect of the Congregation on the Doctrine of the Faith was this:

> This Sacred Congregation has taken the delicate question into study, but it maintains that in working out the texts of the Ritual for marriages contracted between a Catholic party and a non-Christian party, it may not be necessary nor opportune to involve the question of the sacramentality of such marriages. The commission of this Consilium, charged with the preparation of such texts, should therefore carefully avoid every expression that may be interpreted in one or the other sense concerning this point of doctrine.[7]

A final paragraph of this response is quoted in a later draft, where the Protocol number assigned to the communication is given as 1537/66. "This Sacred Congregation, then, asks that you will send here the texts noted above once they have been drawn up, in a way that it may express its own opinion on a concrete suggestion."[8]

Indeed, as the study group prepared the texts, they removed any mention of sacramentality that appears in their other versions of the ceremony, without ever directly affirming that this one is not a sacrament. Even the title, which in the 1614 Ritual was "The Sacrament of Matrimony" became "The Order of Celebrating Matrimony."[9] It made room for either interpretation.

---

[6] Schemata 221, p. 2. Bugnini includes the complete text of the *dubium*; see Annibale Bugnini, *The Reform of the Liturgy, 1948–1975*, trans. Matthew J. O'Connell (Collegeville, MN: Liturgical Press, 1990), 706.

[7] Schemata 221, p. 2.

[8] Schemata 280 addendum, pp. 1–2.

[9] *Roman Ritual*, 454.

In commenting on the final draft of its work, the study group called this one of "the principal pastoral difficulties" and noted that it had consulted the Secretariat for Christian Unity in developing paragraph 8 of the introduction, now OCM 36.[10] There is no record of any drafts the study group may have prepared. The first evidence of the ceremony is in the first edition of the OCM. The second edition has reworked it.

Because of the discrepancy in paragraph numbers from here to the end of the ritual book due to the removal of the original chapter three, both the number in the USCCB's edition and in the *editio typica altera* (ETA) are given in the commentary that follows.

118 (ETA 152).

The wedding of a Catholic and a non-Christian is celebrated in a church or another suitable place. A priest or a deacon presides. The first part of this paragraph is the heading above the former paragraph 55. The Latin original of the second part, describing the presider, says that an approved layperson may assist under approved circumstances. Yet a third part in Latin treats the vesture of this assisting layperson and the form of the nuptial blessing. All this has been removed from the English translation in the United States.

The leader of the ceremony in chapter 3 is called "the one who presides." In the second chapter the presider was called a "minister" because only a priest or deacon may preside, and the missing chapter calls the one leading the ceremony an "assisting layperson." Here, the leader is "the one who presides," through which one can see the original Latin's accommodation that that person might not be a "minister" but an "assisting layperson." The English translation in the United States kept the circumlocution, even though it could have used "minister" for consistency with the second chapter.

Regarding the place of the celebration, Bugnini states that a preliminary draft for this paragraph held that "the church is the preferred place in these cases." But the Congregation on the Doctrine of the Faith changed it to the present rubric: "the celebration takes

---

[10] Schemata 280, I.

place in a church or in another suitable place."[11] This matches the wording in the Code of Canon Law.[12] The code does not explicitly give the local ordinary sovereignty over the pastor in determining the "suitable place" for the wedding between a Catholic and an unbaptized person, but the ordinary is the one who grants the dispensation from disparity of cult, and with that often asserts authority over the question of place as well.

ICEL proposed adding to the opening rubric that this is the ceremony to be used when two catechumens marry, even though the Latin original did not mention it. This does not appear in the English translation, but this is the only logical ceremony to be followed in that circumstance.

THE RITE OF RECEPTION

119 (ETA 153).

The vested priest or deacon goes to the door of the church or to the "place that has been chosen" with other ministers to receive the couple warmly. Then all go to their places. This is the former paragraph 55, which mentioned only the priest as a possible presider. Much of this is carried over from OCM 80, the first form of the reception for a wedding without Mass.

The word "warmly" has been added in the second edition.

120 (ETA 154).

At his place, the presider formally and publicly greets the couple and introduces the ceremony. This is new to the second edition.

Several accommodations have been made for the possible presence of a non-Christian spouse and other non-Christian participants in the ceremony. For example, there is no sign of the cross at the start, nor is there a greeting based on Sacred Scripture or drawn from the Missal. Instead, the presider begins with words addressed to the couple. These explain something about faith that some people in the room understandably may not know: "For believers God is the source of love and fidelity, because God is love."

---

[11] Bugnini, *The Reform of the Liturgy*, 706.
[12] Canon 1118 §3.

This is used as the foundational assumption on which more people in the room may be drawn into common worship on this occasion. The minister invites all to listen to God's word and to pray.

The opening rubric repeats material from OCM 52, 87, and ETA 123. Part of the opening address is from OCM 53.

The Mexican edition provides two other options for this introduction. The first includes this statement: "Those who have faith know that God, the creator of man and woman in his image, considered their union loving and fruitful." The second gives a Christian catechesis on the significance of marriage.[13]

121 (ETA 155).

The Rite of Reception may be omitted, and the ceremony may begin directly with the Liturgy of the Word. This is taken from the second part of the former paragraph 55. It constitutes an extraordinary accommodation to nonbelievers. No sign of the cross, no liturgical greeting, no opening address need begin the ceremony. It may start directly with a proclamation of the word of God. In simplicity and brevity, the rite allows another outreach to nonbelievers by eliminating unessential parts of the ceremony.

In the first edition, the minister could omit the greeting of the couple at the door of the church at a wedding within and without Mass. Now, some greeting of the couple must take place at those weddings, but not in this instance, when one partner may be a nonbeliever.

THE LITURGY OF THE WORD

122 (ETA 156).

For the Liturgy of the Word, two or even one reading may be proclaimed, but one must be from the collection of those that specifically speak of marriage, marked in the list with an asterisk. Most of these rubrics are taken from OCM 90.

This is the former paragraph 56, which permitted three readings, now reduced in number. The first edition in Latin put a single heading for the rite of welcome and the Liturgy of the Word ahead

---

[13] *Ritual* (Mexico), 198–99.

of paragraph 55, though the English translation had separated them. Now the separation of headings appears in the Latin of the second edition.

The original Latin also tells an assisting layperson how to introduce the gospel, as in ETA 125. This has been removed from the translation in the United States.

123 (ETA 157).

A homily should be given, appropriate to the situation. OCM 57 and 91 presume that a homily is given at a Catholic wedding with or without Mass, but here the verb implies that it is advisable, though optional.

The Latin original explains the options for an assisting layperson in keeping with ETA 125. This has been removed from the translation in the United States.

Furthermore, the purposes of this homily have been simplified. For example, OCM 57 and 91 say that the homily should include a presentation on the dignity of Christian marriage, conjugal love, and the grace of the sacrament, but these points are not mentioned in the description of a homily given when the Catholic is marrying an unbaptized person.

THE CELEBRATION OF MATRIMONY

124 (ETA 158).

The presider addresses the couple and opens the celebration of matrimony. A text is supplied from OCM 59, 93, and ETA 127 but now omitting the declaration that both have already been consecrated by baptism. The presider may use these or similar words. This is the former paragraph 58.

The Latin original includes the words that would be spoken by a lay presider from ETA 127, but these have been removed from the translation in the United States.

The Questions before the Consent

125 (ETA 159).

The presider asks the couple about their intentions, and the couple give their answers. This is the former paragraph 59, though with a new heading. It copies material from OCM 60, 94, and ETA 128.

The alternate formula permitted in French Canada is also given here.[14] The specifications proper to England and Wales appear as 159a in their ritual book, where both the first and last names of the couple must be stated.

The Consent

126 (ETA 160).

The presider invites the couple to give their consent, and they join their right hands. This is the first part of the former paragraph 60. It copies material from OCM 61, 95, and ETA 129.

The additional forms of this invitation approved for French Canada's weddings also appear here.[15] In Mexico the community stands for this invitation.[16]

127 (ETA 161).

The groom and the bride exchange their consent. Both forms approved for the United States reappear in this section, as found in OCM 62, 96 and ETA 130. This is part of the former paragraph 60.

The other forms of consent approved for French Canada also appear at this point,[17] as do the ones in Colombia.[18]

128 (ETA 162).

The presider may obtain the consent through questions, as in OCM 63, 97, and ETA 131. Both formulas approved for the United States reappear. This option is not available in England and Wales because of civil law.

This is part of the former paragraph 60. The original included a paragraph explaining that the conference of bishops could approve receiving the consent through questions. This has been removed

---

[14] *Rituel Romain*, 103.
[15] Ibid., 104.
[16] *Ritual* (Mexico), 201.
[17] *Rituel Romain*, 105–8.
[18] *Ritual* (Colombia), 109–13.

from this section because it is included more appropriately in the Introduction to the entire book in OCM 41, section 4.

The Reception of the Consent

129 (ETA 163).

The presider receives the consent using one of the two approved formulas. This is the former paragraph 61, expanded and with a new heading. This repeats material from OCM 64, 98, and ETA 132.

130 (ETA 164).

The presider introduces an acclamation, and all respond. Another acclamation may be used. This is new to the second edition of the OCM, and it repeats material from 65, 99, and ETA 133.

In Mexico, the community is seated after the acclamation, and if it is the custom, the groom lifts the veil of the bride.[19]

131 (ETA 165).

The priest or deacon who presides may bless the rings. This may be omitted if circumstances suggest; presumably, for example, if the nonbeliever would find this offensive. Any of the formulas may be used, including those at OCM 194 and 195. French Canada has its own additional blessing formula, which may be used as an alternative.[20] The presider may sprinkle the rings with blessed water if this seems appropriate. This is the former paragraph 62, and it repeats material from OCM 66, 100, and ETA 134.

The original Latin edition provides an alternate formula for the occasion when an assisting layperson conducts the ceremony (ETA 166). It repeats material from ETA 134. This has been removed from the English translation in the United States.

132 (ETA 167).

If the couple are giving rings, they exchange them after the blessing, reciting a formula, if appropriate. This is the former paragraph 63 with this new distinction: only a Christian spouse

---

[19] *Ritual* (Mexico), 204.
[20] *Rituel Romain*, 110.

may say the complete formula, including the trinitarian sign of the cross. This borrows material from OCM 67, 101, and ETA 135.

The Blessing and Giving of the Arras

133.
  New to the second edition is the option of including the *arras* after the exchange of rings, as in the other celebrations at OCM 67B and 101B. This may be appropriate, for example, if one is a catechumen from a Filipino or Hispanic family. No variations on this ceremony exist as with the rings. Therefore, if it is used, it includes all the parts: the blessing and the giving of the coins.
  In Mexico, the *arras* are not optional. The minister blesses them. The groom pours them into the hands of the bride and recites the usual faith-filled text about the blessing of God. As respectful as the rest of this ritual is to non-Christians, no concession is made for the *arras*.[21]

134 (ETA 168).
  A hymn or canticle of praise may be sung. This is found in OCM 68, 102, and ETA 136.

The Universal Prayer

135 (ETA 169).
  The minister leads the universal prayer. Samples are at OCM 216 and 217. This is copied from ETA 137 and parallels OCM 69 and 103. This repositions material from the first edition's paragraph 64, which combined the petitions with the nuptial blessing. Now they are separate. In French Canada, however, the universal prayer follows the nuptial blessing, the song of praise, and the optional prayer of the couple.[22]
  The universal prayer is not optional. In a way, this is surprising because at Mass it is the prayer of the faithful, and it follows the potential dismissal of catechumens. More appropriate would have been to call these "intercessions" or "prayers," titles that can be

---

[21] *Ritual* (Mexico), 205.
[22] Ibid., 112–16.

found in the RCIA when catechumens or the elect are present for
petitions made on their behalf.[23]

136 (ETA 170).

The presider introduces the Lord's Prayer. The introduction is
new to the second edition of the OCM and is unique in the Catholic
liturgy. It invites the Christians who are present to call on God the
Father. The presider may use these or similar words. The Lord's
Prayer came at the end of the celebration in the first edition's paragraph 66, where the rubric said that it "may" conclude the liturgy,
effectively making it optional. Before the council, the Lord's Prayer
was generally excluded from a wedding without Mass, as noted in
the comments on OCM 109. Now it is always to be included.

A similar introduction occurs at ETA 138, but without the speci-
fication that "those who are Christian" are to offer the prayer.

The rubric preceding the Lord's Prayer indicates that the Christians alone say the prayer. One of the principles of the RCIA is that
the Lord's Prayer is presented to the unbaptized shortly before
their baptism, so that they may pray it after the baptism for the
first time as Christians, adopted children, who call on God as their
Father. "When the elect have been baptized and take part in their
first celebration of the eucharist, they will join the rest of the faithful in saying the Lord's Prayer."[24]

The words for the Lord's Prayer are copied from the Missal.[25]
The introduction, according to Evanou, was worded in a way to
avoid giving offense to non-Christians.[26]

The Blessing and Placing of the Lazo *or the Veil*

137.

The *lazo* or veil may be placed around or over the couple if the
nuptial blessing is to follow and if the custom is consistent with
the family's traditions. This is new to the second edition for use in

---

[23] Samples are in the edition of the RCIA for use in the United States at 65,
153, 167, and 104.

[24] RCIA 149.

[25] OM 109.

[26] Evanou, "Commentarium," *Notitiae* XXVI (1990): 322.

the United States. There is no equivalent in the original Latin. This repeats material from OCM 71B and 103B.

The Nuptial Blessing

138 (ETA 171).

The presider introduces the nuptial blessing. This may be omitted, but as a rule the blessing should be included. If it is omitted, the prayer at OCM 140 replaces it. This is the former paragraph 64a and 65, and it repeats the introduction from OCM 104 with one important change. Instead of calling this the "Sacrament" of marriage, it is called the "bond" of marriage. The OCM leaves ambiguous the question of the sacramentality of this union. The first edition's paragraph 64a permitted the usage of other introductions, but this has been removed, probably because of the care with which this one has been reworked.

The couple kneel, but only if this seems appropriate. Presumably, if the non-Christian does not use this posture for prayer, they may remain standing.

After the introduction, all pray silently.

139 (ETA 172).

The presider gives the nuptial blessing if it is to be part of this ritual. He faces the couple and extends his hands over them. The rubric is the same for the nuptial blessing without Mass, OCM 105.

The blessing is based on the third option from the Missal, which is also OCM 209, but with some important differences. Instead of "the Sacrament of Matrimony," OCM 139 speaks of "the Marriage covenant." Instead of asking that they may "(adorn their family with children and) enrich the Church," the minister prays that they may "be known for the integrity of their conduct (and be recognized as virtuous parents)." The phrase "let them pray to you in the holy assembly and bear witness to you in the world" is removed from OCM 139. All these changes accommodate the nonbelieving partner. This represents quite a change from the days—that some few erroneously think are still here—when the non-Catholic had to become Catholic in order to marry a Catholic.

The OCM includes a chant musical setting of all the nuptial blessings except this one.

ETA 173.

If the one conducting the ceremony is not a priest or a deacon, then the assisting layperson gives a different blessing. Because this circumstance has not been approved in the United States, this paragraph is missing from its English translation. This was new to the second edition of the OCM. Most of this prayer replicates OCM 139 (ETA 172). It opens, however, with praise of God: "Blessed are you, Lord God, creator and sustainer of the human race." The layperson says this prayer with hands joined.

140 (ETA 174).

If the nuptial blessing is omitted, then the presider offers a different shorter prayer. The first edition allowed the omission of the nuptial blessing in this ceremony in its paragraphs 64 and 66. New to the second edition is that a shorter prayer replaces it.

This prayer comes from the Verona Sacramentary, where it appeared among the texts of a wedding just before the nuptial blessing. In the Roman Ritual of 1614, a slightly altered version of the same prayer concluded the marriage ceremony; after this prayer, the Mass began, which included the nuptial blessing. In place of the Verona prayer's first phrase, "Be attentive to our prayers, O Lord," the Roman Ritual's prayer began this way: "Look, we pray, O Lord, upon these your servants."[27] In the Missal, this is also the first of the collects for the ritual Mass for marriage. It reappears as OCM 192. In OCM 140, though, it is not a collect, so it takes the shorter ending of other prayers.

The Mexican ritual clarifies that the couple stand after this prayer, and if they wore the *lazo*, it is removed.[28]

THE CONCLUSION OF THE CELEBRATION

141 (ETA 175).

The one who presides gives a blessing. The first edition's paragraph 66 called for a blessing. Now the words for one appear in the book, together with a cross indicating the blessing gesture.

---

[27] *Roman Ritual*, 464.
[28] *Ritual* (Mexico), 211.

The minister does not greet the people. Although a liturgical greeting such as "The Lord be with you" is reserved to priests and deacons, it presumes a gathering of Christian faithful. There was no greeting at the beginning of this ceremony, nor is there one here.

The words for the blessing are the special ones that apply to the celebration of matrimony. These are taken from the Missal's ritual Mass, and they reappear at the end of OCM 213, 214, and 215.

ETA 176.

If the presider is an assisting layperson, a different text is supplied, and the layperson makes the sign of the cross over himself or herself—not over the people. The threefold blessing invokes the Trinity, and it is copied from ETA 150.

This does not appear in the translation for the United States because assisting laypersons have not been approved.

142 (ETA 177).

A song may conclude the celebration. This is new to the second edition. The rubric is copied from OCM 107 and ETA 151.

In French Canada, after the nuptial blessing and the song of praise, the couple may offer a prayer, as they may do in the other versions of the marriage ceremony. After this comes the universal prayer, the Lord's Prayer, the blessing, and the optional giving of a minister's gift to the couple.[29]

143 (ETA 178).

The minister and witnesses sign the marriage record, but not on the altar. This copies the rubric from OCM 78, 117, and ETA 151.

[29] *Rituel Romain*, 114–17.

IV. Various Texts to Be Used in the Rite of Marriage and in the Mass for the Celebration of Marriage

The title of this section is slightly expanded from the one in the first edition. It includes a direct reference to the title of the ritual Mass in the Missal. The chapter includes a selection of readings and prayers.

I. BIBLICAL READINGS

In both editions, the list of biblical readings goes to the final chapter. The second edition has added several appendices. In French Canada, however, most of the other parts of the final chapter appear elsewhere in the book, so the biblical citations have been placed in the first appendix.[1] In the United States, the complete text of the readings is included in this chapter, whereas the Latin original merely gives the citations.

The scriptural citations were developed after the promulgation of SC by a different study group than the one preparing the ritual for weddings. The ritual study group reported the first list of twenty-seven readings it had received in 1967. The list, which contained no psalms or gospel acclamations, did contain this note:

> Concerning the selection of pericopes, two things should be noted: 1) Most of the pericopes that are proposed here are already present among the pericopes granted to episcopal conferences here and there for the celebration of matrimony, and with very good fruits. Since the selection is extensive, if one pericope is not appropriate

---

[1] *Rituel Romain*, 120–23.

in a certain case, it will be easy to substitute another described elsewhere in the list.

2) For the purpose of doing catechesis, it seemed appropriate to include other pericopes concerning the Christian life in general (for example, Romans 12:1-2, 9-10, 14-18; Matthew 5:1-12; Matthew 7:21 and 24-25).[2]

Early on, this represented a different value from the one expressed in the second edition of the OCM. Now, one of the readings must speak expressly about marriage, not generically about the Christian life. A further explanation accompanied the final draft.

> The last chapter, as has been done for the baptism of adults and funerals, contains a certain number of biblical pericopes, of prayers, prefaces and blessings, which may be used in place of the corresponding texts contained in the preceding chapters, in case they may be deemed pastorally more appropriate, or even to enrich the doctrinal and spiritual context of the rite.[3]

Again, the study group thought that the readings presented opportunities for doctrine and catechesis, spiritual development, and the Christian life. These purposes still exist, but they have been rendered secondary to the inclusion of one passage that expressly speaks of marriage. This requirement is made clear in the rubrical heading before OCM 144, which expands the introduction found in the first edition before paragraph 67.

Before the study group compiled its lists, its members knew that the Vatican had authorized proclaiming the readings in the vernacular[4] and even allowed the local ordinary to approve translations of biblical texts for which no official translation existed.[5]

The list of readings revised for the second edition includes five new passages not in the first edition, but most of which have long been available in the lectionary's fourth volume. When the most

---

[2] Schemata 248, pp. 7–8.
[3] Schemata 280, p. ii.
[4] IO 74a.
[5] Ibid., 74b.

recent English-language lectionary came into force in the United States in 1997, the second edition of the OCM with its expanded list of readings had already been published in Latin. Therefore, the lectionary included the new readings from the OCM; however, inexplicably, one of them was missing, Ephesians 4:1-6.

In the United States, as in Australia, Mexico, and Colombia, the second edition is published not merely with citations but with the full passages, suitable for study and proclamation. Normally, though, it is advisable to use the lectionary for proclaiming the readings.

In Latin, the second edition has updated the other citations to match the new Vulgate, which had been published in 1979. The numeration of some verses has been amended, and Latin words now carry accents. The Latin summaries of each reading are now set in italics. Asterisks designating the group of readings from which one must be selected are assigned to seven Old Testament readings, two from New Testament epistles, and three from the gospels.[6]

In the commentary that follows, an asterisk appears before the paragraph number of the readings so marked in the OCM. One of these readings must be chosen for a wedding, unless the day of the wedding falls within the first four numbers of the Table of Liturgical Days, and the wedding takes place during Mass, as explained in the commentary on OCM 56.

The bishops' conference of French Canada has published its own wedding lectionary in a separate fascicle, and it pairs the psalms with specific readings, though it does not make this obligatory.[7]

The pastoral commentary on the readings published in some editions of the first English translation has been removed. It had no Latin equivalent.

Readings from the Old Testament

The options for readings from the Old Testament can also be found in LM 801. Prior to the liturgical reforms of the Second

---

[6] A commentary on all these passages can be found in Paul Turner, *Preparing the Wedding Homily* (Chicago: Liturgy Training Publications, 2003).

[7] *Lectionnaire pour la célébration du marriage* (Ottawa: Conférence des évêques catholiques du Canada, 2011), 4.

Vatican Council, Catholic weddings contained no Old Testament reading. This entire section was new. Unless otherwise noted, the readings appeared in the first list drafted by the study group.[8]

* 144 (ETA 179).

Genesis 1:26-28, 31a tells of the creation of man and woman and God's command for them to multiply. This was one of the passages in the ninth- to tenth-century Armenian marriage rite.[9] It heads the list of recommended readings from the Consultation on Common Texts (CCT),[10] which has gained broad ecumenical usage at the weddings of Christians. It is the former paragraph 67. The French Canadian lectionary pairs this with Psalm 128 (OCM 171).

* 145 (ETA 180).

Genesis 2:18-24 tells of the creation of woman and the explanation for why two become one. The ninth- to tenth-century Armenian marriage rite also included this option, as does the CCT. It is the former paragraph 68. The French Canadian lectionary pairs this with Psalm 148 (OCM 173).

* 146 (ETA 181).

Genesis 24:48-51, 58-67 tells of the engagement of Rebekah and Isaac. This passage was added to the first edition of the OCM after the study group submitted its original list. It inspired the prayer in the *Liber Ordinum* that mentions the *arras*.[11] Rebekah's veil at the end of this account gives early evidence of the custom of the *velación*. This is the former paragraph 69. The French Canadian lectionary pairs this with Psalm 145 (OCM 172).

---

[8] Schemata 248, p. 7; Schemata 280, p. 16.

[9] Stevenson, *To Join Together*, 59, citing F. C. Conybeare, *Rituale Armenorum* (Oxford: Oxford University Press, 1905), 109–114.

[10] Mark Searle and Kenneth W. Stevenson, *Documents of the Marriage Liturgy* (Collegeville, MN: Liturgical Press, 1992), 273–74, citing Consultation on Common Texts, *A Christian Celebration of Marriage, An Ecumenical Liturgy* (Philadelphia: Fortress, 1985), 23–25.

[11] *Liber Ordinum*, 298.

* 147 (ETA 182).

Tobit 7:6-14 relates the engagement and marriage of Sarah and Tobiah. The father of the bride gives her hand to the groom, showing early evidence of the joining of hands as a symbol of marriage. The CCT also suggests this passage. This is the former paragraph 70. The French Canadian lectionary pairs this with Psalm 33 (OCM 167).

* 148 (ETA 183).

Tobit 8:4b-8 is the prayer that Tobiah offers on his wedding night. This passage appears in the list of the CCT. This is the former paragraph 71. The French Canadian lectionary pairs this with Psalm 103 (OCM 169).

* 149 (ETA 184).

Proverbs 31:10-13, 19-20, 30-31 describes a worthy wife's inward beauty. This passage was part of the study group's initial list, but it was not accepted into the first edition of the OCM. It appears for the first time in the second edition of the OCM, though it has long been among the readings in the lectionary's ritual Mass for marriage in the United States. The French Canadian lectionary pairs this with Psalm 112 (OCM 170).

150 (ETA 185).

Song of Songs 2:8-10, 14, 16a; 8:6-7a is a lyrical love poem sung by a woman and a man. It is the first of the readings in the list not to carry an asterisk because it speaks more of love than marriage. The CCT includes this in its list of recommended readings. This is the former paragraph 72. The French Canadian lectionary pairs this with Psalm 128 (OCM 171).

Listeners will not realize that the reading skips from chapter two to chapter eight of the same book. In Mexico, the final verses of this reading, taken from chapter eight, are presented as a different option for an Old Testament reading.[12]

---

[12] *Ritual* (Mexico), 220.

* 151 (ETA 186).

Sirach 26:1-4, 16-21 describes the virtues of a worthy wife. It appears in the CCT list as well. This is the former paragraph 73. The French Canadian lectionary pairs this with Psalm 34 (OCM 168).

In the lectionary, this reading cites verses 1-4 and 13-16. It is the same reading, however. The numbers in the OCM reflect the verses in the new Vulgate.

152 (ETA 187).

Jeremiah 31:31-32a, 33-34a describes the covenant of God with Israel. It is an image of the marriage covenant but not identical to it, so this reading carries no asterisk. There is no known precedent for this among readings for weddings, East or West. Still, the connection between covenant theology and Christian marriage was an insight favored in the post–Vatican II church. Stevenson calls this reading "a complete newcomer to the marriage liturgy."[13] The CCT accepted it as well. This is the former paragraph 74. The French Canadian lectionary pairs this with Psalm 112 (OCM 170).

The Mexican edition adds another passage, Jeremiah 29:5-7, before this one. Jeremiah reports God's command to the people of Israel upon returning from their exile. The men are to build homes and plant gardens, take wives and have children, their children should have children, and all should seek the welfare of the city.[14]

Following the passage from Jeremiah 31 the Mexican ritual also adds Hosea 2:16, 17[b], 21-22. God speaks to his unfaithful spouse and betroths her again. The end of this passage overlaps with the beginning of a suggested reading for the engagement ceremony in OCM 227.

Readings from the New Testament

This section can be found in LM 802. One passage from Ephesians, however, is missing from that section of the lectionary. Unlike the Old Testament readings, very few of these are listed among the readings with asterisks, so almost all of them need to be coupled with another passage.

[13] Stevenson, *To Join Together*, 148.
[14] *Ritual* (Mexico), 220.

153 (ETA 188).

Romans 8:31b-35, 37-39 affirms that nothing can separate us from the love of Christ. This reading was not on the study group's initial draft list, yet was added for the first edition of the OCM, where it was paragraph 75. The CCT also uses it. The French Canadian lectionary pairs this with Psalm 145 (OCM 172).

154 (ETA 189).

Romans 12:1-2, 9-18 (long form) or 1-2, 9-13 (short form) begs the Christian community to make love sincere. Marital love is a special way of living the ideals of Christian love. The study group's drafts singled this out as one of the readings intending to offer catechesis on the Christian life in general. It is the former paragraph 76.

Although this passage was not among the readings in the Roman Ritual of 1614, it did appear in the tenth-century Roman-Germanic Pontifical.[15] The CCT has accepted it as an option. The French Canadian lectionary pairs this with Psalm 33 (OCM 167).

155 (ETA 190).

Romans 15:1b-3a, 5-7, 13 urges the Christian community to be harmonious and welcoming. This was newly added to the second edition of the OCM, but it has already been in the lectionary. The French Canadian lectionary pairs this with Psalm 112 (OCM 170).

156 (ETA 191).

First Corinthians 6:13c-15a, 17-20 reminds believers that the body is a temple of the Holy Spirit. The oldest known lectionary, the one from seventh-century Würzburg, included this as one of the passages for weddings.[16] Its second suggestion (1 Corinthians 7:2-11), which can also be found in the twelfth-century Roman

---

[15] PRG II: 415.

[16] Adrien Nocent, "The Christian Rite of Marriage in the West," in *Handbook for Liturgical Studies IV: Sacraments and Sacramentals*, ed. Anscar J. Chupungco (Collegeville, MN: Liturgical Press, 2000), 297, citing G. Morin, "Le plus ancient Comes ou lectionnaire de l'Église romaine," *Revue Benedictine* 27 (1910): 4–7.

Pontifical,[17] was not retained in the OCM's list. This passage from chapter 6, though, also appears in the Sarum Missal because it belonged to the Mass of the Trinity, which was becoming associated with weddings.[18] The CCT includes this as an option for weddings. This is the former paragraph 77. The French Canadian lectionary pairs this with Psalm 103 (OCM 169).

The Mexican edition adds another reading here, 1 Corinthians 7:10-14,[19] which barely overlaps one of the earliest passages known for weddings as found in the Würzburg lectionary. Paul teaches that husband and wife may not separate, and that he has this command from the Lord.

157 (ETA 192).

First Corinthians 12:31–13:8a is without fail the most popular reading for wedding liturgies in the modern era, even outside Christian services. Paul's hymn to love is addressed to the entire Christian community, not to engaged couples. It describes how all should live and actually sets a minimum bar for those who are getting married. Note that this carries no asterisk, so if it is used, it must be coupled with another reading or psalm that speaks explicitly about marriage. It can be found in the CCT as well. This is the former paragraph 78. The French Canadian lectionary pairs this with Psalm 33 (OCM 167).

158 (ETA 193).

Ephesians 4:1-6 urges Christians to bear with one another through love. This is the only one of the five readings newly added to the OCM that was never included in the lectionary's collection of readings for weddings (802). It can be found in the first volume of the lectionary as the second reading for the Seventeenth Sunday in Ordinary Time in Year B (110), or in the third volume as the first reading for Friday of the Twenty-Ninth Week in Ordinary Time (477). More conveniently, it is among the New Testament readings for the blessing of abbots and abbesses (807), located in volume

---

[17] *Le Pontifical Romain* I:301.

[18] *Sarum Missal*, 152.

[19] *Ritual* (Mexico), 221.

four only a few pages after the readings for weddings. The French Canadian lectionary pairs this with Psalm 103 (OCM 169).

* 159 (ETA 194).

Ephesians 5:2a, 21-33 (long form) or 5:2a, 25-32 (short form) compares the love of husband and wife with the love of Christ and the church, and it uses the word "mystery" (or "sacrament") to describe marriage. It is one of the few lectionary passages from St. Paul to speak explicitly of marriage.

This passage has one of the most potent pedigrees in the history of lectionary readings. It has influenced many of the prayers and antiphons of the wedding Mass, including the first nuptial blessing (OCM 74 and 105) as well as the first collect (188). It appeared in the ninth- to tenth-century Armenian rite,[20] in Coptic and Ethiopic celebrations,[21] and in the Byzantine liturgy.[22] It was the epistle in the twelfth-century Missal of Troyes,[23] and in the 1570 Missal, which was used at every Catholic wedding Mass until 1969.[24] The CCT also includes it. This was the former paragraph 79. The French Canadian lectionary pairs this with Psalm 128 (OCM 171).

160 (ETA 195).

Philippians 4:4-9 promises that the God of peace will be with those who are kind and think of what is just. This passage, another that speaks of good Christian living, is new to the second edition of the OCM, though it has already appeared as one of the options in the lectionary. The French Canadian lectionary pairs this with Psalm 33 (OCM 167).

161 (ETA 196).

Colossians 3:12-17 asks the Christian community to wear its virtues like clothing and to bind them all together with love. This was the former paragraph 80. It is on the CCT's list of readings

---

[20] Stevenson, *To Join Together*, 59.
[21] Ibid., 72.
[22] Ibid., 75.
[23] Searle and Stevenson, *Documents of the Marriage Liturgy*, 273.
[24] *Missale Romanum*, p. [75].

as well. The French Canadian lectionary pairs this with Psalm 34 (OCM 168).

162 (ETA 197).

Hebrews 13:1-4a, 5-6b asks everyone to honor marriage. This passage is a new suggestion in the second edition of the OCM, though it has already appeared in the lectionary. It has also been part of the Byzantine lectionary.[25] The French Canadian lectionary pairs this with Psalm 112 (OCM 170).

* 163 (ETA 198).

First Peter 3:1-9 asks wives to submit to their husbands and husbands to live with their wives in understanding. This reading was part of the betrothal ceremony in the ninth- to tenth-century Armenian lectionary.[26] It is the former paragraph 81. The CCT includes it, which is somewhat of a surprise because it is broadly considered antiquarian in its description of marital roles. This is one of only two New Testament passages in the wedding lectionary that explicitly speaks of marriage and thus carries an asterisk. The French Canadian lectionary pairs this with Psalm 128 (OCM 171).

164 (ETA 199).

First John 3:18-24 encourages Christians to love in deed and in truth, as Christ commanded. This is the former paragraph 82. It is on the CCT list. The French Canadian lectionary pairs this with Psalm 34 (OCM 168).

165 (ETA 200).

First John 4:7-12 argues that Christians should love one another because God is love. This passage appeared in the study group's drafts together with 1 John 4:12-16, but the second of these was never included in the OCM. The final two of the optional verses for the gospel acclamation, however, come from that part of this letter (OCM 176 and 177). This is the former paragraph 83. The CCT list

---

[25] Searle and Stevenson, *Documents of the Marriage Liturgy*, 273.
[26] Stevenson, *To Join Together*, 148.

includes it. The French Canadian lectionary pairs this with Psalm 145 (OCM 172).

166 (ETA 201).
Revelation 19:1, 5-9a calls those blessed who are called to the wedding feast of the Lamb. A human wedding foreshadows the divine wedding banquet at the end of time.

This is the former paragraph 84. It is part of the CCT's lectionary for weddings. The French Canadian lectionary pairs this with Psalm 148 (OCM 173).

In Latin, the first edition of the *Ordo lectionarium* positioned this passage not among the second readings but as the first reading to be used at weddings in Easter Time.[27] This schema did not carry over into the lectionary's second edition and, hence, not into the vernacular translations now in force.[28] However, OCM 55 does make this the first reading during Easter Time whenever there are three readings at a wedding Mass. On Sundays of Easter Time, the first reading comes from Acts of the Apostles; in Year C the second reading comes from Revelation. The wedding lectionary includes no passage from Acts, so this passage from Revelation steps in as the only selection.

In Mexico, however, two readings from Acts have been added, along with three more readings from Revelation, greatly expanding the selection for Easter Time:

Acts 1:12-14 tells how the apostles remained united in prayer together with Mary, the mother of Jesus.

Acts 2:42-47 describes how the early Christian community shared its possessions and prayers with one another.

Revelation 5:8-10 praises the Lamb of God for making Christians a kingdom of priests to serve God.

Revelation 21:1-5 reports John's vision of the new Jerusalem coming down from heaven like a bride prepared to meet her spouse.

---

[27] *Missale Romanum: Lectionarium, editio typica* (Vatican City: Typis Polyglottis Vaticanis, 1972) III:552.

[28] *Ordo lectionum missæ, editio typica altera* (Vatican City: Libreria Editrice Vaticana, 1981), 373–74.

Revelation 22:12, 16-17, 20-21 reports John hearing the Spirit and the Bride calling, "Come."

Responsorial Psalms

The psalms can also be found in the lectionary (803). The initial list of readings from the study group contained no suggestions for psalms, apart from the recommendation that antiphons and psalms for the wedding come from the Mass for spouses in the *Graduale simplex*.[29] Psalms were included in the first edition of the OCM. There have been no changes to the psalms for the second edition, and only one carries an asterisk. Every one of them is on the list for the CCT.

The Mexican edition has added an "Alleluia" to every psalm refrain if it is sung during Easter Time.[30]

167 (ETA 202).

Psalm 33 (32):12 and 18, 20-21, 22 proclaims that the earth is full of God's goodness. It celebrates God's merciful love, shared now with a couple to be married. This is the former paragraph 85.

The Mexican edition adds the most popular psalm of all, 23 (22), before this one, along with the refrain, "The Lord is my shepherd, there is nothing I shall want."

168 (ETA 203).

Psalm 34 (33):2-3, 4-5, 6-7, 8-9 is a hymn of endless praise to God, who is good and comes to the rescue in times of need. This is the former paragraph 86.

The *Ordo cantus missæ* offers two options for the gradual in the Mass for celebrating marriage. The first comes from verses 10 and 11b of this psalm.[31]

After this psalm the Mexican edition adds two more. Psalm 45 (44) is a wedding hymn on its own, and here it carries a refrain

---

[29] Schemata 248, p. 16.
[30] *Ritual* (Mexico), 338–45.
[31] *Graduale Romanum*, 458.

inspired by a gospel parable:[32] "Behold the bridegroom is coming! Let us rise up to receive Christ the Lord!"[33]

Psalm 100 (99) carries the refrain, "The Lord is our God, and we are his people." This popular psalm is used for a variety of joyous occasions.

169 (ETA 204).

Psalm 103 (102):1-2, 8 and 13, 17-18a praises God who is kind and merciful, and it notes the example of a father who is compassionate toward children. The text here changes the supposedly final translation of the revised Grail Psalms. The word "justice" is now "righteousness."[34] This is the former paragraph 87.

170 (ETA 205).

Psalm 112 (111):1-2, 3-4, 5-7a, 7bc-8, 9 blesses the one who follows God's commands and promises upright and strong descendants. The translation of the revised Grail here has twice changed the word "justice" to "righteousness," and twice changed the word "just" to "righteous." This is the former paragraph 88.

The *Graduale simplex* uses verses 1-8 of this psalm for its responsorial at the Mass for celebrating marriage.[35]

* 171 (ETA 206).

Psalm 128 (127):1-2, 3, 4-5ac and 6a blesses those who fear the Lord and promises a fruitful and multigenerational family. This is the only one of the psalms to carry an asterisk. Hence, if this is chosen as the responsorial psalm, the selection of readings is quite broad. The translation of the revised Grail that appears here has changed the spelling of the word "Sion" to "Zion." This is the former paragraph 89.

---

[32] Matt 25:6.

[33] *Ritual* (Mexico), 340.

[34] For references to the earlier approved version of psalms cited in this section, see *The Revised Grail Psalms: A Liturgical Psalter* (Chicago: GIA Publications, 2010).

[35] *Graduale simplex in usum minorum ecclesiarum, editio typica altera* (Vatican City: Typis Polyglottis Vaticanis 1975), 380–81.

In the preconciliar rite, the gradual was taken from this psalm together with part of Psalm 20 (19). The tract also came from Psalm 128 (127). During Easter, however, it drew from Psalms 20 (19) and 134 (133). Even earlier the pontifical of the twelfth century used this psalm for the gradual of the wedding Mass.[36]

As early as the fourth century Gregory Nazianzen quoted this psalm in the context of marriage, so it has a long history of association with Christian weddings East and West.[37]

The contemporary *Ordo cantus missæ* selects verse 3 of this psalm as the second of its two options for the gradual of the Mass for celebrating marriage.[38]

172 (ETA 207).

Psalm 145 (144):8-9, 10 and 15, 17-18 sings the praises of the Lord who is good to all. The translation of the revised Grail that appears here has changed the word "just" to "righteous." This is the former paragraph 90.

The revised English translation has changed the refrain. The one in the lectionary is "The Lord is compassionate toward all his works." The revision is "How good is the Lord to all."

173 (ETA 208).

Psalm 148:1-2, 3-4, 9-10, 11-13ab, 13c-14a praises God the Creator, in whose act of creation married couples hope to share. The translation of the revised Grail here has changed the word "reptiles" to "creeping things." This is the former paragraph 91.

The Roman-Germanic Pontifical of the tenth century used for its gradual the second verse of Psalm 141 (140), "Let my prayer rise like incense," but this is not among the options in the OCM.

The twelfth-century Roman Pontifical drew its gradual from the votive Mass for the Holy Trinity,[39] as did the Sarum Missal,[40] and

---

[36] *Le Pontifical Romain*, I:260.

[37] Stevenson, *To Join Together*, 75.

[38] *Graduale Romanum*, 646.

[39] *Le Pontifical Romaine*, I:301.

[40] *Sarum Missal*, 153.

the 1570 Roman Missal.[41] The text comes from Daniel 3:55-56 and praises God who looks into the depths and has a throne upon the Cherubim. This does not appear in the OCM.

Alleluia Verses and Verses before the Gospel
   This selection of verses to be sung during the gospel acclamation can also be found in the lectionary at 804. The Lenten acclamation from OCM 56, however, is new. In fact OCM 56 offers two additional verses to the four placed here. When the postconciliar study group prepared its drafts for the marriage rite, it made no suggestions for the gospel acclamations, referring instead to the *Graduale simplex*.[42]
   The Latin original of the first edition made a mistake in listing these verses. It cited 1 John 5:7b as the last of the four. The text, however, matches 1 John 4:7b. The erroneous chapter citation caused the verse to be placed last in the series, following the three verses from chapter 4. The English translation of the first edition corrected the chapter number, which laid bare the problem that the four verses were not listed in biblical order. The second edition now makes what was the fourth acclamation the first and shuffles the others down accordingly. The lectionary caught the error and presented the four in the order in which they now appear in the second edition of the OCM.

174 (ETA 209).
   All four of the gospel acclamation verses in this section come from the fourth chapter of the First Letter of John. So does another one at OCM 56, but it has rearranged several verses from the letter. This verse was paragraph 95 in the first edition, erroneously cited in Latin as coming from chapter 4. It praises all who love.

175 (ETA 210).
   This is the former paragraph 92, where it was the first optional verse in the first edition. It affirms that God is love and urges Christians to love one another.

---

[41] *Missale Romanum*, p. [49].
[42] Schemata 248, p. 16.

176 (ETA 211).

This is the former paragraph 93, the second of the options from the first edition. It argues that if Christians love one another, God's love is brought to perfection in them.

177 (ETA 212).

This is the former paragraph 93, the third in the list from the first edition. It assures those who remain in love that they will remain in God.

The tenth-century Roman-Germanic pontifical offered a different alleluia verse, "O Lord, the God of my salvation, by day and at night I have cried out to you."[43] It is the opening verse of Psalm 88 (87), one of the bleakest songs in the psalter. It does not appear in the OCM.

The preconciliar Mass for spouses used Psalm 20 (19):3 and Psalm 134 (133):3.[44] The second was discontinued for the postconciliar liturgy, but the first is still the one provided by the *Ordo cantus missæ*: "May the Lord send you help from his holy place, and may he protect you from Sion."[45]

Gospel Readings

The selection of gospel readings repeats those from the lectionary (805). Nearly all of these are also in use for the CCT.

178 (ETA 213).

Matthew 5:1-12a is Jesus' much loved Beatitudes. It shows the way of the Christian life to those who wish to follow it and summons an engaged couple to lofty goals. This was among the texts that the study group submitted first, and it was highlighted as an example of one that was selected for the sake of catechesis on the Christian life in general.[46] This is the former paragraph 96.

179 (ETA 214).

Matthew 5:13-16 remembers Jesus proclaiming that his disciples are salt of the earth and light for the world. The message bears

[43] PRG II:415.
[44] *Missale Romanum*, p. [76].
[45] *Graduale Romanum*, 646–47.
[46] Schemata 248, pp. 7–8.

resonance for the broad responsibilities of married life. This is the former paragraph 97.

The Mexican list of readings has added Matthew 6:25-34, in which Jesus admonishes his disciples not to worry about material things.[47]

180 (ETA 215).

Matthew 7:21, 24-29 (long form) or 7:21, 24-25 (short form) tells of the wise man who built his house on rock. It bears a special lesson for those who are starting a new home together. This was on the study group's initial list specifically marked as an example of a reading offered for the sake of catechesis on the Christian life in general.[48] It is the former paragraph 98.

* 181 (ETA 216).

Matthew 19:3-6 is Jesus' teachings on the permanence of marriage. This is one of the most frequently used passages in the history of the wedding liturgy, and it still remains popular with couples. It is listed in the ninth- to tenth-century Armenian rite,[49] the tenth- to eleventh-century Coptic and Ethiopic rites,[50] tenth-century Roman-Germanic Pontifical,[51] the eleventh-century Spanish *Liber Comicus*,[52] twice in the twelfth-century Roman Pontifical,[53] the Sarum Missal,[54] and the 1570 Roman Missal.[55] This is the former paragraph 99.

182 (ETA 217).

Matthew 22:35-40 is Jesus' instruction on the greatest commandments, in which he proclaims the law of love. This is the former paragraph 100.

[47] *Ritual* (Mexico), 223.
[48] Schemata 248, pp. 7–8.
[49] Stevenson, *To Join Together*, 59.
[50] Ibid., 72.
[51] PRG II:415.
[52] Searle and Stevenson, *Documents of the Marriage Liturgy*, 273.
[53] *Le Pontifical Romain*, I:261 and 301.
[54] *Sarum Missal*, 153.
[55] *Missale Romanum*, p. [76].

* 183 (ETA 218).

Mark 10:6-9 is another presentation of Jesus' teaching on the permanence of marriage. Although history does not record its use as much as of OCM 181, it is a parallel to that passage. This is the former paragraph 101.

Although the Mexican lectionary has added quite a number of passages to the selection for weddings, no wedding lectionary includes any pericope from the gospel of Luke.

* 184 (ETA 219).

John 2:1-11 presents Jesus' first miracle at the wedding in Cana of Galilee. Although it was not part of the preconciliar wedding Mass in the Roman Rite, it has broad historical usage in the ninth- to tenth-century Armenian rite[56] and the Byzantine Rite,[57] for example, where—in place of Matthew 19—it inspired the spirituality of many Eastern hymns, chants, and prayers.[58] Other Spanish and Romano-Gallican lectionaries included this passage as well.[59] This is the former paragraph 102.

185 (ETA 220).

John 15:9-12 contains Jesus' words to his disciples at the Last Supper, urging them to love one another. This is the former paragraph 103.

186 (ETA 221).

John 15:12-16 continues Jesus' discourse at the Last Supper, in this case speaking about the cost of love and urging the disciples to bear fruit in his name. This is the former paragraph 104.

187 (ETA 222).

John 17:20-26 (long form) and 17:20-23 (short form) also comes from the Last Supper, but it is Jesus' prayer to his Father that they

---

[56] Stevenson, *To Join Together*, 59.
[57] Ibid., 75.
[58] Ibid., 78.
[59] Searle and Stevenson, *Documents of the Marriage Liturgy*, 273.

may be one. They are one. The couple are becoming one—with each other and with God. This is the former paragraph 105.

II. COLLECTS

The second part of the final chapter begins the presentation of liturgical texts largely drawn from the Missal. The OCM does not carry over the antiphons from the Missal as, for example, the Order of Confirmation does, but it does include the prayers from the ritual Mass. The Missal indicates that these prayers may be mixed and matched: When using the collect from one set, the presider is not bound to use the other presidential prayers from the same set. The eucharistic prayers remain only in the Missal, so the presider needs both books when celebrating matrimony within Mass. The word "collect" refers explicitly to the prayer that concludes the introductory rites of the Mass, but these prayers are used near the start of the other forms of the wedding ceremony as well.

The study group preparing the post–Vatican II ceremony mapped out the questions concerning the collects in 1966.

> *In the Mass of Matrimony there should be found more prayers and readings* ad libitum.
>
> The prayers that are now in the wedding Mass seem of a very general nature, nor do they ever vary. Concerning these there also applies what is said in the Constitution about the rite of matrimony that exists in the Roman Ritual: "let it become richer" (article 77). In the Roman liturgical tradition are found more prayers that may be gathered here, with appropriate adaptations. Perhaps others ought to be developed in order to express the doctrine of the Council concerning matrimony, in the Roman euchological style that has been handed down.[60]

When the study group first presented the collects in an advanced stage of their work, they included an explanation of sources.

---

[60] Schemata 182a, pp. 6–7.

Under this heading are included prayers, prefaces, and blessings to be used *ad libitum* for celebrating weddings. Among the proposed texts are found some both old and new, the genius of Roman euchology indeed having been preserved, to which now also are joined, according to the norm of the new Order of Mass, those Mozarabic-Gallican blessings that are composed with diverse parts.

Among the prayers and prefaces, among which are the blessings of the bride and groom, are proposed texts of the missal and of the Roman Ritual (for example, numbers 86 and 88), and texts taken from the Roman or Latin tradition (for example, numbers 91, 94 and 102), applying some small changes, and new texts.

Adhering to the Roman tradition, with the work of experts, we have observed the rules of meter.

With your helpful observations we hope that our texts may be so perfected that they be worthy of the sacred liturgy of the Roman Church.[61]

Gy singled out Bernard Botte and Anselmo Lentini for their assistance in the style and meter of the prayers.[62] The selection of collects replaces the single one formerly in place for the wedding Mass in the 1570 Missal: "Hear us, almighty and merciful God, that what is administered by our office may be more greatly filled by your blessing."[63] The same prayer appeared in the twelfth-century Roman Pontifical,[64] in the eighth-century Gregorian Sacramentary,[65] and in the sixth-century Verona Sacramentary.[66] The Gelasian positioned it as a post-communion prayer.[67] The prayer made no explicit mention of marriage, and it seemed to underscore the role of the priest in the ceremony. This collect was removed from the post–Vatican II Missal completely, not merely from the Mass for celebrating marriage. The votive Mass for the Holy Trinity may also have been used at weddings, perhaps

---

[61] Schemata 248, p. 9; Schemata 280, p. 17.
[62] Schemata 248, p. 2.
[63] *Missale Romanum*, p. [75].
[64] *Le Pontifical Romain*, 301.
[65] Gregorian 833 (I:308).
[66] Verona 1105.
[67] Gelasian 1455.

upholding the love within the Trinity as an archetype of marital love.[68] The preconciliar collect was rewritten for the post–Vatican II Missal for use on Trinity Sunday, but it is no longer to be used at weddings—unless, of course, one takes place at a Saturday night or Sunday Mass on the weekend of Trinity Sunday.

The Missal has six collects. The first edition of the OCM had four. The second edition now includes all six from the Missal. The French Canadian book has added three more of its own.[69]

188 (ETA 223).

The first option for the collect compares marriage to the sacrament of Christ and the church, inspired by a passage from Paul's Letter to the Ephesians (OCM 159). This is a new translation of the former 106.

The opening lines come directly from the first nuptial blessing (OCM 74 and 105), so it is not to be used in the same ceremony when the minister plans to offer that blessing. The first edition of the OCM permitted the minister to abbreviate the nuptial blessing, so he could omit the identical lines. Now he offers the entire blessing. The third edition of the Missal moved this collect out of set A and into set B in order to separate it from its source, the nuptial blessing that still appears in set A.

The verb "foreshadow" is in the past tense in the blessing and the present tense in the collect, but it is the same Latin word and probably represents a last-minute change to the collect just before the Missal was published, a decision that did not account for the other appearance of these lines in the ceremony. All these prayers were first translated for the third edition of the Missal and then carried over without change into the OCM.

The last lines are inspired from a collect during the Octave of Easter.[70] It was used on Tuesday of that week in the 1570 Missal and was moved to Monday of the Octave in the post–Vatican II Missal.

---

[68] Nocent, "The Christian Rite of Marriage in the West," 296.
[69] *Rituel Romain*, 22–23.
[70] Schemata 248, p. 8.

189 (ETA 224).

This collect prays that those joined in inseparable love may be fruitful. This is the former paragraph 109. It was based on a longer prayer from the tenth-century Fulda Sacramentary for the first edition of the OCM.[71] In the Missal it appears as the second option for the prayers in set A.

190 (ETA 225).

This collect prays that the couple will be confirmed in love for each other. This is the former paragraph 107. The service for a wedding without Mass uses this prayer in place of OCM 89, but other collects may be used for this purpose. In the Missal this is the first of the prayers in set B.

This prayer was newly composed for the first edition of the OCM, and the drafters placed it in the second position after the prayer drawn from the nuptial blessing.[72]

191 (ETA 226).

This collect prays that the couple will grow in faith and share it with their children. It is the first of the Missal's set C prayers. The study group composed it, and it was accepted into the first edition of the Missal, where it is the former paragraph 108.

ICEL debated the translation of the word here rendered "offspring," in Latin *sobole*. Some preferred the word "children" because "offspring" seemed so unusual. Even in Latin, however, *sobole* is an unusual word. The translators tried to show in English the variety of synonyms that exist throughout the Missal in the original Latin.

192 (ETA 227).

This collect prays for the preservation of the couple's union. The prayer is from the Verona Sacramentary, one of the most ancient sources of Roman prayers, but it was new to the second edition of the OCM in Latin. From there it found its way into the Missal,

---

[71] Schemata 248, p. 9, citing *Fulda Sacramentary* 2608.
[72] Schemata 248, p. 8.

where it is the second option in set B. The Missal's English translation was carried over into the OCM.

At one point, ICEL's translators had expanded the second line from "what you have established" to "the bond you have established" for the sake of clarity. It was pointed out, however, that the prayer pertains to the original institution of marriage rather than the union of the couple, which is one of its attributes.

The Verona Sacramentary includes this prayer just before the nuptial blessing,[73] and the Gelasian positioned it as a collect.[74] Perhaps because of its antiquity the second edition of the OCM has restored its use as a collect.

In the event that the nuptial blessing is omitted in a marriage with an unbaptized person, this is the prayer that replaces it (OCM 140 or ETA 174).

193 (ETA 228).

The final collect is a prayer for the mutual affection and shared holiness of the couple. Originally found in the Gelasian Sacramentary, where it served as a prayer for the bride after the Lord's Prayer and before the nuptial blessing.[75] Now it prays for the bride and the groom, and the minister may insert their names into the prayer. Although the first English translation called for the minister to include the names of the couple in all four of its collects, the Latin did not. Now the minister saying the prayers at OCM 190 and 193 (ETA 225 and 228) has the option to include the names of the bride and the groom. In Latin, then, the number of collects that may mention the couple increased from zero to two, and in English they reduced from four to two.

The original location of this prayer before the nuptial blessing means that it performed a function similar to the *Propitiare*, which preceded the blessing in the 1570 Missal and which bears some resemblance to this prayer.[76] In the study group, Wagner had

---

[73] Verona 1109.
[74] Gelasian 1443.
[75] Gelasian 1450.
[76] *Missale Romanum*, p. [76].

proposed turning the *Propitiare* into a collect,[77] which did not happen. The second edition has repurposed this prayer instead.

One of ICEL's drafts opened the prayer with the phrase, "God, who since the springtime of the world," as a closer translation of the Latin. It was thought that "the beginning of the world" was more biblical, so that translation was chosen—even though the original Latin expression *mundi crescentis exordio* itself is not biblical.

The Colombian edition does not include this section because the collects are distributed throughout the book as needed.

The French Canadian edition includes a special appendix on the profession of faith at this point, as noted in OCM 69.

III. OTHER PRAYERS FOR THE BLESSING OF RINGS

In addition to the prayer over the rings that appears in the liturgy, the minister may use one of these. This section does not appear in the French Canadian edition because its prayers are all in the chapters where the minister needs them.

194 (ETA 229).

The minister asks God to bless the rings so that those who wear them may remain faithful to each other. This is the former paragraph 110.

This blessing comes from the Roman Ritual of 1614[78] and the Roman Pontifical of the twelfth century,[79] though in the singular because the only ring was the one that the groom gave to the bride. It is based on a blessing in the eleventh-century Benedictional of Robert of Jumieges, which contained the first description of an entire ring ceremony.[80]

The Latin word for "your" in the fifth line of this prayer could be understood to refer not only to God's will but also to God's peace. If so, the translation would change from a prayer for the couple to "abide in peace and in your will" to something like

---

[77] Schemata 157 adnexum, p. 4.
[78] *Roman Ritual*, 462.
[79] *Le Pontifical Romain*, I:300.
[80] Searle and Stevenson, *Documents of the Marriage Liturgy*, 107 and 110.

"abide in your peace and will." ICEL, however, held that the prayer asks for the couple to abide in peace between themselves (not in God's peace) and to abide in God's will.

195 (ETA 230).
The final choice for blessing the rings is actually a blessing of the couple whose rings will remind them of their love. The draft of this new prayer, composed by the study group, blessed the rings, but it was reworked for the first edition of the OCM and appeared there as paragraph 111.

The Missal contains examples of alternative prayers for the blessing of an object or the blessing of the people who use it; for example, the blessing of ashes on Ash Wednesday, where the first option blesses the people, not the ashes. On Palm Sunday the prayer for blessing branches is followed by an alternative that prays for the people who hold them. On the Feast of the Presentation of the Lord, the priest may bless the candles or say a prayer for the people who are brightened by their splendor. When blessing rings, the minister may bless the people who will wear them.

ICEL struggled to choose here and in other places between "faithfulness" and "fidelity." The words are basically equivalent but have different connotations. In this case, "faithfulness" seemed to embrace more meaning for the prayer.

Words from this blessing may be repeated in a prayer over the rings on the anniversary of the wedding (OCM 243 and 244).

IV. PRAYERS OVER THE OFFERINGS
A selection of three prayers over the offerings are copied from the Missal. The English translations in the Missal are presented again here.

The French Canadian book does not have this section because the prayers over the offerings appear in place within the first chapter, the Order for Celebrating Matrimony within Mass.

196 (ETA 231).
The first selection prays that God will accept the offering made on the occasion of this marriage, which has its origin in God's goodness. Of the three options, this is the oldest. The first

version comes from the sixth-century Verona Sacramentary.[81] It reappears in the eighth-century Gregorian Sacramentary,[82] the tenth-century Roman-Germanic Pontifical,[83] and in two places in the twelfth-century Roman Pontifical.[84] Unsurprisingly, it became the prayer over the offerings (then called the "secret") for the 1570 Missal,[85] which remained in force up to the liturgical reforms of the Second Vatican Council.

Of course, the 1570 Missal still permitted the collect for Trinity Sunday at a wedding Mass, but this was discontinued with the first edition of the OCM, where this prayer appeared in paragraph 112.

197 (ETA 232).

The second prayer asks the Father to receive the offerings brought in gladness and to watch over the couple. This was newly composed for the drafts of the OCM,[86] and it became paragraph 113 in the first edition. The word "gladness" surely results from the study group's desire to acknowledge the festive nature of the wedding day.

ICEL had some concern that the words "fatherly love" sounded too paternal and avuncular, and it considered "steadfast love," but *paterna* is the word composed for the original Latin, so "fatherly" remained.

198 (ETA 233).

The final option asks the Lord to receive the offerings and strengthen the couple in their love for each other and for God. It was newly composed for the drafts of the OCM,[87] and it became paragraph 114 in the first edition. The English translation fails to capture the different types of love in the final lines. More literally,

---

[81] Verona 1106.
[82] Gregorian 834.
[83] PRG II:415.
[84] *Le Pontifical Romain* I:261 and I:301.
[85] *Missale Romanum*, p. [76].
[86] Schemata 248, p. 10.
[87] Ibid.

the priest prays that the couple be strengthened in "charity" for each other and "love" of God.

Although this is a new prayer, it bears some resemblance to the secret (prayer over the offerings) in the Gelasian Sacramentary. That prayer, however, accompanied the offering coming from bridesmaids on behalf of the bride on the day that she was legally of age to marry:

> Be present, O Lord, to our supplications, and peacefully and kindly take up this oblation of your [female] servants (NN.), which they offer to you for your [female] servant (N.), whom you were pleased to lead to the state of maturity and to the day of her wedding, so that what is obtained at your direction may be fulfilled by your grace.[88]

V. PREFACES

The prefaces more properly belong to the Missal, where the revised English translation first appeared. They have been copied into the OCM from there, even their titles, which did not exist in the first edition of the OCM. Musical settings are in the Missal.

The 1570 Missal did not have a special preface for the wedding Mass. These existed in the past, and the study group sought to bring them back into force. The members described their early work in this way:

> *A preface and a* Hanc igitur *are included, proper to the mass for spouses.*
> Both are found in old Roman sacramentaries. Nevertheless, it will have to be considered whether it is appropriate to restore the formulas of the sacramentaries without any change, or to improve them, or to substitute others for them.[89]
>
> The group expanded this commentary as its members continued to develop these prayers.
> *The proper preface and* Hanc igitur.
> A preface and *Hanc igitur* proper to the mass for spouses is included in old Roman sacramentaries (preserved in some places up to the modern age), and thus the connection of Christian matrimony

[88] Gelasian 1445.
[89] Schemata 157, p. 9.

with all of salvation history as well as with the eucharistic sacrifice is expressed in a profound way. It seems that formulas of this kind need to be restored, indeed by adapting those elements that apply less to modern conditions, and by adding new formulas as appropriate.[90]

When the work on the prefaces was completed, Gy thanked in particular Bernard Botte and Anselmo Lentini for their friendly advice and expertise in style and meter.[91]

The French Canadian edition does not have this section because the prefaces appear in place in the first chapter where the priest needs them among the texts to be used when celebrating matrimony within Mass.

199 (ETA 234).

The first of the three prefaces praises God for the gift of marriage, a "sweet yoke of harmony," and an environment in which chaste and fruitful love will increase the children that God will adopt through baptism. The theology is especially rich and still contemporary. This was paragraph 115 in the first edition.

This preface has the longest tradition. Because the Verona Sacramentary has no preface for weddings, the one that appears in the Gelasian is the earliest, and it supplies the source for OCM 199.[92] The Gregorian presents the Gelasian text with a minor variation,[93] as did the Roman-Germanic Pontifical[94] and the twelfth-century Roman Pontifical.[95] The Roman-Germanic Pontifical also recommended it for the Mass on the occasion of a wedding anniversary.[96] The study group adopted the one from the Gelasian, having consulted the Gregorian.[97] It appeared in the same schemata with the note that the group favored drawing "prayers and prefaces"

[90] Schemata 182a, p. 14.
[91] Schemata 248, p. 2.
[92] Gelasian 1446.
[93] Gregorian 835.
[94] PRG II:416.
[95] *Le Pontifical Romain*, I:261.
[96] PRG II:417.
[97] Schemata 248, p. 11.

from the Roman tradition among the texts in their presentation of a revised OCM.[98]

200 (ETA 235).

The second preface praises God for the union of husband and wife, a sign of Christ's gift of grace. This is the first edition's paragraph 116 with the addition of one phrase, translated "in him" in English at the start of the second sentence.

The study group composed this preface for its drafts and used Sermon 22 of Pope Leo the Great as a source.[99] Only the final lines of the proposed preface were drawn from the first part of Leo's Christmas sermon, where he compared the mystery of the incarnation with the union of man and woman. The incarnation, wrote Leo, is "the mystery promised from the beginning, fulfilled in the end, lasting for ever in the heavens."[100]

The initial draft was reworked considerably before its publication in the first edition of the OCM, and the lines drawn from Leo, which had originally inspired the entire preface, were removed. The translation provoked considerable theological discussion at the ICEL meeting in hopes of getting it right. The dense preface that remains is the result of considerable reworking both in Latin and in English.

201 (ETA 236).

The final option praises God for giving an image of his love in the union of husband and wife. This preface was newly composed by the study group, and it was lightly edited to become paragraph 117 in the first edition of the OCM.

This preface notably mines a series of Latin synonyms for love. In the first line, *pietas*, which can mean the kind of dutiful and obvious love that parents have for children, is translated "goodness" to show the quality of God that led to the creation of the human race. A few lines later, *corsortio* is rendered "union" to show the close relationship between husband and wife. Then *amor* is

---

[98] Schemata 248, p. 9.
[99] Schemata 248, p. 11.
[100] Leo the Great, *Sermo* XXII, PL 54:193.

rendered as "love," a quality of God bestowed on the couple. Next, *caritas* appears three times, where the English uses the cognate "charity," to describe the kind of selfless love expected from those who are married. Finally, *dilectio* is translated as "love," though it has a cognate with the English word "delight," to show that human *amor* (love) is a sign of God's "delight." The first English translation rendered all five Latin synonyms with the same word, "love." It built its own rhythm through the repetition of the theme, but the nuances of the synonyms are quite rich.

VI. COMMEMORATION OF THE COUPLE IN THE EUCHARISTIC PRAYER

As noted above in the treatment of the prefaces, the study group wanted to have also a special commemoration of the couple within the eucharistic prayer.[101] This did not exist in the 1570 Missal, but there were precedents earlier in history. At the time of the study group's work, there was still only one eucharistic prayer, the Roman Canon. The first edition of the OCM, therefore, came with only one commemoration for the section of the Roman Canon known by its first words in Latin, *Hanc igitur*. This section, which begins in English with the words "Therefore, Lord, we pray," has a number of variations for special events such as Masses for the scrutinies, baptism, confirmation, or ordination.

After the additional eucharistic prayers were approved, the second edition of the OCM added commemorations for Eucharistic Prayers II and III. None is provided for Eucharistic Prayer IV, which comes with its own unchanging preface. It is not to be used at weddings. Nonetheless, the Mexican edition has an approved commemoration for Eucharistic Prayer IV: "[R]emember . . . those who take part in this offering, those gathered here before you, your children N. and N. who have established a new family today in Christ, your entire people, and all who seek you with a sincere heart."[102] It addresses the circumstance when a wedding takes

---

[101] Schemata 157, p. 9; Schemata 182a, p. 14.
[102] *Ritual* (Mexico), 241.

place at a parish Sunday Mass in Ordinary Time, when Eucharistic Prayer IV could be used.

In the first edition, this section was titled *Hanc igitur,* but those words appear only in the Roman Canon. The more expansive title of the second edition includes the commemoration inserted into all three eucharistic prayers.

The French Canadian book does not include this section because it has incorporated the commemorations in the first chapter with the other texts that pertain to a wedding within Mass.

The English translation of all three commemorations is taken from the Missal.

202 (ETA 237).

The commemoration of the first eucharistic prayer mentions the couple by name among those who are making an offering in this Eucharist. It includes a petition for the gift of children, which can be omitted if, for example, the couple is advanced in years. It also prays for the couple to enjoy a long life together.

The first evidence of such a commemoration is in the Verona Sacramentary, composed not too many centuries after the Roman Canon itself. The prayer, however, presumes that a bridesmaid is offering the bride on the day of her wedding, after she has reached the legal age for marriage:

> Therefore, Lord, we pray, graciously accept this oblation of your [female] servant N., that we offer to you on behalf of your [female] servant N. On her behalf we humbly entreat your majesty, that as you have granted to bring her to the appropriate age for marriage, so through marital union make this now-joined woman rejoice in your gift of the offspring she desires, and in your kindness bring her with her spouse to the length of years for which she hopes.[103]

Isidore of Seville said that "when women who have been married only once accompany these same virgins marrying legally, it is for the sake of an omen, nevertheless an omen of something good,

---

[103] Verona 1107.

namely for monogamy."[104] He may have been referring to a practice presumed by the Gelasian's prayer over the offerings and this *Hanc igitur*.

With some minor variations, this prayer appears in the Gelasian Sacramentary,[105] the Gregorian Sacramentary,[106] the Fulda Sacramentary,[107] the Roman-Germanic Pontifical,[108] and in the twelfth-century Roman Pontifical.[109] In these the role of the presenting bridesmaid is replaced with the "whole family" noted in every usage of this eucharistic prayer.

As the study group prepared its thoughts on a *Hanc igitur*, it made this report of the discussions:

> Bishop Henri Jenny [of Cambrai, France] objected: Private lives are not referenced in the preface and in the *Hanc igitur*, but only the economy of the common salvation of all. Bishop Michele Pellegrino [of Turin, Italy] observed that the difficulty could not be resolved until after considering the question of prefaces in general.
>
> The experts therefore responded. The study group on the Order of Mass unanimously thinks that a proper preface and a proper *Hanc igitur* must be inserted into the Mass for matrimony (Wagner). —Indeed, in the *Hanc igitur*, one does not pray for the whole Church, but for that part of the community that is present (P. Bruylants). —The objection proposed presupposes that matrimony is something merely private; in fact, it pertains to the mystery of Christ himself and the church. Therefore, it has its place in the eucharistic prayer (Prof. Fischer). Bishop Jenny agreed with this final response.[110]

The group agreed to proceed, though Bishop Botero thought that the preface and *Hanc igitur* should not be required but *ad*

---

[104] Isidore of Seville, *De ecclesiasticus offices* II, 20: 5. PL 83:811.

[105] Gelasian 1447.

[106] Gregorian 836.

[107] Fulda Sacramentary, 2609.

[108] PRG II:416.

[109] *Le Pontifical Romain* II:261.

[110] Schemata 182b, p. 3.

libitum.[111] He did not get his wish. The priest is expected to include these in the eucharistic prayer.

The first draft was prepared in 1967,[112] and it was essentially the one that appears in paragraph 118 of the first edition, with minor variations.

203 (ETA 238).

For Eucharistic Prayer II, the priest inserts an intercession in the second half of the prayer, asking God that the couple may abide in mutual love and peace.

204 (ETA 239).

For Eucharistic Prayer III, the priest prays that the couple may be faithful to the covenant they have sealed. As with the commemorations in Eucharistic Prayers I and II, this one mentions the couple by name and affirms that God has brought them to their wedding day. One should not make too much of this, but this is the only one of the three prayers that proclaims that God brought them "happily" to their wedding day.

VII. OTHER PRAYERS OF NUPTIAL BLESSING

The title for this section has changed in the second edition. The first edition called it literally "Prayer over the Bride and Groom," which the first English translation rendered as "Nuptial Blessing."

205 (ETA 240).

Parentheses indicate phrases that may be omitted in circumstances when one partner is not receiving communion or the two are unable to have children. This repeats some material from OCM 72.

The second edition has reworked this material that began paragraph 120 in the first edition. The new paragraph specifies that changes may be made both to the invitation and to the prayer. It also removes the permission to omit sections of the nuptial

[111] Ibid.
[112] Schemata 248, p. 12.

blessing, leaving behind parts that relate to the readings. Now, the entire blessing is to be used.

205A.

The English language edition adds to this section the invitation to the first nuptial blessing as it appears in OCM 73 and 104, now with musical notation. These do not appear in the Latin original, which explains why the title of this section is "other prayers" in Latin. Actually, all the prayers are here in English.

205B.

The nuptial blessing from OCM 74 and 105 is reprinted here with musical notation. The translation copies what already existed in the Missal. It does not appear in this place in Latin, so it carries the same number as the preceding paragraphs, but with the letter B.

206 (ETA 241).

With hands joined, the minister invites all to pray for the couple. This is the former paragraph 120, which gave instructions for a priest presider. Now it clarifies that a deacon may administer this blessing. The first edition also instructed the priest to turn and face the couple, but this rubric has been removed, probably because the minister should already be facing that direction. The English translation supplies chant notation, which also exists in the original Latin. All pray in silence.

This introduction (and the prayer) that follows were drafted by Ligier and circulated through the study group in 1966.[113] The original draft was quite lengthy, nearly twice the number of words in the final version. Ligier called it "Blessing of the bride in which the theme of the Church-Bride encircles the couple." Even his original introduction was prolix by comparison with the final one:

> Humbly and fraternally let us pray for these servants, who, joined in matrimony (or, "entering matrimony today") come before the face of God our Father, like the Church in the presence of the Son, so that in sharing the one bread and the one cup, having been built up

---

[113] Schemata 183, pp. 8–10.

in Christ and on fire through the Holy Spirit, they may be perfected with mutual and holy love.[114]

Mazzarello abbreviated this introduction into the form that came to be used in both editions of the OCM.[115]

207 (ETA 242).
This is the second possibility for the nuptial blessing given by a priest or deacon. It is the former paragraph 120. The second edition has added an epiclesis over the couple and made some minor adjustments for clarity, such as the introduction of parentheses around phrases that may be omitted. The translation here was carried over from the Missal. Chant notation is supplied, as it is in the Latin original at this place.
Here is a translation of Ligier's original lengthy prayer:

Holy Father, who established the human race, created male and female in your image to a full likeness in your Son, so that man and woman, joined in unity of heart and flesh, might fulfill their mission in the world; who also, to reveal the plan of your charity, traced the image of the covenant with the chosen people in the love of spouses, upholding the bride as a kind of new Jerusalem, and the groom as a figure of your only-begotten Son handing over his life on the cross for the Church; look now, and seeing the mystery of the church in these two servants, kindly pour upon them the blessings of that Bride by whom Christ restored to you the universe in the unity of the Spirit.

Kindly extend over both of them the right hand of your blessing, and surround and gladden them at the same time, because, with you as their leader on the road, they have come together, and through the sacrament have mystically become the only bride of your Christ. Grant that, having been rooted in him and mutually opened, knowing and feeling together, they may progress always united in the same charity. Grant that receiving your gifts, one now from another, in the partnership of matrimony, they may be a sign of your presence to each other; that they may faithfully keep the treasure of marital love from all profanation; that, flourishing in the

---

[114] Ibid., 8.
[115] Schemata 248, p. 12; Stevenson, *To Join Together*, 145.

delight by which you created the universe, they may try to increase life from you; that, as parents devoutly returning love, they may rejoice to see their children and their children's children; building a prosperous and worthy home by their own labor, may they delight in the companionship of friends and in conversation with your poor; illumined by your Spirit and devoted to the commandments of Christ with the wisdom of faith, instructing children with the doctrines of the gospel, and attentive to the needs of their neighbor, may they ascend together to the life of holiness; may they be known for the integrity of their actions in good times and in bad; may they bring light to those who are seeking, and show themselves to be examples of the faithfulness of conjugal love and of fraternal affection, and witnesses of your charity.

Be pleased now especially to bless your servant N., as you blessed your Son from eternity, whom you established as the heir of your power and generosity. Make him, who is esteemed as the head of the family, remain firm in goodness, chastity and remarkable obedience, and conduct his duties in the provident and generous spirit of a husband and father.

And endow your servant N., his wife, with most abundant blessings, that her heart may shine with sincere kindness and love for her family, and she may win the reverence of all in her house and be able to fulfill the duty of wife and mother every day. Sanctify her, that she may announce by her holiness and chastity the Christian newness of the world, glorious before your Son, and that she may now be judged worthy to be known as a sole image of the Bride, the Church.

And grant that both, continuous participants in the mysteries of the body and blood of your Son, may draw thanks for the blessing of the Church, the peace and perfection of mutual love, the communion of the Holy Spirit, the desire to increase the complete fullness of the mystical body of Christ, and the firm hope of reaching for ever, after a peaceful fullness of years, the exultation of the heavenly bride, foreshadowed on this day. Through the same Christ our Lord.[116]

Mazzarello simplified this prayer considerably,[117] and that is the version, with minor variations, that appeared in the first edition of the OCM.

---

[116] Schemata 183, pp. 9–10.
[117] Schemata 284, pp. 12–13.

In Latin, the opening lines, recalling creation, refer to the union of "a man and a woman," which is how ICEL translated it. The final English translation changes this to "husband and wife" to specify the kind of relationship the church expects of a sexual union.

One of the pastoral difficulties with the final prayer is that it concludes with a reference to the couple's participation in the Eucharist, yet this is one of the nuptial blessings permitted in celebrating the matrimony of a Catholic with a non-Catholic (OCM 105). It does not make an appropriate choice in that instance.

208 (ETA 243).

This is the third choice to introduce the nuptial blessing. The minister turns toward the bride and groom, and invites all to pray for them. This rubric in Latin and in English, unlike the one in OCM 206, tells the minister where to face. Perhaps the omission in 206 was an oversight.

The translation is carried over from the Missal, and OCM 208 provides chant notation. This is the first part of the former paragraph 121.

The original draft was prepared by Jungmann. His proposed introduction shows how the study group still considered this a blessing of the bride, though expanded. In fact, Jungmann called it, "The Blessing of the Bride, Not Directly Mentioning the Groom."

> Let us pray, dearest brothers and sisters, to God the almighty Father, that he pour out the abundance of his blessing upon the great sacrament of matrimony begun today, and especially upon this bride here present, that by his helping grace she may become and remain a perfect figure of the holy church, which is the bride of Christ.[118]

This introduction was edited to shift its focus away from the bride and to eliminate the reference to the word "sacrament." These changes were evident in the second draft,[119] and they entered the first edition of the OCM only slightly altered.

[118] Schemata 183, p. 8.
[119] Schemata 248, p. 14.

The final translation of this shows another place where ICEL preferred the word "will" to "may." The invitation garners prayers that God will do something; ICEL felt that praying that God "may" do something could make it appear that God may not be capable of doing it. "May" appears in the final translation of the Missal, however, carried over here.

209 (ETA 244).

The third nuptial blessing prays for a fruitful and happy union. This is the prayer that appeared in paragraph 121 of the first edition, amplified with an epiclesis for the second edition. An English translation appeared in the third edition of the Missal and is copied here.

As with Ligier's proposal, Jungmann's also underwent considerable revision. Here is a translation of his first draft proposed to the study group:

> O Lord, holy Father, almighty eternal Father, maker of the human race, who created humans male and female, who gave Eve to Adam as a complement and a helper like himself, and who thus taught that what God has joined together cannot be separated by a human;
> O God, who willed that the covenant of matrimony imitate that blessed union by which your Son, made human, was joined to the Church, from which she might take an example of his fidelity and of an indissoluble partnership, by which you willed that a woman be bound to a man, and a man to a woman, for ever;
> Look kindly upon this your servant N., who today has been joined in the covenant of matrimony, and grant that as the Church, the Bride, clings to your Son in perpetual charity, so she may remain devoted to her husband in unfailing charity through all the challenges of life; may she be a constant helper and concerned for him; may she rejoice with him as a loving mother in the happy flowering of growing offspring;
> O God, who have imparted a stronger feeling of goodness in a woman's heart, give every product of virtue to your servant, that with full faith and charity, she may be an illustrious example to her house, and a never-failing font of love for her household—in the praise and glory of your name, through the same Christ our Lord.[120]

[120] Schemata 183, p. 8.

This was considerably reworked for the first edition of the OCM's paragraph 121. The end of its first section was amplified to include the husband to whom the bride was joined, and the second edition changed this again to "your servants." The transition from the blessing of the bride to the blessing of the couple, so resisted during the discussions in the 1960s, has been complete.

The second edition also introduces places where the minister may insert the names of the couple. This is done more broadly in other vernacular traditions, but the English does not expand on the Latin.

The French Canadian edition has additional options for the nuptial blessing, as indicated above at OCM 74, with optional rubrics. One of the blessings has a repeated acclamation for the people to sing: "Blessed are you, O Lord, your love performs marvels for us."[121]

The Mexican edition presents five different invitations to the nuptial blessing all in one place.[122] These are interchangeable with any nuptial blessing. It also includes a fourth nuptial blessing, which "comes from the ancient Hispanic tradition preserved in the Mozarabic liturgy. It may be used in special circumstances." It includes a series of ten petitions, after each of which the people answer, "Amen." This translates a venerable prayer found in the *Liber Ordinum*,[123] which the study group discussed in its deliberations over the final blessing at the wedding Mass, as shown in the commentary on OCM 77.

VIII. PRAYERS AFTER COMMUNION

The Missal's three possibilities for the prayer after communion have been copied here. In Latin these are identical to the prayers from the first edition of the OCM.

The French Canadian edition does not have this section because the prayers have been integrated into the first chapter on celebrating weddings within Mass.

---

[121] *Rituel Romain*, 134.
[122] *Ritual* (Mexico), pp. 242–43.
[123] *Liber Ordinum*, 299–300.

210 (ETA 245).

The priest prays that God will make this couple one heart in love. This is the prayer from the former paragraph 122, now with parentheses around the phrase that refers to the couple sharing communion. Normally, both partners are Catholic at a wedding within Mass, but sometimes one is not. This prayer may be adjusted if one spouse is not receiving communion.

This is the traditional prayer after communion. It first appeared in the Verona Sacramentary, though at another part of the Mass before the nuptial blessing.[124] The Verona had no special prayer after communion for this Mass, and the one in the Gelasian was one that the Verona had used as a collect.[125] That is the prayer that had served as the collect in the 1570 Missal but has since been completely replaced by six other options.

The Gregorian Sacramentary, then, was the first to take the prayer from the Verona and position it after communion.[126] Both the Roman-Germanic Pontifical[127] and the twelfth-century Roman Pontifical retained it.[128] It remained in place through the life of the 1570 Missal, and now is the OCM's first option. The study group made a few minor changes to the traditional prayer,[129] which were kept for the first edition. Stevenson says that some of this new material came from the 1738 Paris Missal.[130] Most notably among these changes, the study group inserted the very phrase that the second edition now sets in parentheses: "and replenished with the one Bread and the one Chalice." The parentheses are there not to provide a more historically authentic version of the prayer but to accommodate the circumstance when one partner will not be receiving communion.

211 (ETA 246).

In the second option the priest leads all those who have received communion in a prayer that the couple may hold fast to God and

[124] Verona 1108.
[125] Gelasian 1455.
[126] Gregorian 839.
[127] PRG II:417.
[128] *Le Pontifical Romain*, I:262 and 302.
[129] Schemata 248, p. 14.
[130] Stevenson, *To Join Together*, 147.

proclaim his name to the world. This is the former paragraph 123. The study group composed this prayer,[131] and one can see in it the postconciliar interest in evangelization. The Latin word order changed only slightly between the draft and the first edition. This is the prayer that OCM 115 suggests for a wedding without Mass at which some of those present are receiving communion.

212 (ETA 247).
   The final choice prays that the power of communion may grow in the couple, and that all may experience the effects of the sacrifice. This is the former paragraph 124. It was newly composed by the study group[132] and emended slightly for the first edition of the OCM.

IX. BLESSINGS AT THE END OF THE CELEBRATION
   The title of this section has changed slightly in Latin. It used to be "Blessings at the End of Mass." But the second edition realizes that not all weddings take place at Mass, and these blessings may be used in other circumstances.
   In the study group, Lécuyer compiled eight blessings drawn from Ritzer's collection, lightly edited. He indicated the page from Ritzer's book that inspired his list.

   1) May the almighty Lord bless you with the eloquence of his dew and join your heart in a perpetual bond of sincere love (p. 359).
   2) May the Lord bless you with endless blessing and may your seed be a blessing for ever and ever (p. 353).
   3) May the Lord grant long life and endless joy to you whom he has brought to marital joy (p. 354).
   4) As the Lord Jesus Christ, the redeemer of all, gave his disciples the fullness of blessing, may he make it reach your souls and bodies abundantly (p. 355).
   5) May the Lord grant you endless gifts, happily extended times with your parents, and eternal joys with all those present (p. 359, somewhat changed).
   6) May peace, gentleness and tenderness remain in you, so that in one spirit and body you may obtain the fruit you desire from the marriage you have received (p. 360).

[131] Schemata 248, p. 15.
[132] Ibid.

7) May the almighty God (, who created our first parents Adam and Eve by a singular excellence, and who sanctified them with his blessing and joined them into union with him, himself) sanctify and bless your hearts and bodies, and join you in a true partnership of love (p. 361, the parentheses may be deleted).

8) May our Lord Jesus Christ, who consecrated marriage by his presence and by a miracle (when he changed water into wine), himself be pleased to be present at your wedding and to sanctify and bless you (p. 362, the parentheses may be deleted).[133]

Lécuyer recommended three other blessings from page 362 of Ritzer's book, but he did not include these texts in the group's report. None of these blessings ended up in the final edition of the OCM. In the following draft appear the three blessings that ultimately entered the OCM, along with a note that "each blessing is addressed first to the couple, and then to all present."[134]

213 (ETA 248).

The first option for the blessing prays for the unity, fruitfulness, and faith of the couple. It is the same blessing that appears at OCM 77. It was in the first edition as paragraph 125.

214 (ETA 249).

The second choice uses a trinitarian structure. The study group composed this for the drafts, and it was adopted into the first edition at paragraph 126. Its origins are explained in the commentary on OCM 77, which justified the structure from a trinitarian blessing at Matins.[135] Wherever it may have appeared that the study group was proposing something novel, it helped if they could argue from the Roman tradition.

215 (ETA 250).

This third possibility is a christological blessing recalling the wedding at Cana and the love of Christ "to the end." The study

---

[133] Schemata 183, pp. 10–11.
[134] Schemata 248, p. 15.
[135] Ibid.

group included it in its draft as well,[136] and it appeared in the first edition as paragraph 127.

Like the previous blessing, this was newly composed for the OCM. It may have been inspired by a blessing that Lécuyer referenced but did not quote in full when he concluded his list of eight blessings that were all set aside from the first edition. That prayer, from a book of blessings from eleventh-century Canterbury, opened this way:

> May God, who not only willed to come to a wedding, but also to work the first of his miracles there, be pleased to bless this male servant and his female servant about to be coupled in the nuptial bed, as well as the people present.[137]

The reference to the miracle at Cana links these two blessings. It draws a fitting close to the prayers and rubrics contained in the main body of the OCM.

The Mexican edition concludes this section with a suggested dismissal formula.

> *The dismissal may be done with the following words that make evident the mission and marital witness in the church.*
>
> Give witness in the Church and in the world; give the gift of life and love that you have celebrated.
>
> In the peace of Christ, go to serve God and your brothers and sisters.[138]

---

[136] Schemata 248, p. 16.

[137] Korbinian Ritzer, *Formen, Riten und Religiöses Brauchtum der Eheschliessung in den Christlichen Kirchen des Ersten Jahrtausends* (Münster: Aschendorffsche Verlagsbuchhandlung, 1962), 362.

[138] *Ritual* (Mexico), 260.

Appendices

All these appendices have been newly added to the second edition of the OCM. The first edition had no samples of the universal prayer, no order of blessing an engaged couple, and no order of blessing a married couple on their anniversary. Pastoral needs for all three circumstances have led to a welcome addition to the OCM.

I. EXAMPLES OF THE UNIVERSAL PRAYER

As mentioned in the commentary on OCM 69, the study group at first referred people to a collection of prayers called *De oratione communi seu fidelium*, which the Vatican had published in 1966.[1] It contained sample prayers of the faithful in Latin and in French. The ones proposed for weddings are as follows:

> A
> Most beloved brothers and sisters,
> for the peace of all the world, for the happy state of the Church,
> and for the unity of all people,
> let us pray together to Christ the Lord;
> not forgetting those who are joined today by the nuptial covenant in Christ.
> B
> For all Christian people;
> that they may grow in virtue day by day,
> let us pray to the Lord.
> D (C is placed after D here, lest it seem that the state of those getting married appear immediately after the petition for those suffering misfortune)

---

[1] See also Schemata 248, p. 16.

For those afflicted with troubles, or injuries,
or other miseries;
that the One who has mercy may help and free them,
let us pray to the Lord.
C
For the peace of the whole world;
that each one may work carefully according to his or her ability to
    increase it,
let us pray to the Lord.
E
1. For these faithful Christians N. and N.,
now joined in holy matrimony,
and for their perpetual health and well-being,
let us pray to the Lord.
2. That he will bless their covenant,
as he chose to sanctify the marriage at Cana in Galilee,
let us pray to the Lord.
3. That children may be granted to them for the continuance of the race,
we pray to the Lord.
4. That perfect love, peace and strength may be granted them,
let us pray to the Lord.
5. That they may remain happy in strong faith and harmony,
and that they bear faithful witness to the name of Christian,
let us pray to the Lord.
6. That the grace of the Sacrament
will be renewed by the Holy Spirit
in all married couples here present,
let us pray to the Lord.
7. That he may receive all our friends who have now departed from
    this life
into the kingdom of his glory,
let us pray to the Lord.
F
Almighty, everlasting God,
look kindly upon these your servants, and grant
that trusting in you alone,
they may receive the gifts of your grace,
preserve charity in unity,
and after the course of this life,

they may reach the joys of eternal blessedness
together with their children.
Through Christ our Lord.[2]

This set of petitions never received an official English translation, nor was it broadly disseminated for vernacular usage. The
samples in the OCM are the first to obtain that distinction.

The French Canadian publication includes some additional
versions approved for their conference, along with a selection of
responses for the people.[3] In Colombia, the samples were moved
from the appendix into the body of the book, where the presider
can find them more easily. The Mexican edition put nine complete
sample sets of petitions in the preceding section together with the
other texts to be used.[4]

216 (ETA 251).

The first sample of the universal prayer includes petitions for
the couple, as well as for all Christian people. The influence of the
Vatican's 1966 collection is clear. The number of petitions is dimin-
ished and the sequence has been reordered, but all the petitions
were inspired by the 1966 collection.

The introduction is newly composed for the second edition,
completely changing the 1966 introduction. It is a rare instance in
which the bride is mentioned before the groom—even in the Latin
original.

217 (ETA 252).

The second sample includes a more expansive list of petitions:
for the couple, their relatives and friends, all families, family members who have died, the church, and the unity of Christians. This
was freely composed for the second edition of the OCM without a
clear precedent even in the 1966 collection.

---

[2] *De oratione communi seu fidelium: Natura, momentum ac structura, Criteria atque specimina, Coetibus territorialibus Episcoporum proposita* (Vatican City: Libreria Editrice Vaticana, 1966), 148–51.

[3] *Rituel Romain*, 137–38.

[4] *Ritual* (Mexico), 224–34.

The formula that opens the concluding prayer is unusual, "Lord Jesus, who are present in our midst." It is rare for a prayer to address the second Person of the Trinity. Furthermore, an early literal translation had no relative clause: "Lord Jesus, present in our midst," but ICEL members saw that the word "present" could be read as an indicative command verb, rather than an adjective. The extra words "who are" were inserted.

II. THE ORDER OF BLESSING AN ENGAGED COUPLE

The *Book of Blessings* (BB) has long included an order of blessing an engaged couple,[5] and it predates the second edition of the OCM, which now places the ceremony in an appendix with minor variations.

The ritual gives no indications for the posture of the assembly or the leader. The conventions of Mass could be followed—stand for most of the ceremony but sit for nongospel readings and the reflection that follows the readings. But the informality of the situation may suggest that all sit or stand throughout.

218 (ETA 253).

The first paragraph of the introduction gives the rationale for offering a blessing on those who are engaged. This is identical to BB 195, except for the omission of the first phrase in the final paragraph: "In order that the celebration will better achieve its purpose." Perhaps that was thought to be understood. The final line is important: the ceremony may be adapted to accommodate particular needs.

219 (ETA 254).

A family member may preside, especially if only the two families are present. A priest or deacon, if present, should preside but should not give the impression that this is a wedding. This is BB 196.

This paragraph says that even a layperson "presides" at this celebration. The English translation of the OCM in the United

---

[5] BB, 195–214.

States largely reserves that verb for a priest or deacon. But the *Book of Blessings* is comfortable with it in circumstances such as this.

220 (ETA 255).
The leader should adapt the order of service to the circumstances. This is BB 197. It permits a lay presider, which is common in the *Book of Blessings*, though rare in the English translation of the OCM for use in the United States.

221 (ETA 256).
This service could take place as part of the marriage preparation that a parish offers. It is, however, never to be combined with a wedding. This is BB 198.
In the history of the church, however, there have been celebrations that included both the betrothal and the wedding. To cite one example, the Byzantine Rite merged these ceremonies.[6] Nonetheless, the pastoral insight is good: the engagement should precede the wedding by a considerable amount of time.
The ceremony is written with a single couple in mind. Some parishes prepare engaged couples in groups and may prefer to celebrate this with more than one couple at a time. The OCM does not foresee this possibility, even though it does with the celebration of matrimony. The rubrics, however, permit great flexibility, so there would be no problem with a multi-couple celebration.

The Introductory Rites

222 (ETA 257).
The ceremony begins with a sign of the cross and a greeting. This paragraph combines and refines information from BB 199 and 200.
The sign of the cross "is made." Presumably, this happens as it does at Mass, where the minister says the words, all make the gesture, and the people answer "Amen."[7] In fact, that is how it appears in BB 199. But the OCM gives no such details. If all want

[6] Mark Searle and Kenneth W. Stevenson, *Documents of the Marriage Liturgy* (Collegeville, MN: Liturgical Press, 1992), 55.
[7] OM 1.

to say the words together while making the gesture, the rubric permits it.

If a priest or deacon is presiding, he gives the suggested greeting, or another from the Missal. This departs from the Latin edition of the OCM as well as from BB 200, both of which say that the presider may take words from the Sacred Scriptures. This is not Mass, so it is not clear why the greeting must be taken from the Missal, but that is how the English translation of the OCM reads.

The suggested greeting is unique. It relates to the second option of the greeting in the Order of Mass, "Grace to you and peace from God our Father and the Lord Jesus Christ,"[8] but it adds another phrase. The added material comes from Ephesians 5:25, which admonishes husbands to love their wives as Christ loved the church and gave himself up for it. That image of marital life inspired by Christ's life is embedded in the greeting for the betrothal ceremony.

223 (ETA 258).

If a layperson is leading the ceremony, he or she makes the sign of the cross and invites all to praise Christ. All answer, "Amen." This combines the sign of the cross from BB 199 with the greeting in 201.

The Catholic liturgy reserves the usual greeting and the response, "And with your spirit," to a priest or deacon who presides. A layperson uses another formula. This one is inspired by the same passage from Ephesians used in the greeting of a priest or deacon in the previous paragraph.

In reality, people will only answer "Amen" if someone prompts them or if they have a participation aid that they can read.

Because this ceremony is lifted from the *Book of Blessings*, this is the only place that the entire OCM refers to a lay presider as a "minister." The OCM prefers to restrict that word to a priest or deacon. But it is used throughout this ceremony to define the role of the one who leads the service, even a layperson.

[8] Ibid., 2.

224 (ETA 259).

The minister introduces the ceremony, inviting all to pray for the couple as they begin their preparations for marriage. This is BB 202. The rubric is similar to those in OCM 52 and 87.

Reading of the Word of God

The proclamation of the Word of God is dear to the Catholic liturgy in general. The OCM suggests several possibilities for this ceremony. The Latin original gives only biblical citations here, but the edition for the United States provides the entire text of all the alternatives.

The study group working on the *Book of Blessings* at first recommended other Scripture readings for the blessing of those who are engaged: Deuteronomy 30:15-20, where Israel faces the choice of accepting or rejecting the commands of the Lord; Matthew 5:14-16, where Jesus calls his disciples the light of the world; and 1 Corinthians 13:4-13, Paul's hymn to love, the only recommendation to find its way into the finished *Book of Blessings* for this ceremony, recaptured here in OCM 226.[9]

225 (ETA 260).

One of those present or the minister reads a passage; for example, John 15:9-12. This is BB 203. It repeats the reading from OCM 185.

The rubric establishes this order of preference: someone else reads; if not, then the minister who is leading the ceremony. Normally the proclamation of Scripture is not a function of the presider.

The reader introduces the passage with a formula different from the one heard at Mass. Because the reader may be a lay minister, the usual introduction of the gospel, which is reserved for a priest or deacon, is not provided. Instead a different formula positions itself here: "Listen, brothers and sisters, to the words of . . ." This borrows from ETA 125, which describes the entire wedding ceremony when a layperson assists.

[9] Schemata 372, p. 4.

The first suggested passage comes from Jesus' final discourse at the Last Supper. He leaves the command to love, and his command is quite localized: He asks his disciples to love one another. There are other places where he asks them to love their neighbor and even to love their enemy. But perhaps aware of the infighting that can happen within any close-knit group, he asks those at table with him to love the other people at table. The intimacy of this command will give an engaged couple a source of reflection.

226 (ETA 261).

The most beloved of all wedding readings, the hymn to love from Paul's First Letter to the Corinthians, serves as a second option. As noted in OCM 157, this passage has nothing to do with engagement, and everything to do with the normal behavior of Christians toward one another. Still, it strikes a chord with the experience that many couples have. This is BB 204.

227 (ETA 262).

In the third choice the prophet Hosea hears God betrothing himself to his people. A fourth possibility appears here as well: Philippians 2:1-5, where Paul encourages the community to have the same mind. Both these come from BB 205. Neither of these passages is listed among the recommended readings for a wedding. Perhaps that shared distinction explains how they ended up in the same paragraph.

228 (ETA 263).

Following the reading, a psalm or another suitable song may be sung. The OCM recommends Psalm 145 (144). This is BB 206 but with the Grail translation of the verses and a new translation of the refrain. Psalm 145 concerns the goodness of God, who has brought the couple together, and who inspires their goodness.

In pastoral practice, it may seem odd to have a responsorial psalm follow a gospel, but this is fairly common in the *Book of Blessings*. It subtly indicates a difference between this ceremony and the Mass.

229 (ETA 264).

The one who presides may explain the reading and the difference between this ceremony and the celebration of matrimony. This is BB 209.

The rubric avoids using the word "homily," which is reserved to a priest or deacon. A layperson, however, may give some other explanation, for which the liturgy will not assign the same word for a similar event taking place at Mass.

The expression "shedding light" also appears in the description of the homily in Holy Thursday's Mass of the Lord's Supper: "[T]he Priest gives a homily in which light is shed on the principal mysteries that are commemorated in this Mass."[10]

Prayers

The gathered community offers prayers for the couple. Normally this is called the universal prayer or the prayer of the faithful, but this is not Mass, and some of those present may not be among the Christian faithful. Besides, the vocabulary comes directly from BB 208, so it fits the circumstance of a blessing.

230 (ETA 265).

The presider may use, adapt, or replace the petitions presented here for Christians, all people, families, and the engaged couple. This is BB 208, though with the introduction of sense lines and the option for the people to give a different response.

ICEL had discussions about several words here. The introduction has the Latin word *homines*, which ICEL at first translated "men and women" to stress the gender inclusivity of the term. It was insufficient, however, because it seemed to eliminate children. The final decision, "all people," is a fairly expansive translation of the Latin word. Regarding the expression "gentle demands," an earlier translation, "sweet constraints" was more literal but ultimately found too obscure. The word "delight" was also questioned, but the Latin vocabulary for "love' in the OCM is quite varied, and the decision reflected the acknowledgment that "delight" is a property of this stage of a close relationship.

[10] Roman Missal, Mass of the Lord's Supper 9.

The petitions include a number of biblical allusions. The expression "children in Christ" is an oblique reference to Galatians 4:5-6, which says that Christians receive adoption as children. Saying that God revealed people "to the world as witnesses of his love" recalls Acts 22:15, where Ananias gives a similar command to the newly converted Saul. The petition affirming that Christ "loved the Church" refers to Ephesians 5:25, and that the church was "washed clean in his Blood" comes from Revelation 7:14.

231 (ETA 266).
The engaged couple may give some sign of their commitment. They may give rings or gifts, or they may sign a document. This should not, of course, be a kind of prenuptial agreement specifying the results in case of a divorce. This paragraph copies BB 209.

232 (ETA 267).
The minister may say a blessing over the rings or gifts if these are presented. This is BB 210.

In the Mexican edition, this instruction follows the words of this blessing: "Where it is customary, the parents of the engaged couple may present them with a bible or an image of Jesus Christ, the Virgin or some saint."[11]

Prayer of Blessing
The highlight of this ceremony is the actual prayer of blessing, which the presider says at this point. The presider may choose from two alternatives.

233 (ETA 268).
A priest or deacon extends his hands over the couple, but a lay presider, who is the more likely leader of this celebration, keeps hands joins. These are conventions observed throughout the OCM and the BB. The suggested prayer praises God for the love of this couple and prays for their strength. This is BB 211.

[11] *Ritual* (Mexico), 268.

The same study group 23 that worked on the sacramental rites such as matrimony and the initiation rites also prepared the *Book of Blessings*. Their first draft did not contain this prayer.[12] Perhaps it was added for the circumstance when the presider was not a priest or deacon. In some Latin American countries, however, it is common to see parents making the sign of the cross over their children, imitating the gesture of a priest or deacon.

The line about "keeping faith" is possibly an allusion to 2 Timothy 4:7. The phrase "pleasing you in all things" could refer to Colossians 1:10.

234 (ETA 269).

When the presider is a priest or deacon, he says this prayer and makes the sign of the cross over the couple, a gesture that the liturgy reserves for a clergyman and removes from lay presiders. The prayer asks that the couple grow in mutual respect, and love with true charity. This is BB 212.

The final version made a few enhancements to the original one prepared by the study group.[13] Most significantly, it adds the words "sustained by heavenly blessing," and it inserted a red cross, which traditionally instructs the minister to trace the sign of the cross with his hand. The first version prayed for the couple, but it never actually used the word "blessing."

At ICEL's suggestion, the English translation has the leader insert the names of the couple, even though the Latin original simply calls them "these young people." The CDWDS approved this. The decision reflects the reality that not all engaged couples are young and the pastoral realization that stating names makes prayers more personal and precise.

The French Canadian edition has extra alternative prayers of blessing approved for their conference.[14] Both the prayers in OCM 233 and 234 are assigned to a priest or deacon and edited with a red cross, indicating their gesture of blessing. Another locally composed blessing is added to these, complete with the cross. Then the

[12] Schemata 372, p. 5.
[13] Ibid.
[14] *Rituel Romain*, 147–48.

first option and the newly composed prayer are reprinted without the red cross; these provide two alternatives for the lay presider.

Conclusion of the Rite

235 (ETA 270).

The presider says a final prayer for God's assistance. This is BB 213. Even if a priest or deacon presides, there is no blessing at the end. The only blessing is the one over the couple that gives this ceremony its purpose. The French Canadian edition, however, requested and obtained permission for a priest or deacon to give a final blessing over the people.[15]

The prayer has biblical allusions. Paul concludes one letter with a prayer that the God of love and peace will be with his readers.[16] One of the Old Testament proverbs says that one may make plans but the Lord directs one's steps.[17]

236 (ETA 271).

A suitable song may conclude the celebration. Anyone may lead it and participate. Or it may be omitted. This is BB 214. The same direction is found in OCM 107 and ETA 151.

III. THE ORDER OF BLESSING A MARRIED COUPLE WITHIN MASS ON THE ANNIVERSARY OF MATRIMONY

As with the Order of Blessing an Engaged Couple, the Order of Blessing a Married Couple was composed for the *Book of Blessings* after the publication of the first edition of the OCM. The second edition now includes it along with some enhancements.

The *Book of Blessings* puts these two orders of service in reverse order: first the anniversary, and then the engagement. But the outline of this entire section of the book begins with the family, goes to the parents' anniversary, and then moves to the blessing of children and the engaged, positioning this ceremony as a service for the next generation.

---

[15] *Rituel Romain*, 149.
[16] 2 Cor 13:11.
[17] Prov 16:9.

After an introduction (BB 90–93), the ceremony has several
forms: the order of blessing within Mass (BB 94–106), the order
of blessing a couple within Mass on occasions other than their
anniversary (BB 207–114), the order of blessing outside Mass (BB
115–131), and a shorter rite (BB 132–134).

By contrast, the study group's first draft of the ritual had it take
place as a blessing at the end of Mass "in the usual way."[18]

The OCM only includes the situation of blessing a couple on
their anniversary within Mass, the first of the four scenarios in the
Book of Blessings.

237 (ETA 272).

The couple may celebrate a special remembrance of the sacrament of matrimony on special anniversaries. The prayers for the
Mass are found in number 11 of the Missal's collection of Masses
for various needs and occasions. Three sets are provided, one for
a general anniversary, another for the twenty-fifth, and another
for the fiftieth. All those prayers were new to the post–Vatican II
Roman Missal. OCM 237 is BB 90. The translation of this paragraph comes from the Missal.

An anniversary Mass can be found in the tenth-century Roman-
Germanic Pontifical.[19] The 1570 Missal had a Mass for the twenty-
fifth and fiftieth anniversary of marriage.[20] A sign of increased human
longevity, the postconciliar *Book of Blessings* expanded the occasions
to include the sixtieth anniversary as well. The preconciliar Missal
did not have a special set of prayers for this occasion but referred
the priest to use either the votive Masses of the Holy Trinity or of the
Blessed Virgin Mary and then add the prayers from the votive Mass
in thanksgiving. These are no longer recommended because the Missal has developed its own special prayers for this occasion.

The liturgical calendar then and now governs when a votive
Mass may be used. Votive Masses now may be celebrated on weekdays in Ordinary Time.[21] The rector of a church or the priest who

[18] Schemata 372, p. 5.
[19] PRG II:417–419.
[20] *Missale Romanum*, p. [77].
[21] GIRM 355c.

celebrates may permit a votive Mass on days with an obligatory memorial or on a weekday of Advent up through December 16, of Christmas from January 2, and of Easter after the Octave if some real necessity or pastoral advantage calls for it.[22] An important wedding anniversary surely would fall into this category. On other days such as feasts, solemnities, and Sundays, however, the votive Mass cannot be used. The couple may celebrate an anniversary with this ritual and blessing, but the priest recites the appropriate presidential prayers of the feast from the Missal.

To some extent a bishop may determine otherwise. "If any case of graver need or pastoral advantage should arise," the bishop may authorize a votive Mass to be celebrated on a Sunday in Ordinary Time.[23] For example, a bishop could celebrate at the cathedral on a Sunday in Ordinary Time a votive Mass for fiftieth wedding anniversaries, complete with readings and prayers from the votive Mass, not from the Sunday liturgy.

The Roman Ritual also included a service for the silver or golden wedding anniversary.[24] The 1570 Missal said that the celebration takes place after the Mass, but the ritual said that it comes before the Mass. The ritual also said that if the couple never had received the nuptial blessing, the priest could impart it on this occasion. In that case he could use the prayers from the ritual Mass for marriage.

The *Book of Blessings* allowed the celebrant great freedom in the different versions of the ceremony (BB 93), but this does not appear in the OCM, apparently because the order of this service has been reworked, and its outline carries more weight than in the past.

238 (ETA 273).

The readings may be taken from the ritual Mass for marriage or from the Lectionary's Mass for Giving Thanks to God.[25] Again, the liturgical calendar governs the option of choosing other readings.

---

[22] GIRM 376.
[23] GIRM 374.
[24] *Roman Ritual*, 594–99.
[25] LM 943–947.

These may be used on days when the votive Mass may be celebrated. This is BB 94.

The 1614 Ritual recommended two specific readings now found among those for the ritual Mass of marriage: Genesis 2:18-24 (OCM 145) and John 2:1-11 (OCM 184).[26]

239 (ETA 274).

The priest gives an appropriate homily on the mystery and grace of married life. This is BB 95, except that it specifies that "the Priest" not just "the celebrant" gives this homily. Essentially, it is the same person because this celebration takes place at Mass.

This is similar to directions given the homilist when celebrating matrimony within and without Mass (OCM 57 and 91), but the purposes of the homily are applied to the particular circumstance of a couple who have experienced years of married life. Hence it does not need to mention the dignity of conjugal love or the responsibilities of married people.

The Roman Ritual included a lengthy allocution for the priest to use before offering his prayer.[27] It performed some of the function of a homily.

240 (ETA 275).

The priest invites the couple to pray in silence. A text is supplied, but he may use similar words. This is the rubric from BB 96, but the second edition of the OCM has scripted a new invitation that the priest may say. The names of the couple have been added to the English translation.

The word "vows" appears in the last line of the introduction, but the Latin original repeats the word for "promises" that appears in the previous sentence. The only other appearance of the word "vow" in the entire OCM is in the quotation from Tertullian in OCM 11. In the Catholic liturgy, the couple exchange "consent"— not "vows." The word "vows" applies to the promises made in religious life, not in marriage. In the culture, however, people commonly—though erroneously—refer to the marriage "vows." ICEL

---

[26] *Roman Ritual*, 598–99.
[27] *Roman Ritual*, 595–97.

translated the second appearance of the word for "promises" in this introduction as "vows," making a concession to this popular usage. The circumstance is not the wedding itself, but a ceremony recalling it, so a more flexible vocabulary seemed acceptable.

241 (ETA 276).

The couple have two options for renewing their commitment to each other. The first is to do it quietly. This rubric is new. It was implied in BB 96, but it is now made more explicit. Even though the order of blessing a couple within Mass has been part of the *Book of Blessings* since 1989, it has been common to hear couples repeat their matrimonial consent on the anniversary of marriage. The liturgy never promoted this, but in the absence of better guidance, the practice spread. Many couples realized the disconnection of the practice. Their initial consent was permanent and did not require repetition. Now the instructions are clearer. The couple renew their commitment quietly.

In French Canada a further explanation follows this brief rubric: "This is not a matter here of making again the exchange of consent to marry, which is unique."[28]

242 (ETA 277).

Alternatively, the couple may renew their commitment publicly. They offer words of praise to God, not a repetition of their consent to each other. The husband speaks first, and then the wife. Then both together may offer a prayer. The priest summarizes this with a prayer of his own. This is newly added to the material in the *Book of Blessings*.

The formulas recall the original words of consent, putting the verbs in the past tense as the couple recall the day on which they "took" their spouse. The expression "the good and the bad times" recalls another phrase from the consent (OCM 62, 96, ETA 130, and OCM 127). The words also bear a resemblance to the prayers during the preparation of the gifts at Mass. The priest blesses God for the gifts of bread and wine received "through your good-

---

[28] *Rituel Romain*, 150.

ness."[29] Here, the couple bless God for the gift of a spouse received "by your goodness."

The Blessing of Rings

Two options are offered for the blessing of rings, depending on whether or not the couple are exchanging new rings.

243 (ETA 278).

In the first option the priest may say a prayer to bless the couple's rings, the same ones they exchanged on their wedding day. He may then incense them. This is BB 97. It is not clear if the couple have removed their rings or if they continue wearing them for the incensation. The simplest solution is for the priest to invite the couple to extend their left hands together. Inspired by the rubrics of the Mass,[30] he would make a profound bow to the rings, make three swings of the censer, and then bow again.

The rings are not sprinkled with blessed water. This may have happened once before and need not be repeated. The incensation honors the previous blessing, whether or not it involved water.

The English translation has inserted the names of the couple where the Latin original does not have them. This helps personalize the ceremony and the prayer. The words "a sign of faithfulness" and "love for one another" repeat the description of the rings from one of the prayers that may have been used to bless them (OCM 195).

244 (ETA 279).

The couple may give each other new rings. If so, the priest says a blessing over them. This is BB 98, as well as the first part of BB 99, which accounts for the final permission to use OCM 194 instead of this prayer. That formula calls for the priest to bless the rings with a sign of the cross; however OCM 244 does not. BB 99 also permitted the priest to use the blessing found in OCM 195, but this was not carried over into the OCM. Like the previous example,

[29] OM 13 and 15.
[30] GIRM 277.

OCM 244 uses imagery from one of the blessings of rings (OCM 195). In Mexico, though, all three formulas are presented.[31]

These rings are not sprinkled with blessed water. Apparently this is to make a distinction between these and the rings that were given as the original sign of commitment on the wedding day.

245 (ETA 280).

Two options are presented for the petitions. These may proceed with the universal prayer (prayer of the faithful) as usual at Mass. Or the second option, a "prayer in common," may be used, and a sample is provided. In 1966 when the Vatican published sample intercessions, it called the book *Common Prayer, or [the Prayer] of the Faithful*.[32] The *Book of Blessings* frequently uses the term "common prayer" to refer to a set of petitions, often given apart from Mass. The structural difference is that the petitions are addressed directly to God, not announced to the people to elicit their prayer. A similar structure closes morning and evening prayer in the Liturgy of the Hours.

This is BB 100 with only minor variations. In the *Book of Blessings*, for example, each petition is divided in half by a dash, indicating the option that a leader may speak the first half and the people recite the second. That division is not marked in OCM 245.

Although ICEL avoided using the word "partnership" in many places of the OCM because of its connotations with cohabitation, the word remained in these petitions because in context its meaning would be fully understood. The same word is also used to describe marriage in the code of canon law.[33]

246 (ETA 281).

The priest concludes these petitions with a prayer of his own, asking that this family resemble the Holy Family. This is BB 101, although there he may use other words. He has the same permission, nevertheless, as he does at any Mass.

---

[31] *Ritual* (Mexico), 273–74.

[32] *De oratione communi seu fidelium.*

[33] Canon 1055 §1.

This prayer is similar to the collect from the Mass for the Family in the Missal's Masses for various needs and occasions.[34] The English translation of this prayer is based on the one from the Missal.

247 (ETA 282).

During the Liturgy of the Eucharist the husband and wife may carry bread, wine, and water to the altar. This is BB 102.

This is similar to OCM 70, where the evolution of this rubric can be traced in the accompanying comments. Different here is the inclusion of water, which also was mentioned in the 1965 schemata for the Order of Mass.[35] Just as the word "altar" in this rubric can be traced to that early draft, so may the word "water." Today the rubrics for the Mass say that bread and wine are brought to the altar,[36] or that bread and "wine with water" may be carried,[37] but this seems to refer to the custom of the deacon preparing wine with water at the side table and bringing the vessel to the altar.

The Roman-Germanic Pontifical recommended as a preface for the anniversary celebration the one that has been carried over as OCM 199 for the wedding Mass. It also included a *Hanc igitur* for the canon:

> Therefore, Lord, graciously accept this oblation of your servants N. and N., which they offer you on the anniversary day of their marriage, on which day you were pleased to unite them in a shared bond, for whom we humbly pour out our prayers to your awesome care, that they may equally reach the length of days well and peacefully, and may see their children's children to the third and fourth generation, and that they may bless you all the days of their lives. Through Christ our Lord.[38]

No *Hanc igitur* was added to the Missal for this occasion, however—probably to keep it distinct from the wedding.

---

[34] Roman Missal, Masses for Various Needs and Occasions, 12. For the Family.

[35] Schemata 113, p. 5.

[36] OM 22 and GIRM 73.

[37] GIRM 72a.

[38] PRG II: 417–18.

248 (ETA 283).

After the Lord's Prayer the priest omits the "Deliver us" and offers a prayer for the couple. He praises God for the gift of marriage in general and for the blessings bestowed on this couple in particular. He prays for their increased charity and blessing. All answer, "Amen." This is BB 103. The English translation of the rubric comes from the Missal's ritual Mass for marriage.

For the nuptial blessing during a wedding Mass (OCM 72), the priest faces the couple, though he will probably be doing this already. The same rubric appears for the blessing at an anniversary Mass.

Surprising for a wedding anniversary, the Roman-Germanic Pontifical had the priest repeat the Gelasian Sacramentary's blessing over the bride at the wedding.[39] The *Book of Blessings*, however, developed an entirely new prayer fitting for the occasion at hand.

This prayer compares the family life of the couple with Christ's union with the church, an allusion to Ephesians 5:25-33. A similar expression occurs in the first of the collects in the Missal's Mass for a wedding anniversary.[40] The expression "the circle of their children that surrounds them" is optional, depending on the family circumstances of the celebrating couple. The expression is redolent of one near the end of a nuptial blessing (OCM 139 and 209).

249 (ETA 284).

If appropriate, all may offer a sign of peace and charity. In a wedding during Mass, the sign is not optional (OCM 75), but it remains optional here as it is for a wedding without Mass (OCM 110) and in any other celebration of Mass.

250 (ETA 285).

The priest may offer the couple communion under both kinds, as in the celebration of matrimony within Mass (OCM 76).

251 (ETA 286).

The priest blesses everyone in the usual way, or he may use a solemn blessing. A threefold blessing invoking the Trinity is sug-

---

[39] PRG II: 418; Gelasian 1452.
[40] *Roman Missal*, Mass 11, For the Anniversaries of Marriage.

gested. This is BB 106. It is the same as the blessing in OCM 214, though without the reference to children. It includes the broader ending that appears at the end of all solemn blessings for weddings, so that all may make the distinction between the threefold blessing over the couple and the final blessing over the community.

The English translation for the rubric and the deacon's command that open this paragraph are taken from the section of blessings at the end of the Order of Mass in the Missal.

The first draft for the *Book of Blessings* contained only a solemn blessing. It was slightly more elaborate than this one.

BLESSING ON THE JUBILEE OF MATRIMONY
This blessing is given at the end of mass in the usual way.
May God the eternal Father keep you united at heart in mutual love so that the peace of Christ may dwell in you and remain in your home. Amen.

May the Only Begotten Son of God (gladden you always with the crown of children) and stand by you with compassion in good times and in bad. Amen.

May the Holy Spirit of God ever preserve the gift of the grace you have received, and endlessly pour forth his consolation into your hearts. Amen.

And may almighty God bless all of you, who are gathered here, the Father, and the Son, + and the Holy Spirit.[41]

In the draft, this was not just the final blessing. It was the complete order of blessing a couple on their anniversary. The original draft of this ceremony included nothing else—no readings, no other prayers, no rubrics. It has been greatly enriched with a full ceremony.

The Roman-Germanic Pontifical repeats after communion a blessing that first appeared in a similar place in the Gelasian Sacramentary,[42] a prayer noted above in comments about the conclusion of the wedding Mass (OCM 77). The Roman Ritual before the Second Vatican Council had a very simple blessing for the couple,

---

[41] Schemata 372, p. 5.
[42] PRG II:419.

as takes place near the end of any Mass. The priest sprinkled them with blessed water. This action no longer takes place.[43]

The second edition of the OCM published for England and Wales includes an extra appendix for convalidations, the occasions when a Catholic minister presides over a celebration of matrimony for a couple who were already bound civilly.[44] The civil formulas cannot be repeated. The complete ceremony is outlined and the ecclesial formulas are clearly presented.

The French Canadian edition has a brief prayer service for the situation of two catechumens or a catechumen and a non-Christian who have contracted a civil marriage. The church regards the civil ceremony as binding if it is the first marriage of two unbaptized people or if there are no impediments to a Catholic marriage. There is no need for the convalidation of such a union, so the French Canadian edition offers a way for the community to pray about the marriage even though the consent is not to be repeated.[45]

The same edition offers another short prayer for two married neophytes or for a neophyte and a Christian, on the day of baptism in a Catholic church or on one of the following Sundays. If there are no impediments to a Catholic marriage, no exchange of consent needs to take place for the sake of validity, but the ritual supplies prayers that a deacon or priest may offer for the couple.

Appendices in the Mexican edition include excerpts from the Ceremonial of Bishops. This section then suggests pairings of some of the readings in order to centralize a theme. It provides a pastoral commentary on the readings that carry an asterisk. It also includes homily suggestions.

[43] *Roman Ritual*, 598.
[44] Appendix IV.
[45] *Rituel Romain*, 156–58.

Afterword

The second edition of the Catholic Church's Order of Celebrating Matrimony has enriched the first edition and enhanced its vision of the mystery and celebration of married life. It provides better guidance for presiders, couples, and congregations. It keeps its heart focused on the liturgy of the church and the pastoral care of couples.

To be at prayer, standing in the presence of God, always is an awe-filled experience. This experience becomes focused in an excellent way when two people pledge their commitment to each other in the presence of witnesses and in the house of God. They undertake their responsibilities with hearts of joy and a desire to serve. The emotional stress surrounding a wedding picks up on this awe-filled commitment that people are about to experience. Those who in their prayer have encountered the love of God will witness its shining realization in the moments when two people—in one single moment of history and at one single geographical place—profess that they will stand for each other now, everywhere, and forever with inseparable love.

Bibliography

Bugnini, Annibale. *The Reform of the Liturgy 1948–1975*. Translated by Matthew J. O'Connell. Collegeville, MN: Liturgical Press, 1990.

Consilium ad exsequendam Constitutionem de Sacra Liturgia. Coetus a Studiis 22–23: De Sacramentis et Sacramentalibus. Schemata no. 32, De Rituali 2. 17 September 1964.

————. Schemata no. 113, De Missali, 14. 9 October 1965.

————. Schemata no. 157, De Missali, 11. 25 April 1966.

————. Schemata no. 157, De Rituali, 11-Adnexum. 13 May 1966.

————. Schemata no. 182, De Rituali, 14. 8 September 1966.

————. Schemata no. 182, Adunatio Romana Patrum. 17 October 1966.

————. Schemata no. 183. 25 August 1966.

————. Schemata no. 183, De Rituali, 15. 8 September 1966.

————. Schemata no. 204, De Rituali, 17. 8 February 1967.

————. Coetus a Studiis 23. Schemata no. 221, De Rituali, 19. 24 March 1967.

————. Schemata no. 221 bis, De Rituali, 19. 24 March 1967.

————. Schemata no. 248, De Rituali, 23. 11 October 1967.

————. Schemata no. 280, De Rituali, 27. 21 March 1968.

————. Allegato allo Schemata no. 280, De Rituali, 27. 6 May 1968.

————. Schemata no. 372, De Rituali, 40. 9 October 1970.

Driscoll, Michael S. "Marriage and Mozart: Ritual Change in Eighteenth-Century Vienna." *Ars Liturgiae: Worship, Aesthetics and Praxis: Essays in Honor of Nathan D. Mitchell*. Edited by Clare V. Johnson, 77–79. Chicago: Liturgy Training Publications, 2003.

Evanou, Jean. "Commentarium." *Notitiae* XXVI (1990): 310–27.

Fischer, Kathleen, Thomas Hart, Bernard Cooke, and William Roberts. *Alternative Futures for Worship: Christian Marriage*. Vol 5. Edited by Bernard Cooke. Collegeville, MN: Liturgical Press, 1987.

Hellín, Francisco Gil. *Concilii Vaticani II synopsis in ordinem redigens schemata cum relationibus necnon Patrum orationes atque animadversiones: Constitutio de Sacra Liturgica Sacrosanctum concilium*. Vatican City: Libreria Editrice Vaticana, 2003.

291

Huels, John M. "The Significance of the 1991 *Ordo celebrandi matrimonium* for the Canon Law of Marriage." *Studia canonica* 43 (2009): 97–139.

Instituto de Liturgia Hispana. *Gifts and Promise: Customs and Traditions in Hispanic Rites of Marriage.* Portland, OR: Oregon Catholic Press, 1997.

John Paul II. *Familiaris consortio,* On the Role of the Christian Family in the Modern World. November 22, 1981. http://w2.vatican.va /content/john-paul-ii/en/apost_exhortations/documents/hf_jp-ii _exh_19811122_familiaris-consortio.html.

Lectionnaire pour la célébration du mariage. Ottawa: Conférence des évêques catholiques du Canada, 2011.

Liber Sacramentorum Romanae aeclesiae ordinis anni circuli. Edited by Leo Cunibert Mohlberg. Rome: Casa Editrice Herder, 1981.

Merz, Dan. "For Your Marriage." http://www.foryourmarriage.org /marriage-rite-second-edition-whats-new/.

Missale Romanum ex decreto SS. Concilii Tridentini restitutum summorum pontificum cura recognitum. Vatican City: Typis Polyglottis Vaticanis, 1962.

Nocent, Adrien. "The Christian Rite of Marriage in the West." *Handbook for Liturgical Studies.* Vol. 4, Sacraments and Sacramentals. Edited by Anscar J. Chupungco, 275–301. Collegeville, MN: Liturgical Press, 2000.

———, ed. "Il matrimonio cristiano." In *La Liturgica: I Sacramenti: Teologia e storia della celebrazione.* Anamnesis 3/1, 301–64. Genova: Casa Editrice Marietti, 1989.

De oratione communi seu fidelium: Natura, momentum ac structura, Criteria atque specimina, Coetibus territorialibus Episcoporum proposita. Vatican City: Libreria Editrice Vaticana, 1966.

The Order of Celebrating Matrimony. London: Catholic Truth Society, 2016.

The Order of Celebrating Matrimony. Strathfield: St. Pauls, 2015.

Ordo celebrandi matrimonium. Editio typica. Vatican City: Typis Polyglottis Vaticanis, 1972.

———. Editio typica altera. Vatican City: Typis Polyglottis Vaticanis, 1991.

Parenti, Stefano. "The Christian Rite of Marriage in the East." *Handbook for Liturgical Studies.* Vol. 4, Sacraments and Sacramentals. Edited by Anscar J. Chupungco, 255–74. Collegeville, MN: Liturgical Press, 2000.

Rite of Marriage. Toronto: International Committee on English in the Liturgy, 1969.

Ritzer, Korbinian. *Formen, Riten und Religiöses Brauchtum der Eheschliessung in den Christlichen Kirchen des Ersten Jahrtausends.* Münster: Aschendorffsche Verlagsbuchhandlung, 1962.

Ritual del Matrimonio. [Cali: Comisión Episcopal de Liturgia, 2004].

Rituel Romain de la célébration du mariage. Ottawa: Conférence des évêques catholiques du Canada, 2011.

The Roman Missal Renewed by Decree of the Most Holy Second Ecumenical Council of the Vatican, Promulgated by Authority of Pope Paul VI and Revised at the Direction of Pope John Paul II. Collegeville, MN: Liturgical Press, 2011.

The Roman Ritual in Latin and English with Rubrics and Plainchant Notation: The Sacraments and Processions. Translated and edited by Philip T. Weller. Vol. 1. Boonville, NY: Preserving Christian Publications, 2007.

Le Sacramentaire Grégorien, ses principals forms d'après les plus anciens manuscrits. Edited by Jean Deshusses. Freiburg: Éditions Universitaires, 1979.

Sacramentarium Veronense. Edited by Leo Cunibert Mohlberg. Rerum Ecclesiasticarum Documenta. Rome: Herder Editrice e Libreria, 1978.

The Sarum Missal in English. The Library of Liturgiology & Ecclesiology for English Readers. Edited by Vernon Staley. Vol. 9, pt. 2. London: Alexander Moring Ltd., the De La More Press, 1911.

Searle, Mark, and Kenneth W. Stevenson. *Documents of the Marriage Liturgy.* Collegeville, MN: Liturgical Press, 1992.

Stevenson, Kenneth W. *Nuptial Blessing: A Study of Christian Marriage Rites.* New York: Oxford University Press, 1983.

———. *To Join Together: The Rite of Marriage.* Studies in the Reformed Rites of the Catholic Church. Vol. 5. New York: Pueblo Publishing Company, 1987.

Turner, Paul. *The Catholic Wedding Answer Book: ML Answers the 101 Most-Asked Questions.* Resource Publications. Chicago: Liturgy Training Publications, 2001.

———. *One Love: A Pastoral Guide to the Order of Celebrating Matrimony.* Collegeville, MN: Liturgical Press, 2016.

———. *Preparing the Wedding Homily: A Guide for Preachers and Couples.* Chicago: Liturgy Training Publications, 2003.

Index

Abraham, 100–101, 112, 156, 158–59
Acts of Thomas, 136
Adam, 80, 137, 142, 260, 264
adaptations, xvi, xviii, 7–8, 41–50, 57, 81–82, 110, 241
Advent, 32, 34, 35, 36, 73, 280
aisle, 61, 69, 72, 80, 89, 120–21, 161
alb, 41, 53–54, 58, 136, 168–69
alleluia, 76–77, 102, 234, 237–38
altar, 52, 54, 55–61, 67–70, 79–80, 116, 120–21, 124, 130–31, 162, 170–72, 183, 187, 193, 202, 205, 221, 285
Ambrose, 124
anniversary, xix, 155, 160, 247, 250, 267, 278–88
antiphon(s), 5, 63–66, 72, 89, 99–100, 121–22, 151–52, 191, 231, 234, 241
Apostolic See, 26, 42, 43, 49, 210
applause, 161
Armenian Rite, 46, 47, 226, 231, 232, 239, 240
arras, 30, 40, 104, 111–16, 123, 180–81, 200, 217, 226
Arrighi, Gianfrancesco, xv
assisting layperson, 27, 49, 195–205, 211, 214, 216, 220, 221
asterisk, 75–76, 175, 198, 213, 225, 227–28, 230, 232, 234, 235, 288
Australia, xviii, 43, 61, 70, 92, 196, 202–3, 225

"Ave Maria," 153
Aymond, Gregory, 4

banns, 7, 82, 88
Barbeau, Abbey of, 50, 91, 106, 112, 131, 148
bed, 46, 92, 137–39, 143, 147, 265
Belgium, 44, 55, 128
Benedict XIV, Pope, 17
bishop, xviii, 3–5, 8, 14–15, 25–28, 32, 38, 39, 41–50, 54, 56, 58, 75, 81, 84, 96–97, 103–5, 109–11, 116–18, 120, 126, 130, 136, 150, 155, 164, 169, 186–87, 190, 193, 195–99, 215, 225, 280
Blessed Virgin Mary, 35, 153–54, 192, 205, 276, 279
blessed water, 41, 59–60, 98, 102–5, 114, 155, 169, 180, 200, 202, 216, 283–84, 288
blessing, xvii, xix, 11, 13, 15, 25–26, 29–30, 34, 36–38, 40–41, 44, 46–49, 55, 60, 64, 71, 89, 91, 93, 95, 99–102, 102–11, 111–16, 120, 123–25, 125–54, 155–61, 163–64, 166–67, 180–81, 182–86, 187, 189, 192, 200–201, 201–1, 205, 211, 216, 217, 218–21, 230–31, 242–45, 246–47, 255–61, 262, 263–65, 267, 270–78, 278–88
Bobbio Missal, 126

Bonet, Emmanuel, 93, 98–99, 141–42, 196
Book of Blessings, 15, 200, 270–78, 278–88
Book of Common Prayer, 88, 92, 93
Borromeo, Luigi Carlo, xvii
Botero Salazar, Tulio, 84
Botte, Bernard, 242, 250
Boudon, René, 84
bow, 67, 155, 170, 172, 283
bread, 52, 120, 126, 185, 187, 190, 256, 262, 282, 285
Bridal Chorus, 62
bridal party, 52, 54, 56–59, 61–62, 66, 69, 79, 80, 169, 171, 177
bride, xvi–xvii, 1, 5, 10, 27, 38, 44–48, 53–58, 61–63, 65–66, 69–70, 79, 83, 87, 89, 90, 92–93, 95, 102–10, 113–15, 120–21, 124–36, 139–50, 153, 156–57, 167–69, 177–78, 180, 182, 184, 192, 199–200, 205, 215–17, 227, 233–34, 242, 245–46, 249, 253, 255–61, 269, 286
Bruylants, Placid, 128, 254
Bugnini, Annibale, 7, 57, 94, 97, 211–12
Byzantine Rite, 47, 106, 112, 231, 240, 271

calendar, 33–36, 63, 279, 280
Cana, 11, 66, 240, 264–65, 268
candle, 30, 61, 116, 124, 247
cantor, 102, 180
cassock, 58, 169
catechesis, 7, 15, 21–22, 29, 43, 124–25, 146, 213, 224, 229, 238–39
catechumen, 25, 38, 52, 59, 207–21, 288
Cellier, Jacques, xv, 55, 108, 141
chair, 67–70, 170–72

chant, 31, 60, 62–63, 65–66, 70–73, 77, 121, 136, 147, 151, 169–71, 191, 219, 240, 256–57, 259
charity, 12, 38, 81, 143, 148–50, 201, 249, 252, 257–58, 260, 268, 277, 286
chasuble, 53, 58
Chavasse, Antoine, xv
child(ren), 10, 47, 54, 62, 67, 69, 72, 82–87, 100, 112, 125, 137–39, 144–45, 152, 154, 157, 184, 219, 228, 244, 251, 252–53, 255, 268–69, 276–78, 285–87
Ciappi, Luigi, xvi, 10, 20, 86, 209
Cicognani, Amleto Giovanni, 10, 86
Civil Declaration of Freedom, 199
Clement, 105
clothes, 32
Code of Canon Law, xviii, 3, 9, 14–15, 18–19, 22–23, 26–27, 37, 50, 72, 91, 197, 208, 212, 284
collect, 30, 36, 41, 43, 60, 74, 134, 174–75, 192, 220, 231, 241–46, 248, 262, 285–86
Colombia, 43, 61, 73, 84, 89, 95, 104, 119, 122, 146, 172–73, 175, 179, 182, 196, 199, 215, 225, 246, 269
color, 34, 41, 53–54, 168
Columbo, Carlo, xv, 17–20, 85, 94
Communion, 22–23, 37–39, 41, 125–28, 132–34, 149–53, 157, 164, 167, 181, 185–86, 187–92, 196, 201–2, 202–5, 255, 262–63, 286
conference(s) of bishops, xviii, 3, 5, 7–8, 18, 26, 34, 39, 41–50, 56, 77, 82, 107–11, 116, 118, 122–23, 157, 195, 215, 224, 225, 269, 277
confession, 23, 59
confirmation, 22–23, 43, 165, 241, 252
congregation, 36, 39, 66, 131, 289

Congregation for Divine Worship and the Discipline of the Sacraments (CDWDS), xvii–xviii, 3, 5, 22, 45, 60, 82, 111, 120, 134–35, 164, 172, 186, 277
Congregation for the Clergy, 163–64
conjugal love, 9, 10, 13, 77, 80, 105, 199, 214, 258, 281
consecration, 127, 141, 184
consent, xvi, 9, 25, 26–27, 29–30, 34, 37–38, 44–45, 49, 51, 54, 61, 71, 78–80, 82–102, 103, 107–9, 115, 127, 135, 149, 154–56, 176–77, 178–80, 187, 199–200, 214–17, 281–82, 288
Consilium, xv, 2, 7, 10, 17, 57, 78, 82, 84–86, 159, 210
Consultation on Common Texts, 226–34, 238
convalidation, 32–33, 288
Conway, William, 144
cope, 41, 54, 136, 168–69
Coptic Rite, 47, 231, 239
corporal, 187, 203
Council of Trent, xvi, xix, 44, 51, 61, 97
Coutances, 113
covenant, 9, 12, 56, 80, 104, 106–7, 123, 137–39, 182, 219, 228, 255, 257, 260, 267–68
Cranmer, Thomas, 92
creed, 40, 117–20
cross, 12, 41, 54, 59, 61, 67, 70–72, 103–4, 155, 169, 172, 184, 200, 205, 212–13, 217, 220–21, 257, 271–72, 277–78, 283
crown(ing), 44, 46–48, 110, 125
custom(s), xix, 1, 7, 27, 29–30, 36, 40, 42, 44, 46, 48, 49–50, 55, 57, 60, 62, 69, 79, 88, 90, 92–93, 102, 107–8, 110, 111, 115–16, 123,

149–50, 153–55, 159–61, 176, 180, 189, 192, 200, 208, 216, 218, 226, 285

D'Amato, Cesare, 140
dalmatic, 168–69
De Oratione communi seu fidelium, 118, 267
deacon, 25–27, 38, 49, 54, 61, 67, 71, 79, 103, 119, 121, 133, 136, 155, 162, 163–64, 167–71, 173, 186–88, 190, 192–93, 195–96, 198, 200–202, 204, 211–12, 216, 220–21, 256–57, 270–73, 275–78, 285, 287–88
Declaration on Religious Liberty, 19
decorations, 31–32
dialogue, 39, 56, 102, 131, 155, 178, 183, 190, 200, 203–4
Directory for the Application of Principles and Norms on Ecumenism, 39
Dirks, Ansgar, 55, 108
dismissal, 158–59, 161, 192, 217, 265
divorce, 13, 94, 276
document, 162, 193, 205, 276
Dogmatic Constitution on the Church (*Lumen gentium*; LG), 14, 83–84, 143
door, xv, 52, 54–55, 57–61, 64, 67–71, 103, 168, 171, 197, 212–13
dowry, 54, 106
dress, 54, 120
Dwyer, George Patrick, 144–45

East Syrian Rite, 47
Easter Time, 34–35, 74–76, 154, 176, 233–34, 236, 243, 280
Eastern Rite, 48, 51, 91, 135, 186
embolism, 126, 129–30, 132–33, 148–49

engaged, xv, 15–22, 26–29, 37, 58, 60, 71, 90, 93, 123, 195, 205, 230, 238, 267, 270–78

England and Wales, xviii, 43, 61, 70, 73–74, 87–88, 92, 97, 147, 178–80, 196, 199–200, 202–3, 215, 288

entrance chant, 60, 62–66, 70–72, 89, 99–100, 121, 169–71

Ephesians, 12, 76, 85, 139, 143, 151, 225, 228, 230–31, 243, 272, 276, 286

epiclesis, 135, 186, 257, 260

escorts, 57, 69

Ethiopic, 231, 239

Eucharist, 22, 29, 40, 51, 120–54, 162, 165, 176, 185, 188–89, 203, 253, 259

Eucharistic Prayer, 122–23, 126, 241, 252–55

Evanou, Jean, 100, 133, 136, 218

Eve, 80, 142, 260, 264

family, 21, 23, 64, 66, 76, 79, 82, 151, 201, 217, 218–19, 235, 252, 254, 258, 269–70, 278, 284, 286

father, 69–70, 72, 83, 89, 96–97, 153, 227, 258

Felici, Pericle, 17

fidelity, 9, 82, 104, 106–7, 111, 119, 140, 142, 144–45, 147, 212, 247, 260

Filipino, 30, 46, 111, 123, 217

Fischer, Balthasar, xv, 158, 254

flower girl, 69, 116

flowers, 150, 153, 192, 205

French Canada, 43, 61, 88, 95, 101, 104, 107, 111, 116, 119, 122–23, 130, 152, 160, 170, 172, 175, 178, 180–82, 188, 192, 215–17, 221, 223, 225, 282

Fulda Sacramentary, 139, 244, 254

Gallican, 157–58, 240, 242

Gelasian Sacramentary, xviii, 1, 126, 129, 131–32, 138–39, 143, 148, 156–57, 242, 245, 249–50, 254, 262, 286–87

General Instruction of the Roman Missal (GIRM), 30, 53, 66, 67, 70–72, 76, 117, 121, 150, 162, 170, 180, 182, 197, 279, 280, 283, 285

Germanic, 64, 66, 121, 139, 152, 160, 229, 236, 238–39, 248, 250, 254, 262, 279, 285–87

Germany, 44–45, 83–84, 108, 159

Giobbe, Paolo, 78

Gloria, 73, 174

Good Friday, 32, 34

gospel, xvii, 49, 51–52, 66, 74, 76–78, 86–87, 117, 175, 198, 214, 223, 225, 232, 235, 237–41, 258, 273, 274

Graduale Romanum, 65, 121, 151

Graduale simplex, 66, 122, 151–52, 234–35, 237

Grail Psalms, 235–36, 274

greet(s), greeting, 52, 54, 58–61, 67–68, 70–71, 129, 148, 155, 168–69, 172–74, 197–98, 212–13, 221, 271–72

Gregorian Sacramentary, xviii, 1–2, 129, 132, 138–39, 142, 148, 242, 248, 250, 254, 262

Gregory Nazianzen, 46, 90, 236

groom, xvii, 1, 10, 27, 38, 47–49, 53–58, 61–62, 65–66, 69, 72, 79, 87, 89–90, 92–97, 102–6, 108, 110, 113–15, 120–21, 124–25, 128, 130, 135, 139, 143, 145, 148–50, 153, 156–57, 169, 177–78, 180,

182, 185, 192, 199–200, 205, 215–17, 227, 235, 242, 245–46, 255, 257, 259, 269
Guerrero Corona, Jonás, 114
Gy, Pierre-Marie, xv, xvii–xviii, 9, 55, 84, 99, 108, 209, 242, 250

Hadrian Supplement, 2
Hallinan, Paul, 51, 127, 140, 142, 144
Hanc igitur, 249, 252–54, 285
hand(s), 44, 48, 66, 69, 72, 88–91, 97–98, 100, 108, 113–14, 145, 154–55, 160, 178–79, 184, 197–201, 215, 217, 219–20, 227, 256–57, 276–77, 283
Hänggi, Anton, 108, 129
Hervàs y Benet, Joan, 145
Hispanic, 30, 46, 61–62, 123, 217, 261
Holy Office, 48, 108
Holy Saturday, 32, 34
homily, xvi, 21–22, 25, 30, 51, 77–79, 117, 127, 136, 174, 176, 198, 214, 275, 281, 288
Hopfinger, Johannes, xv
Huels, John, 164
husband, 10, 86, 92, 95–97, 104, 106–7, 127, 149, 169, 230–32, 251, 258–61, 272, 282, 285
hymn, 62, 66–67, 71, 76, 115–16, 153, 162, 181, 201, 217, 230, 234, 240, 273–74

"I do," 72, 87, 92, 95–97
incensation, 283
Innocent I, Pope, 1
Instituto de Liturgia Hispana, 112
instrumental music, 62–63, 66, 70–71, 153, 161, 170
Inter œcumenici, 21, 163, 168, 174–76, 181

International Commission on English in the Liturgy (ICEL), 3–4, 24, 10, 15, 26–27, 77, 81, 86, 94, 104, 111, 134, 138, 146–47, 165, 177, 185–86, 212, 244–48, 251, 259–60, 270, 275, 277, 281–82, 284
introductory rites, 16, 52–74, 168–75, 197–98, 241, 271–73
Ireland, 144, 146
Isidore of Seville, 1, 53, 105, 253–54

Japan(ese), 48, 90, 208
Jenny, Henri, 254
Jewish, 137, 209
John Chrysostom, 46, 112
John Paul II, Pope, 8, 12–13, 21, 24, 50
Jounel, Pierre, 128, 149, 196
Jungmann, Joseph, 140, 259–60

kiss, 69, 113, 148–49
kneel, 38, 54, 67, 79, 120, 130–31, 183, 201, 219
Kyrie, 72–73, 183

Latin Rite, 4, 10, 14, 26–27, 41, 47–48, 58–61, 69–70, 77, 81, 86, 89, 94, 96, 104–5, 111, 118–19, 122, 131, 135–36, 138, 146–47, 153–54, 160, 163, 169, 172–75, 177, 182–83, 189, 195, 202–3, 211–14, 216, 219, 223, 225, 233, 237, 243–46, 248, 251–52, 256–57, 259, 261, 263, 267, 269, 272–73, 275, 277, 281, 283
layperson, 26–27, 49, 195–205, 211, 214, 216, 220–21, 270, 272–73, 275
lazo, 30, 38, 40, 120, 123–25, 148, 182, 186, 201–2, 218–19, 220

lectionary, 5, 29–30, 34, 37, 65,
74–77, 145, 176, 198, 224–34,
236–38, 240, 280
Lécuyer, Joseph, xv, 9–13, 21, 133,
142–43, 157, 263–65
Lengeling, Emil, xv, 142, 185
Lent, 32–36, 72–73, 76–77, 117, 237
Lentini, Anselmo, 55, 98, 149, 242,
250
Leo, Pope, 251
"Letter to Diognetus," 9
Liber Comicus, 239
Liber Ordinum, 89, 112, 124, 126,
139, 157, 226, 261
Ligier, Louis, xv, 128, 256–58, 260
Litany of the Saints, 81–82, 119
Liturgy of the Word, 33, 37–38, 52,
74–78, 175–76, 198, 213–14
Lohengrin, 62
Lombard, Peter, 91
López de Moura, Agostino, 84
Lord's Prayer, 111, 120, 125–27,
129–30, 132–33, 181–89, 201,
203, 218, 221, 245, 286
love, xv, xix, 12, 16, 23, 27, 31, 47,
59, 72, 76, 80–81, 83–87, 89,
92–96, 104–5, 111–13, 116, 119,
123, 127, 139, 143, 147, 183, 212,
227, 229–32, 234, 237–40, 243–
44, 247–52, 255, 257–58, 262–65,
268, 272–78, 283, 287
Löwenberg, Bruno, xv
Luykx, Boniface, xv
Lyons, France, 158

Martimort, Aimé-Georges, 55, 93,
109, 128, 141, 158, 185, 196
Mass, xvi–xvii, xix, 2, 25–26, 28–31,
33–39, 41, 50, 51–162, 163–93,
197–98, 202–5, 207–9, 214, 217,
220–21, 223–65, 270–75, 278–88

Mass "For the Celebration of
Marriage," 5, 33
Mass for Spouses, xix, 64, 66, 76,
129, 132, 159, 234, 238, 249
Mass for the Holy Trinity, 63, 236,
242
Mazzarello, Secondo, xv, xviii, 133,
142–43, 257–58
McManus, Frederick, xv, 142, 209
Mejia, Jairo, xv
Mendelssohn, Felix, 161
Menke, Andrew, 5
Metz, France, 51–52
Mexico, Mexican, 40, 43, 59–63,
67–68, 70, 72–73, 75–77, 79, 82,
87–89, 96, 102, 104, 111, 114–16,
119–20, 122–25, 131, 135, 148,
153, 155, 157, 169–70, 172–74,
176–80, 182, 185–87, 189, 192,
196, 198–205, 213, 215–17, 220,
225, 227–28, 230, 233–35, 239–40,
252, 261, 265, 269, 276, 284, 288
minister, 25, 39–40, 49, 54, 58–60,
67–68, 70–71, 81, 86–87, 91, 98,
103, 137, 157, 161, 166, 168–74,
176–92, 195–96, 203–4, 211–13,
217, 219, 221, 243, 245–47, 256,
259, 261, 271–73, 276–77, 288
Missal of Bury St. Edmunds, 54,
63–64, 131, 152
Missal of Troyes, 231
mission(s), xvi, 42, 45, 57, 87, 90,
141, 208–9, 257, 265
miter, 41, 54, 104, 155, 169
Molin, Jean-Baptiste, xv
mortal sin, 17, 23
Mozarabic, 89, 112, 154, 157–58,
160, 242, 261
music, 29–31, 43, 62–66, 70–71, 102,
116, 121, 135–36, 151, 153, 161–
62, 170, 180, 183, 219, 249, 256

Nabuco, Joaquím, 108, 141
Nagasaki Ritual, 48, 90, 103
nave, 69, 80
Neunheuser, Burkhard, 141
New Testament, 75, 173, 176, 225,
    228–34
Nocent, Adrien, 102, 106–7, 146
non-Catholics, 19, 38–40, 94, 134,
    164–67, 185–86, 219, 259
non-Christian, 19, 38, 52, 207–21,
    288
Normandy, 103, 106
nuptial blessing, xix, 11, 25–26,
    29–30, 34, 36–38, 40–41, 47, 29,
    55, 60, 111, 120, 123–25, 125–54,
    156, 163–64, 181–82, 183–86,
    187, 189, 201–2, 211, 217–18,
    219–20, 221, 231, 243–45, 255–
    61, 262, 280, 286

offering, 13–14, 30, 112, 122, 202,
    247–49, 252–54
offertory chant, 122, 151
Old Testament, 45, 64, 74–75, 89,
    141, 143, 175–76, 225–28, 278
Oñatibia, Ignacio, xv
options, xix, 24, 30, 44–45, 52,
    60–61, 63–64, 76–77, 107–8,
    119, 138, 147, 169, 171, 174–75,
    178–80, 191, 204, 213–14, 225,
    231, 234, 236, 238, 247, 261–62,
    282–84
Order of Christian Funerals, xvi,
    40, 45
Order of Mass, 52, 121, 128, 133,
    134, 157–59, 161, 197, 204, 242,
    254, 272, 285, 287
Ordinary Time, 34, 37, 76, 230, 253,
    279–80
Ordo cantus missæ, 65, 121, 151, 234,
    236, 238

Ordo lectionarium, 233
organ, 62–63, 116, 170–71
Our Father. *See* Lord's Prayer

padrinos, 62, 114–15, 123–24, 182
Paprocki, Thomas, 4
parents, 10, 57, 60–61, 67, 69, 83–85,
    101, 116, 123–24, 131, 150, 153,
    170, 219, 251, 258, 263–64,
    276–78
Paris Missal, 262
parish staffs, 16, 33
participation, 28–29, 39, 43, 47, 62,
    102, 115, 132, 164–65, 185, 189,
    191, 259
partnership, 9, 72, 80, 147, 257, 260,
    264, 284
Pascher, Joseph, 98, 108, 128
pastor(s), 15–16, 19–20, 23–25, 27,
    29–30, 32–33, 40, 58, 150, 198,
    208, 212
Pastoral Constitution on the
    Church in the Modern World
    (*Gaudium et spes*; GS), 8–13, 81,
    83, 94
pastoral staff, 41, 54, 104, 155, 169
Paul VI, Pope, xv, 78, 94, 97, 146
Paulinus of Nola, 1
peace, 47, 88, 139, 143, 156, 158, 193,
    205, 231, 246–47, 255, 263, 265,
    267–70, 272, 278, 287
Pellegrino, Michele, 254
penitential act, 72–73
photograph, 161
place, 27–28
pledge, 92, 96, 112, 114–15, 137
Poland, 44, 108
Pondicherry, India, 48, 109
Pontifical of Egbert, 100
Pontifical of Robert of Jumieges,
    100, 246

posture, 68, 131, 164, 187, 219, 270

prayer of the faithful, xvi, 82, 116–18, 167–68, 181, 187, 217, 267, 275, 284; *see also* universal prayer

preface, 30, 122–23, 136, 202, 224, 242, 249–52, 254, 285

preparation, 14–16, 18, 21, 24–27, 28–33, 42, 84, 119, 197, 199, 271, 273

Preparatory Commission, 71, 74, 82, 98, 118, 175, 184, 196

presider, preside(s), 25–26, 43, 49, 54, 73, 75, 115, 117, 136, 153–55, 163–64, 169–71, 175, 182, 186–88, 190, 193, 195–96, 200, 211–12, 214–16, 218–21, 241, 256, 269–73, 275–78, 288

priest, xvi, xix, 2, 6, 18–19, 25–27, 32, 37–38, 44, 47, 49, 52–54, 58–61, 67–73, 76–77, 79–82, 86–93, 96–104, 106, 109–15, 118–19, 121–26, 130–32, 134–36, 139–40, 145, 148, 150, 154–55, 158, 160–62, 163–64, 166–71, 173, 179, 183–84, 186–88, 190, 192–93, 195–96, 198, 200–204, 211–12, 216, 220–21, 242, 247, 249–50, 255–57, 262, 270–73, 275–84, 286, 288

procession, 50, 52, 54, 56–64, 66–67, 69–72, 89, 116, 161, 169–72, 197

promises, 87, 92–96, 119, 151, 231, 235, 281–82

Propitiare, 131–33, 245–46

psalm, 47, 64–66, 71–72, 76n77, 102, 121–22, 144, 151–52, 183–84, 191, 223, 225–33, 238, 274

Rabau, Jean, xv

Raphael, 183

reader, xix, 47, 61, 66, 71, 77, 198, 273

readings, xvii, 21, 29–30, 35–37, 50, 73, 74–78, 135, 145, 175–76, 198, 213, 223–41, 256, 270, 273–75, 280–81

reception, 55–57, 90, 97–102, 176, 179, 200, 212–13, 216–17

Rennes, France, 103

responsorial psalm, 31, 175, 234–37, 274

ring bearer, 69, 116

rings, 29, 38, 41, 44, 48, 56, 102–11, 113–15, 130, 180, 200–201, 216–17, 246–47, 276, 283–84

Rite of Baptism for Children, xvi, 43

Rite of Christian Initiation of Adults (RCIA), xvi, 59, 117, 218

Rite of Confirmation, 43

Rite of Marriage, 1, 3, 223–65

Rite of Pastoral Care of the Sick, 43

Rite of the Dedication of a Church and an Altar, 43

Ritzer, Korbinian, xv, 263–65

Roman Canon, 122, 252–53

Roman Missal, xviii–xix, 26, 34, 60, 65, 67, 72, 75, 77, 134, 152, 163, 173, 237, 239, 279

Roman Pontifical, 63–64, 79, 96, 100, 103, 121, 126, 148, 152, 236, 239, 242, 246, 248, 250, 254, 262

Roman Ritual, xv, xix, 2, 7, 18, 44–48, 50, 53, 55, 78, 90, 92, 97, 100, 103, 107, 109–10, 126, 131–32, 138, 140, 148, 162, 220, 229, 241–42, 246, 280–81, 287–88

Roman-Germanic Pontifical, 64, 66, 121, 139, 152, 229, 236, 238–39, 248, 250, 254, 262, 279, 285–87

Rouen, France, 98

Sacram Liturgiam, 78, 168
sacrament(s), xv–xvi, 2–5, 8, 11–12,
   16–24, 26, 28–29, 32–33, 36,
   38–39, 42, 50, 58, 68, 70, 76, 78,
   84–85, 91, 98–99, 102, 127–28,
   132, 134–36, 151, 166, 177, 192,
   209–10, 214, 219, 231, 243, 257,
   259, 268, 279
Sacred Congregation for the
   Doctrine of the Faith, 20, 94, 97,
   166, 210
Sacred Congregation of Rites, xvii,
   21, 51, 183, 191
sacrifice, 13, 33, 133, 167, 187, 189,
   250, 263
sacrificial, 14
sacristy, 69, 162, 171
Sacrosanctum concilium (SC), xv–
   xvii, 16, 18, 20–22, 32, 42–43, 45,
   49, 78, 92, 140, 165–66, 175–76,
   184, 208–9, 223
sanctuary, 41, 55, 58, 61, 67–70,
   79–80, 124, 165, 170, 172
Sarum Manual, 103, 106, 113
Sarum Missal, 80, 91, 93, 124, 127,
   148, 230, 236, 239
Saturday night wedding, 35, 37, 73,
   117, 243
Schubert, Franz, 153
Scripture, xvii, 21, 74, 115, 173, 212,
   272–73
Second Vatican Council, xv–xvii, 2,
   9, 12, 14, 37, 44, 49, 51, 64, 71,
   74, 92, 97–98, 107, 117–18, 122,
   140, 152, 164, 184, 208, 248, 287
   pre–Vatican II, 5, 42, 64, 105
   post–Vatican II, xix, 1, 5, 7, 22, 31,
      65, 79, 82, 102, 106, 132, 138,
      159, 228, 241–43, 279
Secretariat for Christian Unity, 18,
   211

servers, 52–54, 68–69, 197
Seumois, Xavier, xv, 42, 45, 49, 57,
   110, 159
Sicard, Damien, xv
sick, 32, 43, 91, 93, 95–96, 190
sign of the cross, 59, 67, 70–72,
   103–4, 155, 172, 184, 200, 212–
   13, 217, 221, 271–72, 277, 283
sign of peace, 113, 126, 129–31,
   148–50, 189–90, 203, 286
silence, 59, 69–70, 79, 84, 110, 131,
   134, 182–83, 191, 201, 204, 256,
   281
Siricius, Pope, 1, 124
sitting, 68
solemnities, xvii, 35–36, 128, 280
Solemnity of the Most Holy Body
   and Blood of Christ, 35, 192
song, 31, 66, 71, 73, 101–2, 153, 170,
   181, 186, 191, 204–5, 217, 221,
   274, 278
Spain, 89, 112, 124, 145
Spanish, xviii, 61, 70, 81, 89, 93, 96,
   107, 111–12, 114–15, 124, 135,
   143, 159, 162, 171–73, 179, 182,
   196, 203, 239–40
spouse(s), xvi–xvii, xix, 2, 9–10,
   12, 15, 17, 19–20, 39–40, 44, 47,
   53, 63–64, 66, 74, 76, 80, 83–85,
   90–91, 94–96, 98–99, 105–8, 112,
   115, 119–20, 123–25, 128–30,
   132, 134, 140–41, 144–46, 148,
   159, 179, 212, 216, 234, 238, 249,
   253, 257, 262, 282–83
sprinkle, 41, 59–60, 98, 102–5, 115,
   155, 180, 200, 216, 283–84, 288
Spülbeck, Otto, 84
Stenzel, Alois, xv
Stevenson, Kenneth, 103, 148–49,
   157, 209, 228, 262
stole, 41, 53–54, 58, 136, 168–69

surplice, 53, 58, 168–69
Syrian Oriental Orthodox Rite, 90, 106

tabernacle, 67, 170, 187, 190, 205
Table of Liturgical Days, 34, 37, 75, 117, 225
Tertullian, 13–14, 105, 281
Theodore the Studite, 46
title, 1–6, 50, 53, 124, 135, 163, 167, 196, 207–8, 210, 217, 223, 249, 253, 255–56, 263
Tobit, 63–64, 99–101, 121, 152, 227
Tomizawa, Benedict, 208–9
Trinity, 63–64, 106, 160, 221, 243, 270, 286

unbelieving Catholics, 20–21
United States, xviii, 31, 58, 61–63, 70, 81, 89, 92, 96, 107, 111–12, 114–15, 120, 124–25, 127, 135, 153–54, 161–62, 171–73, 175, 178–80, 182, 195–96, 211, 214–16, 219–21, 223, 225, 227, 271, 273
United States Conference of Catholic Bishops (USCCB), xviii, 4–5, 46, 61, 81–82, 162, 171, 211
unity, 9, 12–13, 30, 39–40, 63, 72, 107, 116, 124–26, 132, 135, 142, 189, 257, 264, 267–69
Universal Norms on the Liturgical Year and the Calendar, 34
universal prayer, 29–30, 40, 60, 82, 116–20, 181–82, 186, 201, 217–18, 221, 267–70, 275, 284; *see also* prayer of the faithful

Vandenbroucke, François, xv

Vatican II. *See* Second Vatican Council
veil, 1, 53, 102, 123–25, 131, 180, 182–200, 216, 218–19, 226
velación, 30, 226
Verona Sacramentary, xviii, 1, 129, 131–33, 137, 220, 242, 244–45, 248, 250, 253, 262
vestments, 33–34, 53–54
Vich, Sacramentary of, 143, 159
virginity, 53
Visigothic, 158
vows, 84, 281–82
Vulgate, 63–64, 89, 99–101, 225, 228

Wagner, Johannes, 55, 93, 108, 128–29, 141, 158, 245, 254
warmly, 59, 169, 172, 197, 212
"Wedding March," 161
white, 33–34, 41, 53–54, 168
"Who gives this woman," 72
wife, 10, 83, 86, 91–97, 104, 106–7, 127, 143, 149, 169, 227–28, 230–31, 251, 258–59, 282, 285
wine, 52, 120, 126, 190, 264, 282, 285
within Mass, xix, 2, 31, 33, 8, 41, 51–162, 163, 166–70, 175, 178–80, 182, 184–87, 189, 191–92, 209, 213, 241, 247, 250, 253, 261–62, 278–88
without Mass, xvii, xix, 31, 33, 37–39, 58, 75, 163–93, 203–5, 212–14, 218–19, 244, 263, 281, 286
witnesses, 26, 60–62, 69, 79–80, 99, 119, 136, 150, 162, 164, 177, 197, 221, 258, 276
Würzburg, 229–30

York Missal, 93